Getting Lost

SUNY SERIES IN THE PHILOSOPHY OF THE SOCIAL SCIENCES

————————————

LENORE LANGSDORF, EDITOR

and

SUNY SERIES

————————————

SECOND THOUGHTS: NEW THEORETICAL FORMATIONS

————————————

DEBORAH P. BRITZMAN, EDITOR

Getting Lost

Feminist Efforts toward a Double(d) Science

Patti Lather

STATE UNIVERSITY OF NEW YORK PRESS

Cover art by Charles Beck

Published by
State University of New York Press, Albany

For information, contact State University of New York Press, Albany, NY
www.sunypress.edu

Production by Kelli W. LeRoux
Marketing by Anne M. Valentine

Library of Congress Cataloging-in-Publication Data

Lather, Patricia Ann, 1948–
    Getting lost : feminist efforts toward a double(d) science / Patti Lather.
        p. cm. — (SUNY series, second thoughts) (SUNY series in the philosophy
    of the social sciences)
    Includes bibliographical references and index.
    ISBN-13: 978-0-7914-7057-2 (hardcover : alk. paper)
    ISBN-13: 978-0-7914-7058-9 (pbk. : alk. paper)
    1. Feminist theory.   2. Social sciences—Philosophy.   3. Social sciences—
Research—Philosophy.   I. Title.

HQ1190.L375 2007
305.4201--dc22   2006019063

10 9 8 7 6 5 4 3 2 1

Contents

Preface

I must destabilize the structures of foreclosure in order to allow passage
to the other . . . With the word *with* commences then this text . . .
Nevertheless, I do not make the other come. The call and the coming
comes from the other . . . the wholly other. It cannot be invented except
by way of the other, by way of the coming of the other who says "come"
and to which the response of another "come" appears to be the sole
invention that is desirable and worthy of interest.

—Derrida, *Acts of Literature*

With a move from *Getting Smart* (Lather, 1991) to *Getting Lost*, this book
marks the trajectory of my work over the last fifteen years. As a feminist
methodologist, my interest in both books has been the implications of the
"post" for research in the human sciences. While the first book took a particular interest in what the post might mean for emancipatory research (and
pedagogy), this book focuses on the methodological learnings from my co-
authored quasi-ethnographic study, *Troubling the Angels: Women Living With
HIV/AIDS* (Lather and Smithies, 1997).

With women living with HIV/AIDS, I first began to learn about getting
lost in terms of what it means to not be in control and to try to figure out a
life, given that. Perhaps more precisely, I learned about getting lost from
trying to simultaneously produce and theorize a book about these women.
There I put myself in an awkward position that was not so much about losing
oneself in knowledge as about knowledge that loses itself in the necessary
blind spots of understanding. This is Walter Benjamin/Jacques Derrida territory, what Paul de Man (1983) termed blindness and insight, where the necessary exclusion is the very organizer of whatever insight might be made and
critical texts always turn back on the very things they denounce/renounce.

The distinction is important. The issue is not the phenomenology of the
researcher negotiating difficult fieldwork. The "proceed haltingly" of my

Knowledge that loses itself in the necessary
blindspots of understanding

Deleuzean stuttering knowledge is about the construction of the research object as what might be termed "concepts of a lesser ontological weight." Bataille captures this move as "including the night from which [knowledge] proceeds only in order to enter it again" (1988, p. 110). This move is also captured in the contrast of my book titles. While *Getting Smart* dealt much with the fundamental tensions between the Enlightenment and postmodernist projects, its very title evokes faith in the knowledge that will set us free via the powers of the reasoning mind. Located at the site of emancipatory research and pedagogy, the book argued that both the seductions of and resistances to postmodernism can help us to "get smart" about the possibilities and limits of critical praxis.

   Getting Lost is a more disabused text. Working the limits of deconstruction, getting lost is theorized as fertile ontological space and ethical practice in asking how research-based knowledge remains possible after so much questioning of the very ground of science. In this book, feminist ethnography is situated as a seismograph of sorts, an index of a more general tension in the human sciences. Grounded in efforts to tell the stories of women living with HIV/AIDS, I explore a logic of mourning and haunting in the context of feminist research methodology. Asking "difficult knowledge" (Pitt and Britzman, 2003) sorts of questions about necessary complicities, inadequate categories, dispersing rather than capturing meanings, and producing bafflement rather than solutions, I put deconstruction to work in unpacking what getting lost might mean as both methodology and mode of representation.

   This book is inscribed into an intertextual web that is enspiriting in being something to rub up against in charting my own course. My sense of web includes, surely, the work of Deborah Britzman. Offering "a psycho-analysis I can bear to learn from" (Weems and Lather, 2000), given my post-Marxist leanings, she is much evident in these pages. The male euro-pantheon is also much evident, particularly Derrida, Benjamin, Foucault, and Nietzsche.[1] Situated "on the interventionist, critical edge of deconstruction" (Niranjana, 1992, p. 161), I also draw from feminist ethnography, qualitative inquiry in the social sciences, and various postcritical theories.

   As those familiar with the tensions between the critical theories of feminism, postcolonialism, and the postcritical moves of deconstruction know, this is no easy place to inhabit. *Getting Lost* seeks to mine such tensions as fertile ground for formulating a kind of feminist research not yet overcoded in the face of received understandings. In a 1993 keynote for the Ethnography and Education Research Forum, I spoke to the early stages of an in-process *Troubling the Angels* and anticipated this second and subsequent book as follows:

   More long term, a methodologically oriented text is envisioned that deals with such issues as narrative strategy and the negotiation of meaning within feminist inquiry; the operations of multi-layered data analysis;

the politics and ethics of doing research on/for/to/with people in general and with PWA's (Persons With AIDS) in particular; and experiential versus interpretive authority, the honoring of participants' voices in a way that problematizes confession, testimonial and the intrusiveness of much social research and how this project has wrestled with such issues. (Lather, 1993)

This "two-book plan" was not well received on several fronts, not the least being concerns that a vulnerable population was being used and abused by deconstruction twice over. As noted by Jane Selby, who heard a version of the talk in Australia, "[t]he paper was an irritant to many" (2004, p. 152) who perceived it as narcissistic navel-gazing at best, unethical at worst, "floundering in the dark, not clearly understanding" what it is doing (pp. 152–53).[2]

This was by no means the only time my work in *Troubling the Angels* troubled my audience, and I will draw considerably in this book on response data across a variety of venues. What is important by way of introduction is that, in attending to how feminist methodology disciplines us with its possibilities, limits, pleasures, and dangers, *Getting Lost* moves in a way that is a search for a form that is pre/simultaneous/post *Troubling the Angels*. Written before, during, and after that book, as an effort to articulate methodology out of practice, my central question in this book is what would practices of research look like that were a response to the call of the wholly other. Some term this "the ethical turn" in the human sciences (Derrida, 1999; Irigaray, 1993; Ziarek, 2001; Critchley, 1992; Gerber, Hanssen and Walkowitz, 2000). As feminist research has never sought to be anything else, I prefer to think of it as gesturing toward the science possible after the critique of science.

"What will have been said" is the future pluperfect tense of the post, its valuable lesson of attention to how that which has been lost in the past might transform the future out of the work of the present (Duttmann, 1993). In addressing "what will have been said," *Getting Lost* brings a Foucauldian "history of the present" to bear on feminist methodology and what it gives us to think in terms of doing inquiry in a postfoundational time.

Early in the project, after a discussion with my friend, Mimi Orner, I wrote the following:

Second text [*Getting Lost*] will fold back into first text [*Troubling the Angels*], but can first text fold forward into book that is not yet? What would that allow me to do? The gesture of revisiting a former text as a form of research is not unusual. But to fold forward, to speculate about an as-yet-not-produced text, showing a work in the making, would be new ground, a sort of dialogue across texts, time, and researching selves. (Research journal, August 31, 1994)

This articulates exactly the sort of future pluperfect thinking that has shaped *Getting Lost*. What is being brought into being through the elaboration of particular practices, the "persistent effortfulness that makes a 'present' " (Spivak, 1993, p. 156)? What are the inclusions and exclusions at work? What uses does feminist methodology see for itself? How does it delimit, constitute, unbind, disharmonize, pervert, rupture, or fit into already established continuums? What are its internal differences and what self-knowledge does it not seem able to bear? What are we "surprised at becoming, pleasuring in this gift of alterability" (Cixous, quoted in Spivak, 1993, p. 156)?

Inhabiting such a polytemporality has had its discomforts. Functioning as both author and (auto)critic of books that did not yet exist, my goal was a reading of my in-process work that produced rather than protected. To this end, the writing assembled here is based on a sort of etch-a-sketch earlier writing that has been erased imperfectly before being written on again. Beginning where I was, where I believed myself to be, my move was toward the need to surrender myself to future deconstructions, given the limits of any knowledge. In Derrida's "The Exorbitant. Question of Method" from *Of Grammatology*, he explicates his choice of subject and lets us in on the lesson learned but, as Spivak notes in the Preface, "in the long run a critic cannot himself present his own vulnerability" (1976, p. lxxv). *Getting Lost*, then, is a palimpsest where primary and secondary texts collapse into trace-structures of one another that fold both backward and forward into books full of concealments, not knowings, and an uncanny time of what "will always have already taken place" (Keenan, 1997, p. 171).

At its heart, *Getting Lost* situates feminist methodology as a noninnocent arena in which to pursue questions of the conditions of science with/in the postmodern. Here we are disabused of much in articulating a place for science between an impossible certainty and an interminable deconstruction, a science of both reverence and mistrust, the science possible after our disappointments in science. Against tendencies toward the sort of successor regimes characteristic of what feminist philosopher of science, Sandra Harding (1991), terms triumphalist versions of science, this book asks how to keep feminist methodology open, alive, loose. Such thinking is within and against Enlightenment categories of voice, identity, agency, and experience so troubled by incommensurability, historical trauma, and the crisis of representation. Given my interest in the science possible after the critique of science, my central argument is that there is plenty of future for feminist methodology if it can continue to put such "post" ideas to work in terms of what research means and does.

Chapter 1 introduces the major concepts that undergird a shifting imaginary in how we think about methodology in the human sciences. Chapter 2 explores double(d) practices via Judith Butler's concept of subversive repetition. Chapter 3 delineates the problems of scientism and the possibilities for an expanded sense of scientificity and concludes by situating feminist methodology in relation to shifts in intellectual movements regarding the human sciences. Chapter 4 unpacks the idea of textuality as praxis by probing an excessive textuality that performs what it announces. Chapter 5 reads the reception of the "post" in educational research and then turns to the uses of deconstruction by way of a reinscription of praxis under conditions of postmodernity. Chapter 6 fleshes out the intelligibility of validity after poststructuralism via an exploration of the usefulness of categories of transgressive validity—ironic, paralogic, rhizomatic, and embodied—and the larger debate about the conditions of science with/in the postmodern. Chapter 7 raises three "postbook" issues: the ruins of ethnographic realism, the masks of authorial presence, and the work of a recalcitrant rhetoric. It concludes with a "methodology of getting lost" by looking at the intersections of research, theory, and politics.

Each chapter is followed by an Interlude designed to elaborate/complicate some aspect of the preceding chapter. These include interviews, letters sent and unsent, updates from Chris and "Linda B," one of the HIV+ women who participated in the study, and, finally, a meditation on what the angel to philosophy of science might be made to mean. This final Interlude draws on Michel Serres's (1995a) theorizing of angels as "quasi-objects" that evoke the anxieties that follow our triumphs when foundations collapse. It draws as well on Walter Benjamin's (1968) angel of history as a way of thinking a nonteleological history, a history thought against the consolations of certain meaning and knowing and toward the thought of the limit as a way to make a future.

The book ends with a textual move intended to break any illusion of mastery via a provocation of something unknown/unknowable, something "still lost" given the nature of the task of representation. Here I present the "riddling quality" of a work-in-the-making that engages myself as reader as much as any audience in the inferential process of solving the puzzle of its meaning by eliciting questions and awkward evocations of things I don't understand about my work.[3]

This sort of textual polyphony or multivoicedness grows out of a "Girlie Day" that I was part of in Copenhagen in the fall of 2003.[4] There, a small group of feminist researchers traded on the stuck places in our work in ways that were particularly fruitful for the structure of this book. My stuck place was whether to write the "easy text" (a collection of already written papers) or the "hard text" that positions the already written as data in working the limits of deconstruction in the context of feminist research methodology. Their urging was toward a both/and form that would identify points in the already written where I did not persuade myself, stuck places, the ruins and runes of the work. This directive finds me stumbling toward a form that deconstructs mastery, including mastery of one's ability to deconstruct the stuck places in one's own work. Hence, the movement of the text is from the already written to something messy that invites further thinking and doing.[5]

Calling on the debates between archeologists and architects on what to do with ruins, the Girlie Day women sent me to Copenhagen's Danish Architecture Centre for the Ground Zero show. This was the first place outside New York City to exhibit the full model and plans for Polish-American Daniel Libeskind's winning entry in the World Trade Center Design Study. There, particularly struck with the holding power of the retainer wall that held out the Hudson River in the 9/11 attack, I thought much of the mix of memory and foundations entailed in building the new out of ruins.

I returned home to filter through the files I had kept over the almost 15 years since the HIV/AIDS study began. Letters and e-mail exchanges, writing from various audiences in response to reading versions of *Troubling the Angels*, transcripts of taped discussions about the book, interviews, all in conjunction with my published and unpublished writing since *Getting Smart*: this was my data. Spanning over a decade, situating this work as a ruin/rune, my goal is to put the post to work to produce useful practices of getting lost as fertile space for shifting imaginaries in the human sciences.

Acknowledgments

I have benefited from a myriad of invitations to speak to early versions of what is presented here. Especially helpful have been extended stays at the Humanities Research Institute at the University of California-Irvine, Goteborg University in Sweden, York University in Toronto, the University of British Columbia, the University of Wisconsin-Madison, the University of Durban, South Africa, Copenhagen University, and the Danish Pedagogical Institute. Especially timely was a Visiting Professorship at the latter in the fall of 2003, thanks to Dorte Marie Sondergaard and Susan Knutsen. Ohio State University provided a sabbatical year. I thank John Struik for readings along the way and, with Barbara Williams, for providing a space on the shores of Lake Ontario at a crucial time in the writing. Deborah Britzman was key in getting a book contract as well as general inspiration. And, finally, I thank my girlfriend, Janet Russell, who, in spite of a tendency to fall asleep when I read to her, listened to the whole darn thing.

Several small grants enabled the work: an Ohio State Coca Cola Grant for Research on Women, 1995–96, an Ohio State Women's Studies Research Grant, 1993–94, and a small money infusion at a crucial time from Jim Pearsol's AIDS Midwest regional center.

The book is a mix of new and old, the latter mostly revised from earlier publications. Parts have been transposed, repetitions minimized, sources updated. I acknowledge prior publication of these fractured parts in the following places and thank the reviewers, anonymous and not, who much improved them along their way:

—Chapter 4, revision of "Responsible Practices of Academic Writing: Troubling Clarity II," from *Revolutionary Pedagogies: Cultural Politics, Instituting Education, and the Discourse of Theory*, Peter Pericles Trifonas, ed. New York: Routledge Falmer, 2000, 289–311, and "Troubling Clarity: The Politics of Accessible Language," *Harvard Educational Review*, 66(3), 1996, 525–45.

—Chapter 5, revision of *Educational Philosophy and Theory*, 35(3), 2003, 257–70.

—Chapter 5 Interlude, reprint from *Educational Theory*, 43(3), 1993, 357–58.

—Chapter 6, excerpted from *The Sociological Quarterly*, 34(4), 1993, 673–93.

—Parts of Chapter 2 and all of Chapter 7, revision of *Signs: Journal of Women, Culture and Society*, 27(1), 2002, 199–227.

Parts of Chapter 1 and Chapter 7 Interlude were previously published in *The Handbook of Ethnography*, Paul Atkinson, A. Coffey, S. Delamont, J. Lofland, and L. Lofand, eds. London: Sage, 2001, 477–92.

The following unpublished selections were used with permission: Chapter 1 Interlude, excerpted from interview by Rubby Dhunpath and Juliet Perumal, and Chapter 4 Interlude, excerpted e-mail from "Linda B." As well, I thank Chris Smithies, Bettie St. Pierre, and Wanda Pillow for their contributions.

Finally, I dedicate this book to Mimi Orner for too few fabulous conversations, to Mary Leach for perhaps too many, and to my father for never enough.

Chapter 1

Shifting Imaginaries in the Human Sciences

A Feminist Reading

A book about a book.—Turns in the social sciences.—Post post theory?—
    (Post)critical ethnography.—A poststructural science 'after truth.'—
    Working the ruins.—Loss and lost, lost, lost.—Derridean rigor as a
    double(d) science.—A praxis of stuck places.—Naked methodology.

Not to find one's way in a city may well be uninteresting and banal. It
requires ignorance—nothing more. But to lose oneself in a city—as one
loses oneself in a forest—that calls for quite a different schooling.

—Walter Benjamin, quoted in Solnit, 2005

This is a book about a book about getting lost at the limits of representation.
Its starting point is the aftermath of poststructuralism. Its central focus is the
sort of practices of critique and inquiry that put the "post" to work in delineating the science possible after our disappointments in science. Grounded in
the instructive complications of a feminist qualitative study of women living
with HIV/AIDS (Lather and Smithies, 1997), *Getting Lost* abstracts a philosophy of inquiry from an archive of work in order to move toward a fruitful
sense of dislocation in our knowledge projects.

My interest in this introductory chapter is in a shifting imaginary for
research in the human sciences.[1] That imaginary has been buffeted about a
great deal over the last several decades. From "linguistic turn" to "science
wars" to "risk society" (Beck, 1992), the end of the value-free notion of
science and the resultant troubling of confidence in the scientific project are

1

much announced. Shifts include the movements of continental and analytic philosophies, varied minoritarianisms, and, of late, a worldwide audit culture with its governmental demands for evidence-based practice and the consequent (re)privileging of scientistic methods.

There is a proliferation of ways to frame these various turns in the social sciences. I position this proliferation within the "science wars" as more traditional scientists take on what they see as the dangerous focus on science as social construction versus "truth" about "nature."[2] The claims of science to a certain privilege in terms of authoritative knowledge are much debated. The myriad turns that have characterized research in the human sciences over the last few decades are not so much linear as multiple, simultaneous, and interruptive. Rather than evoking nostalgia for a lost world of certain knowledge, to engage and transvalue[3] these shifts is to move toward a thought of dissensus rather than consensus, a dissensus not easily institutionalized into some new regime of truth. This is about the "ruins" of methodology, the end of transcendent claims and grand narratives: methodology under erasure.[4] In such a place of thought, inquiry is seen as a social practice, and what is at stake is not so much the nature of science as its effects. Questions of accountability and responsibility are ethical and social. Hence, my central argument is the need to rethink the terms in which we address, not the end of science, but the end of a narrow scientificity.[5]

Surveying the various turns in the social sciences, one is struck by the difficulties of deciding on even what terms to feature.

---

*linguistic (Rorty, 1967; Derrida, 1978; Norris, 1996)
*structural (Althusser, 1971)
*critical (Fay, 1987; Angus and Langsdorf, 1993)
*deconstructive (Derrida, 1976; Norris, 1984)
*rhetorical (Nelson et al, 1987; Simons, 1990)
*cultural (Clifford and Marcus, 1986; Jameson, 1998)
*narrative (Polkinghorne, 1988; Casey, 1995)
*historical (McDonald, 1996)
*ethnographic (Van Maanen, 1995)
*postmodern (Best and Kellner, 1997; Clarke, 2005)
*ethical (Garber, Hanssen and Walkowitz, 2000; Baker, 1995)
*visual (Laspina, 1998)
*pragmatic (Hanssen, 2001; Ockman, 2000)
*policy (Bennett, 1992; McGuigan, 2001)
*theological (Derrida, 1989; Caputo, 1997c; Ward, 2000)

Figure 1. Turns in the Social Sciences

To complicate matters even further, there is of late the language of "return." This includes a return to the real (Foster, 1996), the empirical (Seidman and Alexander, 2001), and to objectivity, whether after deconstruction or after feminist and postcolonial critiques of objectivism (Stanfield, 1994; Harding, 1987, 1991, 1993; Cudd, 2001). Feminist philosopher of science, Sandra Harding (1993), for example, argues for "strong objectivity" based on "systematically examining all of the social values shaping a particular research process" (p. 18). Art historian Steven Melville (1996) argues for an "objectivity in deconstruction" that emphasizes how " 'deconstruction is not what you think' " in its moves of reversing, undoing, and complicating the linguistic turn. To turn everything into discourse is not exhaustive of our engagement with things and how they happen. There is a being in excess of our languages of knowing, whether we know it or not. This is a deconstructed objectivity that refuses "to let its notion of objectivity be constrained by the dominant paradigms of truth" (p. 140).

Across this dizzying array of in-movement shifts, one might think it is, finally, as if the critiques of truth in Nietzsche, self-presence in Freud, referential language in Saussure, and metaphysics in Heidegger were coming home to roost in the social sciences. But there is a new scientism afoot that belies such a linear narrative. Growing out of a worldwide audit culture with its governmental demands for evidence-based practices (Strathern, 2000), scientistic methods are being (re)privileged as if the last several decades of the critique of positivism had not existed (Lather, 2004a, b; Lather and Moss, 2005). Add to this much talk of "post-post" and "the end of theory" (Antonio, 2000; Payne and Schad, 2003; Hoy, 2004) and one begins to feel lost, indeed, in negotiating what it means to (re)think critique and practice in such "dark enough" times (MacLure, 2004).

This book explores what it might mean to claim getting lost as a methodology for such times. Theorists from Walter Benjamin to the modern French masters of posthumanism have long theorized what opens up in the face of the loss of absolute knowledge. Yet it seems that the social sciences have not much attended to a problematic of loss as "an experience of mourning and promise" (Derrida, 2001, p. 67). To take fuller account of the fall into language and the consequent loss of the unmediated referent is to "place hope in this disappointment" and "general shake-up" (ibid., pp. 73, 69) in order to negotiate the mourning and melancholia, pathos and nihilism attendant upon the loss of pure presence.

This raises considerably the stakes of critical practice in our day. Situated in the present postcritical period, *Getting Lost* delineates the open-endedness of practical action as a structure of praxis and ethics without foundations in a context of demands for practices with more to answer to in terms of the complexities of language and the world. In sum, through a development of getting lost as a way of knowing, the book will posit research approaches that no longer confidently assume that we are "in the know" in moving toward a new generation of postcritical work. What enablements can we imagine from loss? What Spivakian "setting-to-work" (1999) might help us engage the limit of the saturated humanist logics that determine the protocols through which we know? These are the questions at the center of the book.

While the "view from nowhere" is much contested, traditional foundations of knowledge continue to undergird much of contemporary research in the human sciences (Spanos, 1993). Rather than focusing on the persistence of this traditional world view in the face of its loss of plausibility, my interest is to explore how feminist research methodology registers cultural shifts and intellectual movements in order to situate itself as a rich ground from which to ask my questions of a less comfortable social science. In this chapter, I introduce the major concepts that undergird twentieth-century turns toward epistemological indeterminacy so as to underscore contemporary interest in situatedness, perspective, relationality, narrative, poesis, and blurred genres (Greene, 1994).

My sense of task is to delineate the weakening of any "one best way approach" and to foreground, instead, how discourse-practices of methodology enter into the circulation and dialogue that make up the ongoing interplay of the field. From poststructuralism to (post)critical ethnography, across methodological practices of working the ruins, a praxis of aporias or stuck places, and naked methodology, I delineate the central terms of my title: getting lost and double(d) practices. Trying to enact a text that both "interrupts itself and gathers up its interruptions into its texture" (Derrida commenting on Levinas in Bennington, 2000, p. 203), I use a Deleuzean sort of plateau format to fold and layer concepts in ways that are multiple, simultaneous, and in flux rather than presenting them as linear and discrete.[6]

Such a style that enacts what it announces describes, as well, my paradoxical desire to "eschew any deconstructive coquetry or stylistic ambition." Instead I produce a rather straight-ahead "if unsatisfactory" movement of the text (Bennington, 2000), given the sort of reader I am hoping for, a reader with "severe" demands of academic work that it make a difference in struggles for social justice. While chapter 4 will be much occupied with issues of accessibility in academic work, my effort here is to introduce a hybrid textual style that mixes the experimental and the straightforward. My guide in this is Helene Cixous:

> The only book that is worth writing is the one we don't have the courage or strength to write. The book that hurts us . . . Writing is writing what you cannot know before you have written it . . . a book stronger than the author. (Cixous, 1993, passim)

Plateau 1: Post-Post Theory?

What are we calling postmodernity? I'm not up to date.

—Michel Foucault 1998

The central investment of this book is in coming to terms with the complexities involved in the "post" turn in the human sciences. Talk of "post-post" (Marcus, 1994) and "post-theory" (McQuillan et al., 1999) makes the issues even more complicated. This plateau is framed by "the many obituaries for postmodernism" (McHale, 2004, p. ix), and begins with a cursory overview of postmodernism and poststructuralism.[7]

Whatever postmodern and poststructural mean these days, they are pervasive, elusive, and marked by a proliferation of conflicting definitions that refuse to settle into meaning. Indeed, refusing definition is part of the theoretical scene. While the terms poststructural, postmodern, and, sometimes, even deconstruction are often used interchangeably as code names for the crisis of confidence in Western conceptual systems, there are distinctions to be made. Postmodern generally refers to the material and historical shifts of the global uprising of the marginalized, the revolution in communication technology, and the fissures of global multinational hyper-capitalism. In art and architecture, it refers to a juxtaposition of classic and modernist elements, sliding meanings and contested boundaries in ways that challenge "uniqueness, authenticity, authority and distance" where "*this new intensity of dis/connection is postmodern*" (Foster, 1996, pp. 219, 221, emphasis in the original).

Poststructuralism refers more narrowly to a sense of the limits of Enlightenment rationality. It particularly foregrounds the limits of consciousness and intentionality and the will to power inscribed in sense-making efforts that aspire to totalizing explanatory frameworks, especially structuralism with its ahistoricism and universalism.

Deconstruction is both a method to interrupt binary logic through practices of reversal and displacement, and an antimethod that is more an ontological claim. Deconstruction "happens," Derrida says, as an outcome of the way language undoes itself (Derrida, in Caputo 1997a, p. 9).

Some call for the end of theory, by which they mean poststructuralism. John Schad, for example, in a book entitled *life.after.theory* writes that "the moment of 'high' theory appears to have passed" including "Lacanian psychoanalysis, Kristevan feminism, Althusserean Marxism, Derridean deconstruction and Foucauldian history" (2003a, p. ix). This death is attributed to many things: the excesses of "careless readers of Nietzsche everywhere" (Payne in Norris, 2003, p. 79); the ethical unintelligibility that results from the leveling of distinctions between truth and falsity (Norris, 2003); a "hopeless skeptical impasse" (Norris, 2003, p. 113) quite unprepared to deal with the shifting terrain of right-wing political and neo-Christian movements.

The death of theory is held to be hastened by neoliberal audit culture and its demand for a new scientism of transparent and quantifiable value.[8] "[B]usy declining in a university 'near you' in the second half of the nineties," Schad cites books with such titles as *After Theory*, *Beyond Poststructuralism*, and *Post-Theory*.[9] In the subsequent interviews with Jacque Derrida, Frank Kermode, Toril Moi, and Christopher Norris, such linear thinking is interrupted, complicated, doubled, and, especially in Moi's case, endorsed.[10]

Getting Lost explores how to live in such contradictory times by arguing that we are not so much at the end of theory as at "neither the beginning nor the end" of what Derrida terms "the age of . . . [impossible] formalization of deconstruction into methods" (2001, p. 69). Such an age is part of a general "seismic tremor . . . within the culture and within the University" given the "identification crisis" around decolonization (p. 61). Gayatri Spivak (1999) calls this moment, usefully, "the setting to work of deconstruction" in struggles for social justice. It is here that *Getting Lost* is located. Writing against the authoritative voice of the kinds of knowledge we are used to, knowledges of demarcation and certitude, this book challenges the social imaginary about research in the human sciences and addresses the problem areas where contemporary researchers are stuck. Its sensibility is toward that which shakes any assured ontology of the 'real,' of presence and absence, a postcritical logic of haunting and undecidables.[11] A central claim is that such aporetic suspension is ethical practice in disenchanted times.

Plateau 2: (Post) Critical Ethnography

I hope that the truth of my book is in the future.

—Foucault, in Dillon, 1980

In this shifting definitional field, philosopher John Caputo prefers the term postcritical to postmodern, given the latter's "opportunistic overuse" (1997c, p. 119). In earlier writing on pedagogy, I delineated postcritical as that which foregrounds movement beyond the sedimented discursive configurations of essentialized, romanticized subjects with authentic needs and real identities, who require generalized emancipation from generalized social oppression via the mediations of liberatory pedagogues capable of exposing the "real" to those caught up in the distorting meaning systems of late capitalism. Within postcritical practices, emancipatory space is problematized via deconstruction of the Enlightenment equation of knowing, naming, and emancipation. "Especially placed under suspicion are the philosophies of presence that assume the historical role of self-conscious human agency and the vanguard role of critical intellectuals [via] crusading rhetoric [stuck in a framework that] sees the 'other' as the problem for which they are the solution . . . [This] may have more to do with the end of some speaking for others than the end of liberatory struggle" (Lather 1992a, pp. 131–32).

For Caputo (1997c), postcritical means post-Kantian in the sense of a continued commitment to critique and demystification of truth but with a meta layer of being critical of demystification itself. He posits a postmodern modernity that mimes the Enlightenment desire for universals and demystification, a new Enlightenment of testimony and witness that differs from the authoritative voice of verification, proof, or demonstration (p. 154). Out of engagement with Derrida's *Specters of Marx*, Caputo sees poststructuralism and postmodernism as ways to continue emancipation but by another means.

As the last turn in the preceding box of turns, Caputo (1997c) calls on a shift from a Kuhnian to a more Benjaminian/messianic sense of crisis that calls on the resources of theology as a way through the aporias of modernity. Caputo elaborates that, in positing a shift from Kuhn to something more messianic, Derrida writes not about a paradigm shift in understanding but about "a more Jewish . . . ethico-political" grasp of difference that "shatters understanding, that underlines the saliency of the incomprehensible, something we confess we do not understand." This is not a new way of seeing but, rather, "a blindness, a confession that we are up against something . . . to which we can only bear witness" (p. 74).

"Past the post" (Knauft, 1994) of the new ethnography of epistemological wrestling with representation, blurred genres and the ethics of the gaze, such a shift asks how we come to think of things this way and what would be made possible if we were to think ethnography otherwise, as a space surprised by difference into the performance of practices of not-knowing. Meaning, reference, subjectivity, objectivity, truth, tradition, ethics: what would it mean to say "yes" to what might come from unlocking such concepts from regularizing and normalizing? A postsecular, postcritical, post-Enlightenment undecidability becomes not the last word, but the first in making room for something else to come about. Motored by a desire to stop confining the other within the same, this is a sort of preparation that is more about not being so sure, about practices of deferral while entire problematics are recast and resituated away from standard logics and procedures (Caputo, 1997c).

Plateau 3: A Poststructural Science 'After Truth': Ethnography as Index

[P]ost-modernism involves the development of new rhetorics of science, new stories of knowledge 'after truth.'

—Tomlinson, 1989

Poststructuralism understands structures as historically and reciprocally affected by practice within contingent conditions of time, particularly conceptual practices and how they define disciplinary knowledges (Prado, 1995, p. 154). It is about complicating reference, not denying it, through a profound vigilance regarding how language does its work. It is a skepticism not about the "real," but about "when a language is taken to be what being itself would say were it given a tongue" (Caputo, 1997c, p. 17). What do we speak of when we speak of a poststructural science 'after truth'?

The theoretical and methodological competitiveness of "successor regimes" (Harding, 1991) that continues to characterize social inquiry often positions the "new" ethnography as some sort of savior. To the contrary, Deborah Britzman (1997) points out that such research is filled with sacred objects to be recovered, restored, centered. There is a tendency to avoid the difficult story, to want to restore the good name of inquiry with these "new" and "better" methods. But research "can't seem to get it right," Britzman writes (p. 35), and too often our efforts fall back into the too easy to tell story of salvation via one sort of knowledge practice or another.

Rather than heroism or rescue through some improved methodology, Britzman argues that we may be in a time and place where we are better served by ethnography if it is positioned as a means to see the need to be wounded by thought as an ethical move. "Incited by the demand for voice and situatedness" (1997, p. 31), she writes about the curious history of ethnography's mistaken identities and asks whether it can be a mode of thought that refuses to secure itself with the consolations of foundationalism and nostalgia for presence, the lost object of correct knowledge, the security of understanding (Britzman, 1998). This is a move out of a "devotional scientism" and toward what Nietzsche (1974) termed a "gay science."[12] A gay science is based in the very splintering of the mechanisms of control and the resultant incredulity about salvation narratives of scientific progress, reason, and the overadministered world. Such a move uses poststructuralism to distinguish between scientism and a more expanded notion of scientificity.

The received and familiar story of ethnography is that it studies the production of everyday life by often "othered" people analyzed at the level of meaning, social structure, power relations, and history. Its specific disciplinary claim is its ability to situate culture as relative in order to denaturalize via cultural comparison. Because of both its subject and its process, often despite itself, ethnography has escaped, perhaps a bit, the sort of scientism that haunts other disciplinary methodologies. As a double practice, both science and a wanderer outside of the scientific paradigm it unevenly purports to follow, it exists between travelogue and science, narrative and method, story and data in a space Harry Walcott has termed "the most humanistic of the sciences and the most scientific of the humanities"

(Mehan, 1995, p. 242). Now, at the cultural moment of the decanonization of science, this marginal scientific status well situates ethnography as a productive site of doubt if one can manage to avoid the "too strong, too erect, too stiff" (Caputo, 1993, p. 161) in working the inside/outside of ethnography. This entails being adept at its practices and moving within its disciplinary habits while disrupting its tendencies to congratulate itself on being the knowledge-producing practice best situated in the contemporary scene to learn from its instructive complications.

In the last decade or so, the "new" ethnography has turned on itself and a sort of "self-abjection" has come to characterize the field (i.e., Behar, 1996). Full of a sense of failed promises, charged anxieties, and mourned history, ethnography is trying to think its self-estrangement as a way out of a mimetic relation to the natural sciences with their mathematized empiricism in the face of the refractory object of its study (Albanese, 1996, p. 9). If, as Foucault (1998) states, we are freer than we feel, how can we feel freer in this space? How might we think ethnography as "an art of being in between," of finding ways of using the constraining order, of drawing unexpected results from one's abject situation (de Certeau, 1984, p. 30), of making the dominant function in another register, of diverting it without leaving it? What does ethnography give us to hear and understand about the force needed to arrive at the change to come, that which is, perhaps, underway?

Here, one might begin to speak of a "new" new ethnography or a (post)ethnography,[13] deferred and diffused across disciplines and working borders and wrestling with urgent questions in moving into postfoundational practices. In postfoundational thought, as opposed to the more typical sort of mastery project, one epistemologically situates oneself as curious and unknowing. This is a methodology of "getting lost," where we think against our own continued attachments to the philosophy of presence and consciousness that undergirds humanist theories of agency. Methodologically assuming no privileged signifier, no exclusivity, no priority or predominance, here is where the journey of thinking differently begins: moments in the politics of truth (Foucault, 1970).

Such counternarratives of science help to situate ethnography with/in the postmodern as a science "after truth" (Tomlinson, 1989). Here the discipline of science becomes the rigor of staging and watching oneself engage with the question of knowledge and the production of the object, the referent. The object is bottomlessly resistant to nomination, attached to its specificity and its surfaces of visibility. As noted by art historian Steven Melville (1996), things are present and complete, but the "truth" of them depends on what is visible/knowable via highly troubled knowledge practices, including ethnography itself under conditions of postmodernity. It is to that that I turn next: not ethnography *among* the ruins, but the ruins of ethnography.

Plateau 4: Working the Ruins

The object of philosophical criticism is to show that the function of
artistic form is as follows: to make historical content . . . into a philosophical truth. This transformation of material content into truth content
makes the decrease in effectiveness, whereby the attraction of earlier
charms diminishes decade by decade, into the basis for a rebirth, in
which all ephemeral beauty is stripped off, and the work stands as a ruin.

—Walter Benjamin, 1977

What opens up when inquiry is situated as a ruin? In an address to the
American Historical Association, Judith Butler (1993a) draws on Walter
Benjamin's "Theses on the Philosophy of History" in order to gesture toward
the value of taking the failure of teleological history, whether Marxist, messianic, or, in its most contemporary formulation, the triumph of Western
democracy (e.g., Fukuyama) as the very ground for a different set of social
relations. It is the ruins of progressivist history, naive realism, and transparent
language that allow us to see what beliefs have sustained these concepts; only
now, at the their end, Butler argues, does their unsustainability become clear.
Hiroshima, Auswitz, Mai Lai, AIDS, for example, make belief in history's
linear unfolding forwardness unsustainable.

In such a time and place, terms understood as no longer fulfilling their
promise do not become useless. On the contrary, their very failures become
provisional grounds, and new uses are derived, "the site of an attempt to
trans-value" in Bill Readings words (1996, p. 129). The claim of universality,
for example, "will no longer be separable from the antagonism by which it
is continually contested" in moving toward a configuration of ethics and
sociality that is other to the Hegelian dream of a reconciliation that absorbs
difference into the same (Butler, 1993a, p. 6). Butler terms this "the ethical
vitalization" (p. 7) of the failure of certain kinds of ideals, a Nietzschean
tranvaluation of working the ruins of such ideals as the very ground of what
playwright Tony Kushner has termed "non-stupid optimism" in struggles for
social justice (de Vries, 1992).

Moving across levels of the particular and the abstract, trying to avoid
a transcendent purchase on the object of study, we set ourselves up for necessary failure in order to learn how to find our way into postfoundational
possibilities. The task becomes to throw ourselves against the stubborn materiality of others, willing to risk loss, relishing the power of others to constrain our interpretive "will to power," saving us from narcissism and its
melancholy through the very otherness that cannot be exhausted by us, the
otherness that always exceeds us. To situate inquiry as a ruin/rune is to

foreground the limits and necessary misfirings of a project, problematizing the researcher as "the one who knows." Placed outside of mastery and victory narratives, inquiry becomes a kind of self-wounding laboratory for discovering the rules by which truth is produced. Attempting to be accountable to complexity, thinking the limit becomes our task, and much opens up in terms of ways to proceed for those who know both too much and too little.

In her debate with Benhabib, Butler writes,

> For that sphere [of politics] will be the one in which those very theoretical constructions—those without which we imagine we cannot take a step—are in the very process of being lived as ungrounded, unmoored, in tatters, but also, as recontextualized, reworked, in translation, as the very resources from which a postfoundational politics is wrought (1995, p. 131).

In this move, the concept of ruins is not about an epistemological skepticism taken to defeatist extremes, but rather about a working of repetition and the play of difference as the only ground we have in moving toward new practices (Butler, 1993a).

Plateau 5: Loss and Lost, Lost, Lost[14]

> In a certain way, there is perhaps no voyage worthy of the name except one that takes place there where, in all senses of the word, one loses oneself, one runs such a risk, without even taking or assuming this risk: not even of losing oneself but of getting lost.
>
> —Derrida, in Malabou and Derrida, 2004

My interest in this book is in a sort of historical/philosophical take on loss that particularly draws on Walter Benjamin's ideas about mourning. While the work of mourning in the context of science will be addressed in a later chapter, in this section, I introduce what getting lost might mean as both methodology and mode of representation.

At its simplest, getting lost is something other to commanding, controlling, mastery. At its most complex, in a Lacanian register, we spend our lives with language trying to make it register what we have lost, longing for lost wholeness. Lack, lost, missing, absence: in the Lacanian world, the referential function is subject to endless substitutions of multiple self-losses, usually unconscious. In this linguistic sense of constitutive loss, meaning enters with the loss of the real, with lost objects, the mother's breast being prime (Cohen, 1998, p. 96).

In a more historical sense of loss, a structural loss, Nietzsche spoke of the death of the old god as unspeakable loss. "How many new gods are yet possible?" was Zarathustra's bewildered cry and today we know this includes the loss of an innocent science too. Other losses include: the unitary, potentially fully conscious subject; researcher self-reflexivity as a "way out" of impasses in ethics and responsibility; and transparent theories of language. Lost also is the clear political object. The frame of our present has shifted across the postcommunist era to a state of "endless war" between neoimperialism and a terrorism without borders and, perhaps, even leaders (Hanley, 2005). Basic categories that have defined and animated oppositional discourses have lost their political purchase. Enlightenment categories of rationality, individual autonomy, and historical development are under suspicion, along with such terms as revolution, socialism, and proletarian democracy. Even feminism becomes a "dinosaur" discourse, the enabling fiction of an earlier generation. Duncker (1999), for example, refers to a "Jurassic feminism" meeting up with queer politics.

History, too, has "lost its way." The grand ideals that allowed us to read history in a particular direction, as a story of progress and emancipation, from the Industrial Revolution and the triumph of science over nature, to the emancipation of the working class, the victory of socialism, and the equality of women, no longer persuade. "All bets are off" as the social history of the 1970s "has lost its coherence as an intellectual project . . . and it has lost its prestige as the natural location for the more radical, innovative, and experimental intellectual spirit in the profession" (Eley, 1996, pp. 213, 225).

Across the disciplines, how to deal with such losses in ways other than nostalgia means accepting the disfigurations of language, loving what we do to ourselves with language (Cohen, 1998, p. 189) including the creative quality of loss itself. Derrida (1995) argues that knowledge that interrupts or derails absolute knowledge is knowledge that loses itself, "gets off the track" in order to expose itself to chance. This is Derrida's "as if to the being lost" (p. 289) in order "to learn by heart," knowledge from and of the other, thanks to the other, "where what it promises always leaves something to be desired" (p. 291).

Over the course of the book, the concept of getting lost functions as a paradox. It is a means of critiquing a certain confidence that research must muster in the audit culture. It is a metaphor for a new generation of postcritical work (Hoy, 2004). It is a way to engage a new interdisciplinarity that is able to question not just the nature of knowledge but its grounds of practice in postfoundational times. Here loss bears the very possibility of Foucault's (1970) idea that, finally, we can begin to think again. Given Derridean theories of the interminability of knowing in the face of the ineffability of the known, new losses are incurred by the necessary stabilization of science. Such losses are just beginning to be thought about, in addition to a more Freudian sense of mourning and loss in the context of the social sciences (Britzman, 2003) and a more Benjaminian sensibility where to be lost is "to be capable of being in uncertainty and mystery . . . a chosen surrender" in order to find what goes beyond what we know (Solnit, 2005, p. 6).

Getting Lost mines such concepts to track an ontology that circumvents foundations. From power and discourse in Foucault, justice and messianicity in Derrida, to being "lost in the Other" as ground of "future transfiguration" in Judith Butler (2004, p. 240), the book delineates the open-endedness of practical action as a structure of praxis and ethics within the context of postfoundational discourse theory.

In theorizing distinctions between loss and lost in working toward research practices that take into account the crisis of representation, how can writing the other not be an act of continuing colonization? To risk writing otherwise is not to find an innocent place, but to use the tensions as a way of learning how to live in de-authorized space. Texts that do justice to the complexity of what we try to know and understand include the tales not told, the words not written or transcribed, the words thought but not uttered, the unconscious: all that gets lost in the telling and the representing. My argument is that a stance of "getting lost" might both produce different knowledge and produce knowledge differently in working toward more Deleuzean "stumbling" practices that take such losses into account.

What to be "rich in loss" might be made to mean is perhaps best evoked in Pitt and Britzman's concept of "difficult knowledge" (2003), knowledge that works otherwise than to secure claims through data. Attempting to theorize the qualities of difficult knowledge, they distinguish between "lovely knowledge" and difficult knowledge. The former reinforces what we think we want from what we find, and the latter is knowledge that induces breakdowns in representing experience. Here, accepting loss becomes the very force of learning, and what one loves when lovely knowledge is lost is the promise of thinking and doing otherwise.

Plateau 6: Derridean Rigor as a Double(d) Science

Deconstruction cannot limit itself or proceed immediately to a neutralization: it must, by means of a double gesture, a double science, a double writing, practice an *overturning* of the classical opposition *and* a general *displacement* of the system. It is only on this condition that deconstruction will provide itself the means with which to *intervene* in the field of oppositions that it criticizes.

—Derrida, 1982

The concept of "doubled" is key in deconstructive logic. A doubled reading offers itself without guarantee or "counter" axiology. Authority becomes contingent, "as an expression of a deeper and fundamental dispute *with authority as such*" (Radhkrishnan, 1996, p. 106, emphasis in original). Hence, a doubled practice must disable itself in some way, unmastering both itself and the pure identity it offers itself against, theorizing the double as a way to move in uneven space. Sometimes referred to as "under erasure," what Derrida (1982, p. 329) writes of as "a double gesture, a double science, a double writing" intervenes in what it critiques by not only overturning the classical opposition but by a general displacement of the system (Nealon, 1993a, b). My interest in a feminist double(d) science, then, means both/and science and not-science, working within/against the dominant, contesting borders, tracing complicity. Here, the doubled task is to gain new insight into what not knowing means toward the telling of not knowing too much, and rigor becomes something other than asserting critical or interpretive mastery.

Derrida speaks of "deconstruction, if there is such a thing" (Caputo, 1997a). Invested in a nonauthoritarian mode of knowledge production, he stages knowledge that de-authorizes itself, that undermines itself through its own operations. Such knowledge recognizes that it differs from itself and will never arrive at plenitude. What is lost here is the unmediated referent that has historically authorized representation as well as certitude and instrumental transparency. Something other than cure and rectification, such knowledge is both affirmation and negation, critique and postcritical valorization, growing out of counterpractices of nonauthoritarian authority that are precisely what I hope to delineate.

It is here that I encounter the double(d) of the Derridean double session: "the deconstructive and the affirmative in an impure, tactical, and nonsynchronous coalition" that aligns projects of affirmation with destabilization of master discourses (Radhkrishnan, 1996, p. 115). Doubled logic cannot abdicate its referential purchase on history and experience. What it abdicates is an axiomatic attitude to representation. Instead, it endorses a problematic attitude, a double reading that is both critique and complicity, a way to move beyond inside and outside. Key to a different logic, it is "the double necessity of working from within the institutional constraints of a tradition even while trying to expose what that tradition has ignored or forgotten" (Nealon, 1993a, p. 101). Rather than essence or origin, the double(d) marks the trial of undecidability as dispersion, dissemination, groundless ground, the always already divided origin, that which can never be mastered, sublated, or dialecticized (Derrida, 1981, p. 221).

One example of this double gesture is Foucault's support of the resistance of people for their "rights," where he paradoxically endorses such protest while simultaneously "submitting the same word to the theoretical and rhetorical work of decapitation, undoing, and reinscription" (Keenan, 1997, p. 166). This "ethico-political" gesture combines practical intervention in the existing relations of force with a philosophical problematizing of the very terms in which the gesture is made. Such a double move is undertaken "while refusing to allow either gesture to escape unscathed . . . Each moment of the double gesture undoes the other" (p. 170). Here, the risk, the chance of the political, is undertaken without guarantees, without opposition, without resolution, truly temporal, unprogrammable, necessary, and inevitable: an impossible praxis.

Plateau 7: A Praxis of Stuck Places

> Morality, politics, responsibility, if there are any, will only ever have begun with the experience of the aporia. When the path is given . . . the decision is already made . . . The condition of possibility of this thing, responsibility, is a certain experience of the possibility of the impossible: the trial of the aporia from which one may invent the only possible invention: the impossible invention.
>
> —Derrida, 1992b

Classically, praxis is the self-creative activity through which we make the world, *the* central concept of a Marxist philosophy that did not want to remain a philosophy, philosophy becoming practical (Bottomore, 1983, p. 386, emphasis in the original). For the Greeks, *praxis* was the realm of free action of citizens (free men), as distinct from *poiesis*, the servile action of necessity. Marx put together a practice of material transformation that brought these together in a relationship of reciprocity with a theorizing quite other to contemplation, "proposing to philosophy that it view itself in the mirror of practice" (Balibar, 1995, p. 41).

The idea of praxis has long given me much to think about and to do. My earlier articulation of "research as praxis" (Lather, 1986a) sought that intersection of material transformation through theory's practice and practice's theory. Reprinted in *Getting Smart* (1991), the chapter on research as praxis is the most cited part of the book, even though I now see it as full of unproblematized assumptions about the role of "transformative intellectuals," ideology critique, a voluntarist philosophy of consciousness, and pretentions toward "emancipating" or "empowering" some others.[15] The failure of most readers to trouble the foundationalism of my concept of "research as praxis" speaks, I think, to the yearning and unsettlement of the academic left, given the demise of humanism and regimes of transcendent generality on the one hand and the "conservative restoration" (Apple, 2001) on the other.

Refusing the much that must be refused in the Hegelian enclosure of dialectics, negative or not, is a tempting move in the face of the much that must be rethought: the concepts of certainty, morality, meaning, and praxis;[16] resistance and agency (Pitt, 1998); the unconscious (Britzman, 1998); empowerment (Orner, 1992); rationalism and dialogue (Ellsworth, 1989, 1997; Leach, 1992): the list goes on. But I am entirely persuaded by poststructural theory that it is what seems impossible from the vantage point of our present regimes of meaning that is the between space of any knowing that will make a difference in the expansion in social justice and the canons of value toward which we aspire. That is precisely the task: to situate the experience of impossibility as an enabling site for working through aporias. Ellsworth calls this "coming up against stuck place after stuck place" as a way to keep moving in order to produce and learn from ruptures, failures, breaks, refusals (1997, pp. xi, 9).

Hence, my interest is a praxis that attends to poststructural suspicions of rationality, philosophies of presence, and universalizing projects, a praxis that moves away from the Marxist dream of "cure, salvation and redemption" (Felman and Laub, 1992, p. 177). Learning to see the imperialism of our continued investments in teleology, "persuasion," consensus, and ideology critique premised on some "real" outside of discursive renderings, the task becomes not so much to invent or incite as to use praxis as a material force to identify and amplify what is already begun toward a practice of living on.

Plateau 8: Naked Methodology

> We no longer believe that truth remains truth when the veils are withdrawn; we have lived too much to believe this. Today we consider it a matter of decency not to wish to see everything naked, or be present at everything and "know" everything.
>
> —Nietzsche, quoted in Kofman, 1988

My interest in nakedness comes from the very material practice of time in hot tubs that has characterized Chris and my methodological wrestling in our study of women living with HIV/AIDS.[17] Grounded in the hours spent in my co-researcher's hot tub where we discussed the project, my interest in nakedness also comes out of a small research retreat in Wisconsin when this project was at its beginning. There, structured around each of seven women having two hours of "exquisite attention" for her work in any way she wanted, I stripped and sat in a jacuzzi in a bathroom surrounded by six dressed women who fired questions at me about the ethics and politics of what I was undertaking.[18]

.   As was evident at that session, such work pushes a lot of buttons for those invested in the politics of knowing and being known. This is as it should be. While naked methodology became a situated practice toward an ethical encounter with the women in our study, it is not about presenting myself as transparent, vulnerable, and absolutely frank. Based on Nietzsche's strong thesis that every word is also a hiding place, an apparent nakedness is but a mask that conceals a will to power. Any illusion of presence unmasked is interrupted by the difficult task Nietzsche invites us to: not to unmask and demystify but, rather, to multiply perspectives toward an affirmation of life as a means to knowledge without guarantee (Kofman, 1993). This is a rigor of staging and watching oneself subvert and revalue the naked truth in order to learn to live without absolute knowledge, within indeterminacy. Based on Derrida's thesis of necessary complicity and what Foucault cautions as the invasive stretch of surveillance in the name of the human sciences, such a project is situated in the loss of innocence of qualitative research, particularly feminist ethnography (Stacey, 1988; Van Maanen, 1995).

To situate inquiry as a laboratory for discovering the rules for the production of truth, I trouble the possibilities for "coming clean" in practices of researcher reflexivity. As June Nash (1997) notes, the first calls for reflexivity in anthropology came in the mid-1960s (p. 18), well before postmodernism appeared on the disciplinary scene. Visweswaran (1994) distinguishes between interpretive/reflexive and deconstructive ethnography. Reflexive ethnography authorizes itself by confronting its own processes of interpretation as some sort of cure toward better knowing, while deconstruction approaches "knowing through not knowing" (p. 80). In delineating reflexivity as a modernist practice, Felman's (1987) distinctions between Hegelian, Nietzschean, and Freudian philosophies of knowledge are useful. The former *"believes it knows all there is to know";* a post-Nietzschean philosophy of knowledge is that "which *believes it knows it does not know*;" and a Freudian philosophy of knowledge is that where authority is given "to the instruction of a knowledge that does not know its own meaning, to a knowledge . . . that is not a mastery of itself" (p. 92, emphasis in original). Mindful of the dangers of reinscribing the potentially fully conscious, individualized, humanist subject, the possibilities of nakedness are theorized as a way to sketch the theory of representation that structures my methodological imperatives.

In this effort, Nietzsche invites us to learn to read well, to decipher the text in order to discover the drives toward mastery in a time when all concepts have lost their meaning, become dislocated, fragments of ruins, no more foundation. How does one manage to live in such as place where desires for the "naked truth" will not do? Nietzsche's best answer was an affirmation of the will that wills itself to illusion, knowing it will not perish without absolute knowledge (Kofman, 1993). The necessary multiplication of perspectives can work toward the solution of the problem of value, "a pragmatism directed toward a use which is yet to come" (p. 127) that turns life into a means to knowledge, fuller of future by risking not being understood as one writes outside traditional norms.

> No cure.
> Immanent value.
> Necessary perspectivalism.
> It's a good thing too (Fish, 1994).

Conclusion

This chapter has delineated what McWilliam (1993) terms "galloping theory" as we try to stay abreast of perpetually reforming knowledge problematics. About more than critical fashion, the motivation for such an effort is to engage in a transvaluative moment regarding the purposes of the social sciences: to further change the terms of the legitimation of knowledge beyond discrete methods and toward the social uses of the knowledge we construct. Caught between a rock of responsibility and a soft place of the received claims of scientism to one-best-way production and legitimation of knowledge, we live out these tensions.[19] Now, in our time of the "rage for accountability" (Lather, 2004a, b) the "methodological fundamentalists" are having their moment; critical researchers are being written off as "ideologues" (Howe, 2004). What is at question is the adequacy of standard methods, the desirability of research and policy goals, and the philosophies of science that prescribe narrow views of these issues.

The crisis of legitimation occurring across knowledge systems is registered in a cacophony of postpositivism, nonfoundationalism, kinds of realism and postrealisms, warranted assertability, logic of inquiry, construct validity, carefully controlled inference, objectivism, situational validity, and Cronbachian insights regarding the decay of generalizations (Garrison, 1994). As will be discussed in subsequent chapters, feminist knowledges, too, are experiencing a crisis of legitimation as they face not just external critiques, but internal debates, critiques, and reflections on the meaning and scope of feminist methodology (Fonow and Cook, 2005).

Suffering from our categories of science and research and the failure of their promise to deliver, our practices are overcoded by the normative, our procedures and operations too much configured into repetitions of banality. To ask what makes certain possibilities impossible for us is to press our uncertainties and to calculate the apparatuses of our capture. What would it mean to create a different space in which to undertake other thinking, an aesthetic space, a political space? What would it mean to create new solidarities, fragments of other possibilities, to experiment differently with meanings, practices, and our own confoundings?

The geography of such questions is very different from opposing a dominant culture considered radically other. It is, as well, to face "a loss that [is] no longer to be undone by willful reflection" (Hanssen, 2001, p. 78). This is about working within/against the dominant, contesting its borders, tracing our complicity, moving toward a double(d) science in order to capture the vitality of the deviations that elude taxonomies in addressing the question of practices of science within a postfoundational context.[20]

Asking what becomes possible when *all* research is positioned as distressed and exceeded, I raise questions about the difficulties and limitations of the categories we use to do our work. Much thinking has been going on in such a place, particularly in the tensions across our paradigmatic divides. For those who have moved out from under a narrow scientificity, other practices are being rehearsed toward changing the social imaginary about research. Moving beyond the normalized apparatuses of our own training, a social science more answerable to the complications of our knowing is beginning to take shape. Feminist methodology has been no small contributor to "the changing shape of the thinkable" (Gordon, 1991, p. 3) and it is my fondest hope that this book can contribute to this continuing invention of ourselves into "the surprise of what is not yet possible in the histories of the spaces in which we find ourselves" (Rajchman, 1991, p. 163).

Interlude

(Excerpted) Interview with Patti Lather

conducted by Rubby Dhunpath and Juliet Perumal
21 November 2001, Durban, South Africa

Rubby: We would like to begin by asking you to share with us, briefly, something of your academic life history.

Patti: I went to Indiana University and got a doctorate in Curriculum Studies and I was fortunate that Egon Guba was there at the time. He had made this paradigm conversion into qualitative research. Because he was so famous as a quantitative researcher when he started talking about qualitative research, people listened to him. That was in the late '70s and early '80s. I was fortunate enough to be able to do a qualitative dissertation, one of the first, in the program there.

And I was also fortunate that when I had to declare my minor, the Women's Studies doctoral minor had just been approved, so I was in the first group of women to get that and that was a very fertile combination for me. At one point Guba asked me how I got so smart and I said it was because of that combination. And I developed my first theoretical/methodological thinking, and I was 30 after five years of public school teaching when I began my doctoral work.

I finished the doctorate in 1983 and went off for my first university job. I went up to [Mankato] Minnesota for five years and taught Women's Studies and it was a very heavy teaching load but it was a wonderful program. It was a praxis Master's program and women came from all over the world, from all sorts of feminist activism and they wanted their Master's for a variety of legitimating purposes and, I think, just understanding themselves and their work better. It was a very fertile place for a young academic to get started and I developed some wonderful habits that have served me very well. And then I've been at Ohio State since 1988.

Rubby: If you were to reflect on your own life as a researcher, who and what were the sources of your inspiration?

Patti: Well, obviously with Guba and he was a force of fire and zeal. Watching someone who was not a young man and watching someone who could change was inspirational. He had a huge paradigm shift in his late career and became very open to feminism, for example.

And then the other big influence on me was feminist work. I became a thinker with feminist work and I got into it when I was teaching. I taught high school American History and I was desperate to bring in women's perspectives and there was at that time very little literature, so I learned to be a learner. But when I went to university and got into feminist research methodology, I was very motivated and, again, because of what I was getting from both Guba and the feminists, I was able to put it together in a way that was extremely energizing for me. And in some ways that energy is still here.

I was energized by the whole set of questions and critical perspectives from feminists on doing science. It was just all new and when I went into doctoral work I knew I had to do research and I assumed it would be quantitative, that was all I knew of science. I was an English major, I did literary criticism, I analyzed novels, that was what I knew. But the idea that I was going to have to do science! I saw it as a bitter pill I had to swallow. I figured I'd take some classes and sew some numbers together, but I wasn't very thrilled about it. And then after feminist research methodology opened up, I started getting thrilled.

I was also fortunate in that probably the biggest single help at that time for me was when the National Women's Studies Conference came to town. And I got in on the organizational committee and then when the program came out I very deliberately tracked the feminist research methodology sessions. I found seven sessions on feminist research methodology and I went to every one of them. I had developed a bibliography so I had a sense of the issues. I got to hear the big women in the area and they were all very excited too, because of course this was the first time they had ever gathered together themselves. So it was like being in on the front end of a newly born baby where the energy was just palpable and the freshness of it was very exciting.

Juliet: Is that what inspired your book *Getting Smart*?

Patti: Sure, and then I was just lucky that education was ready and hadn't had much feminist poststructural work, so I was able to be one of the first voices in education to bring these ideas to bear. Of course, there were certainly other women working in those areas including early feminist work in education.

Juliet: What are some challenges that you face as a White woman researcher and as a researcher working within the paradigm that you do?

Patti: Well, I think the race issue, as you well know, is very compli- cated and a Black woman told me "I thought you were a Black woman!" She was just shocked. She said, "It took me half your session to get over the shock." I said, "Well, what made you think I was a Black woman?" She wasn't exactly sure, but she said just . . .

Rubby: But isn't that interesting . . . many of us at UDW thought you were a Black woman . . . before we saw your photograph . . . because you give such an articulate Black perspective, on issues that do not really concern a White woman.

Patti: Oh, this is so interesting. And I'm thrilled with this, but also bothered because it says . . . it makes me wonder if I've falsely represented myself somehow. Everybody's supposed to say 'as a White woman,' when you're writing which I agree with to some extent—but not too much. I thought, well God, maybe I've misrepresented myself. And I went back and looked at *Getting Smart* and there's a place in there where I say 'as a White woman.' Well she must not have read that part.

That's one sort of unexpected complication with race—when you actu- ally get mistaken for a different race than what you are in ways that are both pleasing and worrisome, but disorienting in some ways.[1] I mean very, very simply, the big challenge is access in terms of who tells whose story. We're doing our work at a time of fierce identity politics and these issues about insider or outsider, and who has the right to tell these stories are just huge and complicated. Here I am in the angels book trying to do work on women and AIDS and many of those women were women of color as well as HIV positive. I was like a double outsider. So how do you access those sorts of things, and in a way earn your stripes? According to the qualitative literature, you do this by learning, building trust and rapport and each research project has a different shape around that.

Rubby: What are some of the challenges that you face as a re- searcher working within the paradigm that you do? How do you nego- tiate these challenges?

Patti: I'm a full professor, so I don't have to negotiate much at all. I can do anything I want to, which is quite a wonderful freedom. Nonetheless, trying to get the angels book published was a challenge because it has a very marginal sort of layout. This was actually one of the biggest worries of my professional career. I had done this work, I had worked with these women, they had trusted me with their stories, they were very invested in having the book come out—I couldn't find a publisher! Unbeknownst to me at the time the publishing world was going through a shake up. I had thought that be- cause my first book was successful that I would have carte blanche and that they would be lined up at the door to publish my second book, but quite the opposite. I was just getting sick about it, until I finally found a publisher that would publish it as long as we paid for the layout. So Chris and I, we just bit the bullet and went ahead and split the costs and paid upfront for it to be published. That was the only way that we could get it done.

Rubby: How does the research supervisor maintain the integrity of scholastic rigor while encouraging experimentation with alternative research genres?

Patti: I insist with my students that they learn the interpretive paradigm first. In order to deconstruct something you've got to have something to deconstruct. I won't let them just come in and start doing experimental work. They need to understand what the center of the field has been and once I feel like they've got that, then I'm encouraging of them to start experimenting. I make them write what John van Maanen calls the "realist tale" in his *Tales of the Field* where he talks of 13 ways you can tell data stories. The big one, he says, and about 85% of all fieldwork, is what he calls realist tales. And then you have the confessional tale and the critical tale and the feminist tale, etc. Then if they want to tell another kind of tale or three other kinds of tales, or some like to do videos or write poems and whatever, they can do all of that, anything they want after they've done the standard thing.

Then it comes to how do you bring the quality criteria to bear on the more experimental? I make them give me their framework for evaluating. So, for example, I had one student, Wanda Pillow, she was researching programs for pregnant girls and she came up with what she called "the validity of discomfort" (Pillow, 2003). And then she had to articulate that and evaluate her own work based on her own validity criteria that were immanent and accessible within her own work. She ended up with a lovely paper that included this "validity of discomfort" and contributed to the validity literature. That's one way to do it.

Juliet: What, from your perspective, makes feminist research distinctively feminist?

Patti: Is there a distinctive feminist methodology? I used to think the answer was no, but I'm starting to think maybe it's more complicated than that. All these emancipatory identity-based methodologies, they end up looking pretty much the same. So then you ask, is there a distinctive Afro-centric methodology or feminist methodology? And now there's gay and lesbian. I went to an AERA session a couple of years ago on Latina research methodology and they all sound Freirerian to me when it comes right down on the ground.

One of my former students, Jim Scheurich, has co-written a wonderful piece called *Coloring Epistemologies: Are our Research Epistemologies Racially Biased?* Now not only have you got a certain distinct methodology, but is there a distinctive epistemology? So I've been discussing with him around this issue for a couple of years and I say to him, "But what's the difference between coloring epistemology and feminist epistemology?" I can certainly listen to arguments that at particular points in history particular groups of people need to be able to claim their own this or that. That's strategic and as long as you go about the strategic well, I think you're doing just what you need to be doing. But don't get confused and think that strategic epistemological claims are anything other than an historical strategy. Also don't forget that there's something to be said for joining forces and recognizing that you're involved in the same project as opposed to somehow thinking that you've got to have an absolutely different thing going on.

Rubby: In your mind Patti, has there been any tangible, physical ways in which feminist research has contributed to the field of research?

Patti: I think it's been part of this multisited effort to shift science. Feminist methodology started bubbling up in the late '70s, early '80s and I'm trying to think if there were any identity-based alternative methodologies before that. So it might have been at least one of the first to articulate a system around identity-based ways of knowing. I think in terms of the number of women that were in the academy, particularly in the social sciences, who went through feminist experiences—that excitement I was talking about in the early days spread like wild fire. If you were a woman in the academy it was pretty hard not to be aware of it. Although not all women went along with it, you had to know about it.

So whatever the contribution feminism has made I think it opened doors, it shook things down, it was extremely marginal and you had to fight for legitimacy. But enough good work kept happening in the middle of the struggles so that at a certain point there was an accumulation of work that was, even if you thought it was crap, there was just so much of it. And it was across the disciplines. It was everywhere and you just couldn't get away from it. I think that accumulation of things ends up buying you some legitimacy, even if it's very begrudged.

Juliet: Feminists who are critical of feminist discourses/practices are often construed as enemies within, who dilute the political solidarity necessary to effect social emancipation. What is your response to this allegation?

Patti: I hope we're past it. I think in any kind of movement there's a period of fragility where you argue that you can't air your dirty linen in public because it undercuts the strength and unity. You must present a unified front to the outside, which is "the enemy" trying to attack us and keep us from breathing.

But as the movement gets stronger it shifts and you start being self-critical. You've always got internal critique and at some point you start feeling strong enough that the internal critique becomes part of your strength and being able to be public about that is part of growing legitimacy.

Also, one of my investments is post work. Post work doesn't let you set yourself up as somehow this innocent successor regime that's got the right answers. It makes you face complicity; it makes you face internal critique, self-reflectivity. Then of course the post could be its own celebration of itself. We can fall back into those patterns of successor regimes and truth claims and I think we are so deeply enmeshed in competitive truth games that it's hard to break out.

Juliet: In your book *Getting Smart*, you speak of the 'possibilities of critical social science' and 'the politics of empowerment.' Jennifer Gore, among others, has critiqued such a positionality by arguing that feminist pedagogues/researchers *assume* that they are *already* empowered and are therefore in a position to empower others. How would you respond to this charge?

Patti: Well I thoroughly agree. I find it very interesting that in *Getting Smart,* chapter 3 on research as praxis gets cited the most. That piece is the oldest work in there and by the time I wrote the book I was already very critical of it, but Michael Apple was my series editor and he very clearly said to me, "It's that chapter that made us want you to write the book in this series."

So I left that chapter as it had originally been published and in the next chapter on feminist empowering research, I do a self-critique. I think that was what the post does too, it does make you look at these impositional tendencies that I think are the big danger of critical perspectives. Critical theory has been a very strong and important force in bringing the idea to bear that there is no neutral knowledge and it is politics all the way down. But I think it's like a hammer, it's pretty sure it's right, and it has taken the posts to make that clear.

Rubby: What makes *Troubling the Angels* distinctively different from your previous work?

Patti: *Troubling the Angels* was very unusual in that it was research by invitation. I was invited in to do a job and get a story out. That profoundly shaped what I did. These women didn't want socioeconomic analysis of macro forces of empire. They wanted their stories told. I had a huge shaping influence on the story and how it got told and insisted on the angel intertext as a place to bring history and sociology and a little political theory to bear, but it's mostly the story of their voices, because that's the job that I was brought in to do. So I think that makes the project pretty different from most social science research.

Rubby: Have there been any spin-offs for you in terms of how it has shaped your own research?

Patti: Well I'm in the process right now of writing *Getting Lost*. It is essentially a methodology book. It will be like *Getting Smart* 10 years later (probably more like 15 years by the time it comes out). And it's all coming out of my learning experiences from doing that book. It is a profound shaping influence. I had already gotten into poststructuralism by the time of *Getting Smart* where I was pretty much asking: "Well what difference does poststructuralism make in terms of our research approaches?"

But the angels book forced me into dealing with voices. Poststructuralism makes you suspicious of voices as some innocent uncomplicated story. There were these 25 voices and my suspicions, and my seductions and my wanting to get in the way and interrupt the romance of voice and my wanting to get out of the way and let the power of voice go forward. And those sorts of tensions were littered throughout that work and, I think, I'm the better researcher for it.

I experienced very keenly the idea of doing something under erasure. I was doing voices under erasure and to work under erasure means to both do it and trouble it at the same time, hence the title *Troubling the Angels*. It was about troubling methodology. And I was the troubled researcher. My co-researcher was a much more straight-ahead kind of girl and would have been very happy to have a more straight-ahead Susie's story, Mary's story, Gloria's story, sort of unproblematic telling of the women's stories. As we worked, our actual negotiation was how to both do that and trouble that at the same time. Given our negotiations around our very different ideas about what this book was going to be, the form of the book became a sort of organic outgrowth of our negotiations about her wanting a straight-ahead story and me wanting to trouble the straight-ahead story. It demonstrates how fertile working such tension can be. It would have been a very different book without the two of us. We came to have great appreciation for our differences because it was actually the negotiation of our differences that profoundly changed the book. And for the better, I think.

Rubby: You have co-authored *Troubling the Angels* with Chris Smithies who is a psychologist, who comes from a medical background, which ostensibly draws from clinical models of research. How have you negotiated the fundamental differences in ideologies and philosophies that characterize your respective approaches?

Patti: Chris is a feminist but she knew nothing about qualitative research although she knew that's what she had to have. She knew she didn't want statistics. It was about telling the women's stories. She knew nothing about the crisis of representation, nothing about post sorts of stories, nothing about suspicions of the innocence of the seeming straight-ahead story and I was deeply into all of that. Also Chris is not particularly interested in having me educate her about it, and I guess the flashpoint would be the angels. She hated the angels. I got into them fairly early in the study and we fought—not awful—but very productively from the beginning, around these angels. She just could not understand why they would be in there at all! What were they doing in there? And I would have to try to explain it to her. And I never, never successfully explained it to her. But through our efforts to try to negotiate that, we made spaces for both of us in the book and the angels kind of became Patti's thing, and I was given space although the angel intertexts were originally much longer and she made me shorten them down.

Juliet: She clipped its wings?

Patti: Yes, she clipped the wings considerably and so that negotiation with her, particularly around the angels and how much of them and how little of them and what they were doing in there, and why we should care and whether they added or subtracted, interrupted, or deconstructed was a big part of the project. In her quest (and I think she would actually agree with this) she got inside deconstruction a little bit, although I never called it that. By troubling the angels, troubling became my code word for deconstruction. That was a word that could travel outside the academy and do deconstruction, but never have to say the word. I don't think the word 'deconstruction' is in the book at all, and yet I would argue that this is an extremely deconstructive book. It enacts deconstruction.

I was wrestling with how to do this and, of course, the big pressure was how to do justice to the women's stories. How can a deconstructive girl do justice to the enormous weight and richness of these 25 women's stories? How can you both do justice to these stories and interrupt the idea of the transparent, innocent voicing of stories? My definition of justice became enacting deconstruction in a way that didn't shut the women out from reading their own stories! I mean, surely whatever doing justice to their stories was, it meant they had to be able to read and understand their own stories—that was pretty clear. And a broader audience had to be able to read and understand and get access to those stories—that was pretty clear. So how was I to bring deconstruction to bear given that sort of a mandate? At one point I realized enacting was the key. I needed to do deconstruction instead of talking about deconstruction. Once I figured that out then things started to fall into place.

Juliet: In critical ethnographic research, researchers are sensitive toward not violating the realities of research participants. This sometimes means constraining the researcher's analytical voice, manipulating data representation, etc. Is this manipulation and analytical quietude an abdication of interpretative responsibility?

Patti: This question cuts right to the heart of the major problems I had with trying to honor the women's stories and also bring my interpretive responsibilities (which in this case happen to be deconstructive) to bear. Frankly, that's why we did the split text with the women's stories at the top and then voice, voice, voice, voice, voice all over the place—a lot of it. Yet I was able to come in at the bottom and do my thing. So it's a both-and instead of an either-or. What I didn't do much in the book was theorize the data. I certainly theorized the method—it's very methodological. One of the criticisms of the book is that I didn't really analyze the data that much. The data does sort of speak for itself. There is one part in the book where I theorize the data; it's only a few pages and I do it and then I trouble the doing of it. Exactly what does it mean for me to come in with my interpretive voice and say what things mean and how can that not be a sort of imposition of somebody else's framework? Could it possibly be a gift? I wrestled with those issues in the book. I basically walked away from it and didn't do very much of it. I think if I were redoing the book now I would do more interpretation, still troubling what it means to do that, but I would do it and trouble it, instead of trouble it and not do it. One of my worries about the book is that it will actually feed this idea that data can speak for itself which I see students doing too much of in the narrative turn. I won't allow my own students that. Some of my students will say, "Well, but in your book you don't do that so how come we have to?" And then my answer is, "Because I'm a full professor and you're not."

Juliet: You talk about *Troubling the Angels* as a gift to these 25 women whose stories get told. In the light of the Gore et al. criticism regarding feminists and empowerment, does the word *gift* not become a synonym for empowerment?

Patti: I think that you have to be careful around situating yourself as the great emancipator. Foucault has this wonderful phrase, I'm not going to remember it all but he says, "People know what they do, they often know why they do what they do, but what they don't know is how what they do fits into larger frameworks." And that's the gift an academic can give, that is to situate the stories within these larger frameworks. That's our work. And if it's done sensitively it can be a gift.

I think sometimes constraining the researcher's analytical voice is a good thing to do. I call it getting in the way, getting out of the way—there's that dance—getting in the way of the data, getting out of the way of the data. In manipulating the data, we can't not do that, there's no way. Even if, like in *I, Rigoberta Menchu*, where it looked like Menchu just sat there and unreeled her story, what you've got there is the invisible manipulation of data. There's always the manipulation of data. So, whether you want to make your manipulations visible, whether you want to foreground or background that manipulation, that's the decision you have to make as the researcher. But you can't get away from manipulating the data. That's what we do!

Juliet: *Troubling the Angels* 'is a book about the limits of what can be said and known about the lives of others.' While acknowledging the limits of what can be said about the researched, what are your views about the trend for researchers to resort to what Goodson refers to as 'pornographic narratives' (i.e., narratives that are prone to explicit self-disclosure and exposure of the researcher so that the research product takes on the status of a confessional)?

Patti: John van Maanen calls it vanity ethnography and that's a phrase that I've used quite a bit in my own work. This is another one of those really serious concerns about the direction that, in this case, educational research is going. I'm very happy to have the embodied researcher foregrounding the moves they're making and the wrestling they're doing with the project, but being careful not to take over the story with that sort of stuff is a big tension in work right now.

In fact, a sort of common understanding of qualitative work is that the researcher is the instrument, and who you are, and how you are in the world is a huge part of the study and Foucault says it is all autobiography anyway, and I think that's not untrue. But I think we do fieldwork in order to get outside of ourselves and we have to be careful in this particular moment to not get too enamored with reflexivity. If we say we're going to study so-and-so, then let's make sure that the focus is on so-and-so, not to leave our stories out, but to contain them and milk them for what they can add to the depth of analysis.

Juliet: In *Troubling the Angels* you are sensitive to the fine line between 'making a spectacle of these women's struggles and wanting to speak quietly . . . in the hope that it will make it better for others.' From personal experience, we observe what may be construed as an extreme pendulum swing towards privileging emotional data. Is this tendency sliding into a simple opposition to what we have critiqued positivism for: the shift from a preoccupation with rationality to extreme emotionality?

Patti: Again, this is a big concern of mine as I read across a variety of, particularly student work, but also some more advanced academic work. To a certain extent the answer is yes and it's necessary. I mean a very classic move of deconstruction is you identify the binaries, you reverse them and then you use the energy of the reversal to try to get to the third place which is both-and AND neither-nor—both rational and emotional and something that is neither rational nor emotional. And I think we've done the reversal and we're trying to get to the third space. We've got to remember that we're trying to get beyond the necessary reversal. But you can get stuck in the reversal and the point of the reversal is to use the energy of reversal to make that very difficult move into new space. What we're trying to do is get beyond the binary of rationality and emotionality into a place that is both of them and yet some place that is beyond both of them.

We wrestled with this in *Troubling the Angels*. We spent a lot of energy, for example, trying to make sure we focused on the day-to-day and not just the sensational aspects of living with HIV/AIDS. We spent a lot of energy trying to show that these women spent time, helping their kids with homework and having to wrestle economically with how do you feed your kids when you don't have enough money and the day-to-day issues that are "just like lots of people." When the story of their lives was presented to a reading public, the reading public could see that these women were just like them in a lot of ways, but also different from them in a lot of ways.

And the text had many purposes, some of which I've alluded to here, but one of them I haven't talked about yet is to get a less voyeuristic gaze. You start feeling like you're getting closer to these women and knowing these women and then that is interrupted by the layout. In fact you can't ever quite get your hands on them and so you get frustrated because we want to consume, we want to do what bell hooks calls "eating the other" in the culture of consumption. The book is actually set up to try to interrupt that easy consumption of the other. One of the problems with walking a fine line is you don't know if you were successful or not. There are places in the book where I think we fall off this way, or we fall off that way, but walking that fine line was a big part of the work of the book.

Rubby: Does *Troubling the Angels* court the danger of romanticizing and exoticizing AIDS sufferers and the pandemic?

Patti: Sure, sure it courts that danger. It tries to walk that fine line between neither demonizing nor angelizing. The not angelizing was our insistence on bringing the not-so-pretty parts of their stories in and including the woman who had sex with men without protection and never told them.

Not demonizing them was easy. The struggle I, and Chris particularly had, she's nuts about these women—she's been working with them for many years and is just in love with them—a love affair of great enormity. I had to struggle with her, for example, to make sure the not-so-pretty parts were in there. It was not difficult to convince her. She knew that it had to happen, but it was a part of the book that didn't make them look so good, so we had to negotiate it to make sure it got in there.

The larger question about the field in general is yes, I think there's a romance of the marginal, there's a certain cultural capital in working with the marginal in terms of the academy. If I don't bring race to bear on work I get criticized, but if I do bring race to bear I get criticized. Normally you're going to get it from both sides anyway, even if you do try to negotiate with a certain sensitivity—that's just where we're at.

Chapter 2

Methodology as Subversive Repetition

Practices toward a Feminist Double(d) Science

> The book experience: *Troubling the Angels.*—Methodological responsi-
> bility.—Feminist experimental ethnographies.—Double(d) practices of
> representation.—Getting lost: Textwork, headwork, fieldwork.—Disap-
> pointment as a rubric.

Michel Foucault has spoken of "the book experience" as "designed to change
what one thinks and perhaps even what one is" (Ransom, 1997, p. 175).[1] This
chapter is about research into the lives of others as a troubling, as an ethical
move outside mastery, heroism, and the wish for rescue through some "more
adequate" research methodology. It is grounded in both the "new" ethnography, that which comes after the crisis of representation (Marcus and Fischer,
1986), and the ethnography to come, what Jacques Derrida refers to as the "as
yet unnameable which is proclaiming itself" (1978, p. 293). In this, I look for
the breaks and jagged edges of methodological practices from which we
might draw useful knowledge for shaping present practices of a feminist
ethnography in excess of our codes but, still, always already: forces active in
the present.

   In this chapter, I introduce *Troubling the Angels* as an example of
feminist experimental ethnography and then discuss issues of methodological
responsibility and double(d) practices of representation. I address such issues
via "the thinking that writing produces" (St. Pierre, 1997a, p. 178) out of the
efforts of Chris and myself to write a book about women living with HIV/
AIDS. As much limit case as model, what I offer in our work is not so much

privileged example as a "doxology" (Foucault, 1998, p. 329): the description of the uses that might be made of a conceptual ensemble as a particular play of form on the ordering of the empirical. Additionally, the exemplary moment of returning to the HIV study, where science meets philosophy in the face of the other, enacts what might be termed the latest turn in the social sciences, an "empirical turn within postmodernism." Seideman and Alexander (2001) term this a "downward shift" where "theoretical concerns increasingly have become expressed in investigations of an empirical kind" (p. 3). My goal is to situate feminist methodology in relation to shifts in intellectual movements regarding the human sciences, shifts to which it has so profoundly contributed.[2] Using a particular study as index and resource, this chapter explores practices of representation via moves of getting lost across textwork, headwork, and fieldwork.

Troubling the Angels: Women Living With HIV/AIDS

The research project on women and HIV/AIDS began for me in January of 1992. Chris Smithies, a feminist psychotherapist with four years of experience with women and AIDS support groups in Ohio, broached a qualitative research colleague of mine about a feminist research partner who could serve as a "chronicler." What became clear to me at this initial meeting was the fruitfulness of this study for my own struggles with the methodological and theoretical implications of poststructuralism for the doing of qualitative inquiry. I saw an opportunity to wrestle across the "extreme constructionism— especially deconstruction" characteristic of some poststructuralisms via the political responsibility to "real bodies and political rage" entailed in such a study (Stockton, 1994, pp. 16, 6). Hooked on the possibilities, I attended a women and HIV/AIDS retreat in May 1992 at a rural convent where Chris and I presented a research opportunity to the women. Serving as access and immersion, the retreat seared me into some different understanding of the politics of knowing and being known.

As the project took shape, Chris and I interviewed 25 women, largely in meetings of women and HIV/AIDS support groups in four major cities in Ohio, but also, as is not atypical of even quasi-ethnographic work, at holiday and birthday parties, camping trips, retreats, hospital rooms, funerals, baby showers, and picnics.[3] We desktop published the results in late 1995. It was distributed to the participants, with whom we met in their support groups in early 1996 in order to revise toward what the women called "a K-mart book." By this, they meant a book widely accessible to them, those they care about, including other HIV+ women, and the wider community. The revision was published in trade book format in 1997.

From a publicity flier for the book:

Based on an interview study of twenty-five Ohio women in HIV/AIDS support groups, *Troubling the Angels* traces the patterns and changes of how the women make sense of HIV/AIDS in their lives. Attempting to map the complications of living with the disease, the book is organized as a hypertextual, multilayered weaving of data, method, analysis, and the politics of interpretation.

Because of the book's unconventional narration, it invites multiple entries and ways of reading. Interspersed among the interviews, there are [angel] inter-texts, which serve as "breathers" between the themes and emotions of the women's stories; a running subtext where the authors spin out their tales of doing the research; factoid boxes on various aspects of the disease; and a scattering of the women's writing in the form of poems, letters, speeches, and e-mails.

Enacting a feminist ethnography at the limits of representation, *Troubling the Angels* mixes sociological, political, historical, therapeutic, and policy analysis along with the privileging of ethnographic voice.

As I originally thought of the project, I wanted to bring together three interests. The first was my abiding interest in research as praxis (Lather, 1986a). How could such a study contribute to struggles for social justice in a way that would be of use to the study's participants? This interest mandated a combination of critical ethnography and participatory action research and led to inquiry that was "openly ideological" (Lather, 1986b) in its advocacy of support for those with HIV/AIDS and interactive and negotiated in terms of research design.

My second interest was my desire to contribute to the, at that time, small pool of feminist experimental ethnographies. What would such a text look like that combined the poesis of the sort of work that James Clifford and George Marcus called for in their 1986 *Writing Culture* and feminist commitments to social change? In this particular case, invited in to chronicle stories, my sense of task was to write for a broad public audience, particularly the women participating in the study, but to do so in a way that troubled habitual frames of representational space that too often offered such women up for consumption and voyeurism.

The third interest that propelled the study was my investment in empirical work as a site to learn how to find our way into postfoundational possibilities. The closeness that fieldwork allows to the practical ways that people enact their lives confronts us with the materiality of others, in this case, the complicated experiences of living with HIV/AIDS. Situated in the ambivalent tensions of feminist ethnographic traditions, *Troubling the Angels* is much about philosophical argument, rhetoric, typography, and ethnographic voice. Chris and I deal with this through such textual practices as a horizontally split

text where the women's words are on the top of the page in bigger font and
researcher narratives are on the bottom in smaller font. Most pages combine
a top two-thirds that appears to be unmediated interview transcript that foregrounds insider stories and a subtextual bottom under-writing that both decenters and constructs authorial "presence."

In terms of what is lost and found, settled and unsettled, done and
undone in such practices, as Henri Lefebvre (1991) noted about architecture
around 1910, "a certain space was shattered" but, nonetheless, "did not
disappear . . . without leaving any trace in our consciousness, knowledge or
educational methods" (pp. 25–26). Traces, fragments, and ruins survive,
embedded in common sense, perspective, social practices, and political power.
Given such historical sedimentations, how might one look for places where
things begin to shift via practices that exceed the warrants of our present
sense of the possible? Such doubled practices would be within/against a
disciplining space of returns and reversals, knowings and not-knowings. In
such a place, what might feminist knowledge projects look like that work
within and against identity categories, visibility politics, and the romance of
voice? How might such projects enact a way to use the ruins of correspondence theories of language as a fruitful site for doing and reporting feminist
ethnography in ways that attend to the complexities of our desire for "realist
tales" (Van Maanen, 1988) of women's experiences? Juhasz (1999), for example, takes a sort of post-post turn by arguing that the "feminist realist
debates" represent only one side by disallowing realism and identification as
"viable theoretical strategies toward political ends" (p. 194). Against a decade
of antirealist theory, both "molded and frustrated by feminist film theory"
(p. 194), Juhasz, grounded in her efforts to make a documentary about women
and HIV/AIDS, notes both the deconstructive uses of realist style and "the
political efficacy of realism" (p. 196). While tending to conflate political
effectiveness and mimetic representation rather than theorize their relationship, Juhasz's essay enacts a complex desire to use realism "toward a more
noticeably self-aware theoretical/political practice" (p. 197).

This exemplifies how the sort of "trace structures" that Lefebvre notes
in his analysis of architectural remainders shape contemporary inquiry. What
does methodological responsibility look like in such a space? What are the
possibilities and limits of feminist ethnography in addressing such issues?

Within/Against: Methodological Responsibility within Noninnocent Space

What is scientifically possible is determined by science, not by reflection
on science. It appears that the only method of proving that an alternative
science is possible is actually to make it.

—van den Daele, quoted in Redner, 1987

The new ethnography grew out of a literary turn in the 1980s with concerns over "textuality, disciplinary history, critical modes of reflexivity, and the critique of realist practices of representation" (Marcus, 1997, p. 410). What George Marcus (1994) has termed "messy texts" announce the new: partial and fluid epistemological and cultural assumptions, fragmented writing styles, and troubled notions of ethnographic legitimacy, including the "ethnographic authority" of fieldwork (Clifford, 1983). Feminist work both challenged and built on this move, particularly in terms of a sense of failed promises, charged anxieties, and a "self-abjection" at the limit as a way to live on in the face of the loss of legitimating metanarratives.[4]

Kathleen Stewart characterizes the new ethnography as too much about "a discipline of correctives" (1996, p. 24), too much within assumptions of "cure," particularly via the "solution" of experimental writing.[5] More interested in what Kamala Visweswaran argues for as ruptured understandings and practices of failure as "pivotal" (1994, p. 100), Stewart calls on James Agee's *Let Us Now Praise Famous Men* as instructive in its imperfections. "Nothing worked," Stewart notes, and yet his palimpsest of layered evocations still carries force (Quinby, 1991; Rabinowitz, 1992; Lofaro, 1992). Textual solutions, hence, offer both limits and possibilities. This calls for a doubled epistemology where the text becomes a site of the failures of representation and where textual experiments are not so much about solving the crisis of representation as about troubling the very claims to represent.

This might, then, be the contemporary problematic of ethnography: "double, equivocal, unstable . . . exquisitely tormented" (Derrida, 1996b, p. 55), an ethnography of ruins and failures that troubles what Visweswaran calls "the university rescue mission in search of the voiceless" (1994, p. 69). Given the demise of master narratives of identification, objectivism, and linear truth, such ethnography draws close to its objects in the moment of loss where much is refused. It is this drawing close, "as close as possible," that has long been the seduction of fieldwork (Dirks, Eley, and Ortner, 1994, p. 16). This closeness to the practical ways people enact their lives has been the promise for understanding how the everyday gets assumed. The reflexive turn has broadened such understanding to include the very space of ethnographic knowing. It is not enough, as Judith Butler notes (1993b, p. 52), to focus on the limits of our knowing. The task is to meet the limit, to open to it as the very vitality and force that propels the change to come.

In terms of feminist methodology, Audre Lorde's "the master's tools will never dismantle the master's house" has been much noted. First articulated in her 1984 *Sister Outsider*, Lorde called for tools of knowledge production based on subaltern ways of knowing that had heretofore been excluded from legitimate knowledge. Feminist methodology discussions sought these counterpractices of knowing in personal voice, archival resources such as diaries and journals, dialogic and interactive interview formats, reflexivity regarding interpretive imposition, practices such as co-writing: the list goes on. The point is that such a search was conducted under assumptions of finding a less exploitative, more innocent way of proceeding. Judith Stacey's 1988 essay interrupted this drive to innocent knowing, with its focus on the inescapable power imbalances of inquiry situations, feminist or not. By setting itself up as better intentioned, Stacey argued, feminist ethnography risked even greater violation of the researched than the more distanced "objectivity" of conventional research methods.

Visweswaran (1994) has termed this the loss of innocence of feminist methodology. Given the realization of the limits of representation and the weight of research as surveillance and normalization, Visweswaran advises the workings of necessary failure versus the fiction of restoring lost voices. Here, the feminist researcher is no longer the hero of her own story. At a moment when feminist intentions fail, the conventional move of most methodological texts in providing strategies and problem-solving advice, premised on the assumption that "better" methodology will mean better accounts, breaks down. Methodology often diverts attention from more fundamental issues of epistemology. Hence, Visweswaran wants to track failure not at the level of method, but of epistemic failure (1994, p. 98). All is not well in feminist research, she argues, and the problems cannot be solved by better "methods." Faced with its own impossibilities, the practice of failure is pivotal for the project of feminist inquiry in negotiating the crisis of represention, the loss of faith in received stories and predictable scripts.

Failure is not just a sign of epistemological crisis, but also an epistemological construct that signals the need for new ground versus repetition on the same terms (Butler, 1993a). Visweswaran seeks a trickster agency that makes a distinction between success and failure indeterminate. To give voice can only be attempted by a "trickster ethnographer" who knows she cannot "master" the dialogical hope of speaking with (p. 100), let alone the colonial hope of speaking for. Here, the necessary tension between the desire to know and the limits of representation lets us question the authority of the investigating subject without paralysis, transforming conditions of impossibility into possibility where a failed account occasions new kinds of positionings. Such a move is about economies of responsibility within noninnocent space, a "within/against" location.

Butler's (1993b) work on iteration or subversive repetition is of use as a way to keep moving within the recognition of the noninnocence of any practice of knowledge production. Within/against, then, is about both "doing it" and "troubling it" simultaneously. In this both/and move, "subversive re-iteration reembodies subjectivating norms while at the same time redirecting the normativity of those norms" (Schrift, 1995, p. 55). This is a moment of dispersion, a proliferating moment, within the relations of overdetermination.

The argument is that agency exists in the possibility of a variation within a repetition. In order to be intelligible, we need to repeat the familiar and normalized. The task is not whether to repeat but how to repeat in such a way that the repetition displaces that which enables it. While Butler's work was on gender performance, it can be used to rethink practices of feminist methodology in displacing the idea that the work of methodology is to take us to some noncomplicitous place of knowing. Instead, the work of methodology becomes to negotiate the "field of play" of the instructive complications that knowledge projects engender regarding the politics of knowledge.[6] Here method is resituated as a way into the messy doings of science via risky practices that both travel across contexts and are remade in each situated inquiry.

Fleshing out the web of contradictions within which feminist researchers work, given the indignity of being studied, the violence of objectification (Karamcheti, 1992), what are the ethics of such pursuits? What work do we want inquiry to do? To what extent does method privilege findings? What is the place of procedures in the claim to validity? What does it mean to recognize the limits of exactitude and certainty, but still to have respect for the empirical world and its relation to how we formulate knowledge? What is left for science in an era of blurred genres? Such questions are about the politics and ethics of feminist research with/in the postmodern, research that probes questions of narrative authority and the possibilities of generative research methodologies. To address such questions, I turn to the research practices of Chris and myself in our study of women living with HIV/AIDS.

Double(d) Practices of Representation

Troubling the Angels incited much "fieldwork, textwork and headwork" (Van Maanen, 1995). Particularly interested in what it means to tell the stories of others in a way that takes into account the crisis of representation, it assembles a set of practices that include decentering authorial voice via relatively unmediated participant voices, authorial confession, autobiography, "epistemological ruminations" (Foley, 1998, p. 117), and participant response data in disrupting its own truth claims. Such a text offers situated, partial knowledge via a movement toward the sort of doubled practices that would allow us to neither assume transparent narrative nor override participant meaning frames. This is a representational practice that uses the breakdown of meaning and the illusiveness of signification to foster our capacity to notice what Britzman (2000) calls "the vantage of the other and the obligation of our own implication," all that betrays us in the telling as well as that which cannot be said and that which cannot be heard in the saying.

Surrendering the claim to any simplicity of presence, Chris and I function as agents of displacement, making representations only to foreground their insufficiencies. We do this in order to resist the women in our study being consumed without remainder by some sense-making machine. Our task is not so much to unpack some real as to enact the ruins of any effort to monumentalize lived experience. Such reflection on ungraspable meaning is not about ineffability but about how the ambiguities of knowing are the structure of our grasp. This is a kind of failed engagement with the ontological question of the status of the object after poststructuralism.

The effects of *Troubling the Angels* as a book and the process of its making are and will continue to be knowings based in an uncompromising insistence that the truth cannot be spoken directly. Moving well outside of formerly comfortable holds on sense-making, Chris and I use the laboratory of this project to address what it is that we have come to it to understand and what it means to know more than we are able to know and to write toward what we don't understand.

Getting Lost: Textwork

> T]he point of *Glas* is to confess the loss of autonomy, the loss of self, of the author, of the subject, of self-creation . . . Derrida would never want something purely unreadable . . . But it is true up to a point . . . which is its point . . . to experience unreadability, undecipherability . . . Derrida wants us to get a little lost.
>
> —Caputo, 1993

In her book, *The End(s) of Ethnography*, Patricia Clough (1992) recommends that we give up on data collection and "the defenses and compulsions of methodology" and turn, instead, to decoding representations (p. 137). On the contrary, like Nietzsche, my turn is not away from but into the grounds of science, respecting the limits of language and interpretation in what I term feminist efforts toward a double science, a version of what Nietzsche has called the "unnatural sciences" (Nietzsche, 1974, p. 301). Having wanted to never be an armchair methodologist, I am much about the seductions of fieldwork. My interest is precisely in the attachment to its procedures that rub us up against the sort of stubborn materiality that Benjamin (1968) was so interested in rescuing from abstraction.

Theoretically situated in poststructural theories of meaning-making and subject formation, Chris and my project focused on how the participants constructed themselves in relation to the categories laid on them, demanded of them as women with HIV/AIDS. Methodologically grounded in qualitative/ethnographic research approaches, the study enacted an interest in what it means to tell the lives of others, an interest much pursued across poststructural

Struggle

anthropology, feminist methodology, and critical ethnography. Both within and against conventional notions of social science research, the goal was not so much to represent the researched better as to expore how researchers can "be accountable to people's struggles for self-representation and self-determination" (Visweswaran, 1988, p. 39).

In taking the crisis of representation into account in practices of data analysis, what is one to make, for example, of what poststructural anthropologist George Marcus (1993) has referred to as a move toward evocative portraits, a type of data reporting that "emphasizes a direct exposure to other 'voices' . . . unassimilated to given concepts, theories, and analytic frames" (p. 13). "We are," he says, in a moment "when the need to chronicle the world seem[s] to outstrip the capacity to theorize it . . . What we're saying . . . is kind of old-fashioned: that it is possible to present the voices of others in a more or less unmediated way" (pp. 14–15).

Troubling the Angels marks my getting lost in the relations of textwork, turning both into and away from the conventional move of researchers positioned "behind [the] backs [of informants] to point out what they could not see, would not do, and could not have said" (Britzman, 1995, p. 237). To struggle against omnipotence in making sense of participant efforts to make sense of their experiences of HIV/AIDS, I trouble the ethics of reducing the fear, pain, joy, and urgency of people's lives to analytic categories. Exploring the textual possibilities for telling stories that situate researchers not so much as experts "saying what things mean" in terms of "data," the researcher is situated as witness giving testimony to the lives of others.

Britzman (1995) raises the dangers of such a posture: the reification of experience and identity, agency and voice,[7] and unmediated access to some "real" that reverts back to humanist pathos, empathic caring and a longing for transcendence, some way out, in the face of human struggle. There is no exit from the lack of innocence in discursive stagings of knowledge. With a deconstructive goal of keeping things in process, keeping the system in play, fighting the tendency for our categories to congeal, my textual practices move toward some place of both/and and neither/nor, where I trouble the very categories I can't think without.

Looking for ways to make the text say more and other about something as absurd and complicated as dying in the prime of life toward understanding in the shadow places of history as loss, we developed several practices. If Chris and I were to not use AIDS to tell the story of how difficulties are our tutors in overrehearsed ways, we needed multiple layers that folded both backward and forward, a multilayered weaving of method, the politics of interpretation, data, analysis—all embedded in the tale. One example would be the member check in *Troubling the Angels* and its layering of further data into the text. This is an enactment of what I termed "a necessary condition

weaving method

of tentativeness" in my construction of authorial voice in the book. Here we are "standing open to the inconclusiveness" of our work (Gallagher, 2000, p. 152). Inviting the women in our study to see themselves being studied, "looking-at-being-looked-at-ness" becomes both "a way of seeing and a way of representing" (p. 154) that is "troubled, exalting, particular and communal," where not only researcher and researched but also readers are "left open for scrutiny" in what we think we know (p. 155).

Getting Lost: Headwork

Based on Walter Benjamin's "Angel of History," the angel was used to interrupt salvation narratives of science and rationality as well as to turn sentimentality against itself. Benjamin believed that truth and justice were theological in being ultimately incalculable and unknowable. He invested the angel with historical significance as a means toward philosophical truth content about the ruins of aura and the possibilities of disenchantment (Rochlitz, 1996, p. 266). As a "willfully underdetermined category," the angel worked to turn history into philosophy, to make historical content into philosophical truth (Benjamin, 1977, p. 182). In a time of ascendent secularization, it was to an image from the ruins of the sacred that he turned to interrupt the socially dominant in order to spark an ethical order for the sake of an imperilled present. The secularized discourse of post-Kantian modernity is not as different from earlier theological discourses as modernists would like to believe—this was Benjamin's turn to theology, against the devaluation of truth in the name of knowledge. This is about subversion and the limits of knowledge. And we are left not with truth but with the knowledge of our search for what we cannot find. This positions the angel as the ghost of unassimilable otherness that haunts the house of Reason, self-reflexive subjectivity, and historical continuity. Gesturing toward a force other than individualized and psychologized motivations, the angel helps organize a much broader, less bounded space where we do what we can while leaving a place for what we cannot envision to emerge.

Modulating from argumentative to poetic registers, *Troubling the Angels* unfolds across a range of voices that stage how nothing can deliver us from our misrecognitions. Such a practice is about the ways we are struck by what we try to understand, captured by it, and then attempt to grasp the limits and possibilities of our grasp, a dream of science outside mastery and transparency (Melville, 1996). Our hope for readers is something other than a reading that can only find what it is looking for, perhaps a reading that surprises, a place where disjunction occurs, obliged by the text to see how we see, out of the overdetermined habits of reading, a reading that is other or more than we should like it to be, always more and other, protean. Purposefully not intelligible within standard frames, it is a book about multiple,

Only find what you are looking for   *why protean*

Protean - Diversity

Destabilize Categories

shifting reals, a stubborn book that rubs against the desire for interpretive mastery and implicates an audience rather than persuades or seduces.

Delineating practices both within and against the "new ethnography" with its reflexivity, multiple voices, and textual experimentation, my interest is in practices that enact a stammering relationship toward the incompletely thinkable conditions and potential of given arrangements. Such practices include works that "mesh and collide" registers of information, mappings that destabilize the categories of explanation, enactments of the inadequacy of a frame (Levinson, 1998, p. 289). "Show yourself not getting all you could out of the opportunity and not making a virtue from the restraint," Levinson writes in her evocation of such practices (p. 290). All of this is by way of illustrating ". . . the inevitable . . . unimaginable breakdowns in the machinery of representation" (p. 291).

Here, Walter Benjamin's (1968) "Theses on the Philosophy of History" uses the irreducible resources of theology to break with ossified discourses (Rochlitz, 1996). Benjamin's "messianic Marxism" or "secular messianism" argued both the limits of secularized reason and the intertwinement of theology and philosophy. But this is theology present "as form rather than content," the hunchback who stays out of sight in order to better guide the hand of the puppet of historical materialism (Nagele, 1991). Benjamin's thinking is neither Marxism nor theology but a contesting of both while twisting their resources for practices of living on. Rather than the epistemological concerns that characterize modernity (Greene, 1994), this is about "the discontinuous, catastrophic, nonrectifiable, and paradoxical" crisis of the self-regulation and purpose of ethnography (Lyotard, 1984, p. 60).

Just as Derrida, and before him Benjamin, has called upon Jewish mysticism as a way to think against secular humanism, in this move, angels are of use as a (post)critical gesture in shattering the sorts of rationalities that have shaped our negotiation of previous crises. Something other to the reductionisms of secularism, rationalism, and transformationalism, the angel is not so much about opposition as *perversion*.[8] This takes " 'the form of the unacceptable, or even of the intolerable, of the incomprehensible, that is of a certain monstrosity' " in delivering us from the certainties of science, just as science delivered us from the certainties of religion (Derrida, quoted in Caputo, 1997c, p. 74). Welcoming the angel/monster into where we are is to use Derrida's move of repetition forward as a way through aporia, but a disloyal repetition, a risky business that produces what it repeats in order to see this not as loss but as letting something new come. This is more about Benjamin and Derrida's justice to come than Kuhn's theory of normal and revolutionary science. It is about bending the rules with respect for the rules, a certain respectful mimicking in order to twist and queer science to come up with a less formulaic story of itself.

Exhibiting Diversity

Bending Science

Getting Lost: Fieldwork

In trying to generate new practices out of the methodological concerns that
I bring to this study, what are the limits of textual strategies in doing research
for social justice in a way that takes the crisis of representation into account?
Two problems arise: the anxiety of voyeurism that can so easily entangle the
researcher in an ever more detailed self-analysis, an implosion into the self,
and secondly, the displacement of more interactive social relations of research
by an exclusively textual focus.

John van Maanen (1988) has raised the dangers of "vanity ethnography" in efforts to include the researcher in the telling of the tale. While I
disagree with Daphne Patai's (1994) conflation of postmodernism, self-
reflexivity, and identity politics as a solipsistic self-implosion and her turn to
a kind of neorealism, I share her concerns regarding the dominant confessional, psychoanalyzing approach to self-reflexivity that reinscribes the philosophy of consciousness and voluntarism that so characterizes humanism.
Looking for ways out of bourgeois interiority, rather than this individualized
angst, posthumanist reflexivity is about the micropolitical practices of representation, the metanarratives within which inquiry is embedded, the relation
of its questions, and the effectivity of its practices to the sociocultural horizon. Foucauldian genealogical questions of who speaks and the force of
desire and investment that produces power/knowledge foreground the origins
of one's concepts, the weight of tradition, the ways current codes of traditional political problematics are insufficient, and the construction of complicated, disturbed answers.

In a focus on textual strategies, however, questions like who is speaking
to/for/with whom, for what reasons and with what resources are displaced
with what is the object of my analysis? How have I constructed it? What are
the conventions of disciplinary practices that I seek to put under erasure?
Empirical bodies can get lost here. As Whitford (1991) notes in her book on
Irigaray, "Playing with a text . . . is a rather solipsistic activity; it is not a
dialogue with the other which includes process and the possibility of change"
(p. 48; see, also, Lutz, 1993, p. 145). It is one thing to ask whether new voices
are being heard, quite another to ask whether voices are hearing themselves
and one another fruitfully. What can be done to create more interactive social
relations in a study as well as the more typical poststructural move of devis-
ing textual strategies that disrupt illusory notions of found worlds?

What the women thought of all this is represented in the Epilogue, and,
suffice it to say, they were both "for" and "against" our textual moves. "Who-
ever thought when we started all of this that it would ever be a book" was
the strongest part for me of what they said, as testimony to the something that
was more than nothing of our efforts. But in addressing issues of responsible

engagement, was the member check sufficient as an effort to speak "*to/through*" rather than from the "position of mastery" of "speaking *about*" (Picart, 1999, p. 171)? What is at stake in replacing invisibility with visibility in a way that refuses seemingly self-evident, transparent stories, as if voices "speak for themselves" (Piontek, 1999)? What can such uses be made to mean?

In terms of what the women gained from their participation in this study, pizza was part of our enticement for them to come and speak to us at the support groups, and book profits will be shared with funding women and HIV/AIDS support groups in Ohio. As well, at the end of each group interview, they responded to our questions about the effects of our presence on their group and they reported that it helped them deal with some of the harder issues that they have a tendency to avoid in the sociality of the groups. Not uncommon to interviews, then, our work with them became a site for their reflection, particularly with one another. It also gave them a site to articulate a further purpose in their attachment to seeing their stories in book form, to helping other women. For several of the women, participation was also about payback for Chris and her work with the support groups over the years. Finally, the "member check" solicited their reaction to our storying of their lives.

This entailed visiting each of the groups after they had read the desk-top-published version of the book. The following excerpts from my research journal during this process give some feel for how Chris and I negotiated issues of exploitation and appropriation in what it means to use other people's lives as data.

[**From my research journal, November 4, 1994:**] I handed out the table of contents page plus sections from the story series to which this group of women had made particularly visible contributions. It took almost an hour to get through the overview, with many questions and many stories bubbling out, especially from the new women who seem sad to miss the opportunity to get their stories in the book. Those who had participated seemed thrilled to see their own and one another's words, corrected some of the attributions, wanted to know where some of their own words had gone, commented on what a long way I had come, how I was so much smarter now than when they had first met me at the retreat, over and over "confirmed" the pertinence of the major themes we had featured,[9] and were much more interested in the sexuality section than the death and dying one. I asked what they thought of the angels, and one woman answered, "It's what holds us. I think it's beautiful." Another said that spirituality is such a part of this, that it makes sense. The facilitator showed her guardian angel pin that was on the inside of her collar and talked of how she was formerly pretty uninterested in spiritual matters, but that this work had led her to great

interest in— angels! One woman wanted to know, "But why 'troubling'?" I said: because these are not the romantic ladies tripping around
in nighties that are so popular right now. These are angels who trouble
our sense that all is right with the world, that AIDS is something "out
there," unrelated to each one of us, that we can afford to distance from.
The biggest learning of this trip for me was that they want to read the
whole thing and how much they trust that we will do the "right thing"
by them. This underscored our earlier decision to do the desktop publishing in order to get a "real book" into their hands in a timely fashion.

[**From my research journal, February 7, 1995:**] I joined the group
the last half hour, overviewed the table of contents, walked them through
handouts from selected story series to which their group had made a
large contribution, and passed around the angel images which drew
some interest, but not much. One woman couldn't stop reading; she
gulped it down, talking about how much she liked the format. She said
the angel images were good, "not fat little white babies," but images
that "fit the topic." She said the format catered to a general reader, but
also breaks the conventional style, a different style that will get attention. A doctoral student, she noted that the split text was "postmodern"
with its multiple voices, dialogue within dialogue, its "not presenting a
master narrative . . . It's not just one woman's story, but a playing back
and forth across the stories, stories that break into each other, providing
relief. I think it's great. I'm proud of you. Who would have thought
when we did the taping [for the interviews] that it was really going to
be a book." I talked to this woman about writing a few pages of her
reaction to the text; she responded with how busy she was. The facilitator noted that the format, in not being just one person speaking at a
time, captured the support group motif and was "feminist" in the way
we took a "backseat" with our researcher narratives and worked
collaboratively with one another and the research participants. Again, I
was struck with all the stories we're not telling, both the shifts in the
lives of the women we have interviewed and the stories of women who
have newly joined the group.

Recognizing the instrumentalism attendant upon the research task that
we must both "practice and deconstruct at once" (Chow, 1991, p. 112), Chris
and I moved softly with urgency, trying to not pounce too quickly, to seek
some widened space to speak beyond our means, as we got on with the task
with which we were charged. Power is inherent in relationships and intrinsic
to inquiry. Viewing power as capillary, nomadic, and circulating rather than
as unidirectional creates the possibility of spaces in which no one is as yet

the master versus the "giving" people power more typical of "emancipatory" projects. Here, the researcher is assumed to hold all the cards in spite of a kind of Baudrillardian revolt of the object that typifies poststructuralist theories of power. Scheurich (1995), for example, in his writing on new imaginaries of interviewing, argues against ideas that human interaction is unitary and oriented toward joint construction of meaning. "Instead, interactions and meaning are a shifting carnival of ambiguous complexity, a moving feast of differences interrupting differences" (p. 14). The idea of a benevolent, empowering interviewer is displaced by the interview as a space where interviewees "carve out space of their own" (p. 24), where "meanings of words continually migrate and change" (p. 27), where "the interview always exceeds and transgresses our attempts to capture and categorize" (p. 28).

The work of the angels was essential in bending this inevitable use of the women's lives to address what Rilke termed the Too Big. The Too Big is about confronting the loss of transcendence, whether through god or the proletariat or science, and the immensities of the ordinary: of birth and change and death. This slowed everything down, but the risk was that it would be worth it in producing a text that does justice to these women's lives, a text that exceeds our own understandings. My hope was that the women would react to the angels like Derrida did to Geoff Bennington's (1993) writing about him in a split text format where the bottom of each page is Derrida's running commentary, "a sort of internal margin," designed to escape, to surprise, the systematization of his work proposed by Bennington in the top 2/3 page. Bennington refers to the "hypertext" dimensions of the text that open it to multiple paths of reading (p. 14). Derrida writes of "what is written 'up' there, beside or above me, on me, but also for me, in my favor, toward me and in my place . . ." (p. 26).

Conclusion: Disappointment as a Rubric

In unpacking the textwork, headwork, and fieldwork issues involved in *Troubling the Angels*, my move is toward a "philosophical ethnography" (Mol, 2002) from which to address a science that is empirical without being narrowly empiricist, a science possible after the questioning of the grounds of scientificity. Such a science is rooted in a disappointment that is neither the disappointment that undergirds the neopositivism urged of late by those who want knowledge directly useful in policy arenas (e.g., Oakley, 2003) nor that which characterizes those disappointed by this fall back into positivism. It is, rather, a disappointment that is a kind of rubric in foregrounding the ontological consequences of a structure of lack and deferral and the costs of forgetting a fundamental negativity (Rajan, 2002, p. 240). This ontology of the unthought structures is what Derrida has referred to as the necessity of the human sciences to pass through "the detour of philosophy" in a way that, as well, exposes philosophy to its margins via the double(d) sciences that arise (Rajan, 2002, pp. 28, 29). Such sciences address "the problem of how one thinks in the absence of foundations" (p. 132) and "track the way in which [a] field meets its breaking point, the moments of its discontinuities, the sites where it fails to constitute the intelligibility it promises" (Butler, 2001, p. 12). This is the disappointment of a "thought that returns upon itself" (Rajan, 2002, p. 18) in both opening philosophy to a wider cultural field and using philosophy to mark all knowledges with "the negativity of being what they are not and not being what they are," serving as "the unconscious of the sciences" (p. 194).

Interlude

Naked Methodology

In August 1992, I met with six other women in a rural area outside Madison, Wisconsin for a research retreat. In terms of format, each of us had two hours of "exquisite attention" for our work, in any way we wanted. I chose to be naked in the jacuzzi, surrounded by the other women, all dressed, as they asked questions of me about the very early conceptualization of Chris and my project on writing the lives of women with HIV/AIDS. What follows is excerpted from the tape recording of that conversation.[1]

Patti: The working title of my project is *Standing With Angels: Women and HIV/AIDS*. My interest is in a double science, double gestures, double writing that has something to do with what Liz said about Mimi's dissertation.

Mimi: One of Liz's comments to me was that I did a very good job explaining feminist postmodernism and that was a problem, like you killed something, that there is something wrong with that gesture. It's about word play—

Patti: It is also about the text performing what it announces.

Mimi: And destabilizes meaning as it goes. There is something problematic about continuing to write about what we are writing about in the same old way.

Patti: All of that has to do with this thing I am calling the double gesture. And I am interested in figuring out what it means to do data in these ways, to do data in doubled ways given my interest in the politics of knowing and being known.

Liz: At the moment when violence and culture come together, maybe in the act of your research, how could your research also be witnessing and testimony to this violence that has been done in the culture right now to women with AIDS so that these lives will not be forgotten?

49

Patti: What does it mean to see these women as data, as victims, as AIDS patients, as all these labels? Whatever doubled is, it is doubled on multiple levels. Personally, it is a chance to get myself into a situation where I cannot use my poststructuralist affiliations to undermine emancipatory intentions and practices. Like the work my co-researcher is doing in support groups and the work these women are doing with each other, and then what it meant for me to be at the retreat where I first met the women. I went to this three-day retreat, the first all-women's retreat in Ohio. I could see that it was really powerful on a whole lot of levels and there is something about my poststructural glasses that leads me to not look at some of the powerful things that are happening.

I am particularly interested in the question of emancipation given who these women are. I mean who is going to get emancipated here? They've got AIDS and they brought me into the project to get their stories out to help other women. I mean where is the emancipatory intention, where is the direction of the intention, for whom is this emancipatory and in what way?

But my position is actually a suspicion of emancipatory intentions on a researcher's part. It is like something is happening to those women; they are brought together. Whatever was going on at that retreat, it was something that brought out the best in them. What is all this emancipatory stuff? How does it play itself out in this particular situation?

Mimi: And what do you mean "where I can't undermine emancipatory intentions"?

Patti: That's my agenda, I want to bring my high theory and its suspicions of emancipatory intentions to some kind of crisis.

Mimi: So you want a situation in which you suspect you can't deconstruct emancipatory intentions.

Patti: Certainly not totally.

Mimi: That what you do doesn't fuck up what they are doing. That whatever the academic thing is that you are doing—because things are so extreme in this situation because these people are dying—as much as you would like to know these people and be friends, you don't know these people and you wouldn't be friends outside this academic situation. So whatever it is that positions you as an academic outsider—and you just don't want to destroy or distort or do anything harmful.

Patti: Well, I can't not distort at some level. Given this, how can I position myself?

Liz: That is still putting yourself at the center, because you are saying that it is all turning on you, you are either doing a lot of damage or you are doing a lot of good. So you are still in the center of the story somehow; it is still the dilemma of the researcher. If that is what you want it to be, that is great, it can be a reflection of your dilemma as a researcher. But it is not going to be about them and women and AIDS.

Patti: What I want to do is try to create a space where it will be all those things.

Mimi: So what is your greatest fear about all of this?

Patti: That I will kill them with my high theory, that I will eat away their stories—

Mimi: Double science, double death—

Patti: Somehow do them injustice—that is a big part of it. I was so struck by their generosity toward one another.

Janet: Why did they agree to be in this project? How have you explained the difference between the research project and the support group? What is motivating them to say yes to participating in the research?

Patti: They are motivated to say yes because they want to tell their story in such a way that what they see as the relative silence on women surviving with AIDS is broken.

Liz: And it seems like the way we are talking about them now has also been the language of us/them. Yet with AIDS—all of us are one blood cell away from HIV, one injury. Who knows—you might also want to play with the us/them thing.

Patti: I know that when I started writing about my reflections on the retreat, my litany was, "I do not now, to my knowledge, have AIDS."

Liz: So that might help with this we/they, to bring it down from the generalized abstract discussion of researcher/researched, us/them, emancipatory fucking them over, to the specifics. In this specific situation, there is something a little different about researcher/researched because you could very much become one of them very easily. And maybe you are already. Which is very different than any other researcher/researched relation. So to deal with the specifics of this situation—

Patti: Then I think of the James Agee book and I want to do something with the physical nature of the book toward some kind of merging with the reader and the author, in Agee's words, some kind of effort in human actuality. I don't really know what that means. His book is a compilation of quotes, his own assessment, and photographs with no captions. I might use photographs and the women's writing. Chris, my co-researcher, says that you have to be really careful, that many of these women are sick, that they are women who have very complicated busy lives and they have a lot of things going on. And whatever it is that you are going to ask from them, you have to remember this. But she does think that some will want to put some of their writing into the book—maybe letters and poems. Instead of being a master discourse about passing judgment, I want to create a sense of space for another person, some different forms, complexly intertextual, so that readers will be moved by the texture of the writing.

Janet: What do you expect from them, what are they going to do for you?

Patti: At a minimum they are going to tell stories.

Janet: No, I mean to you—you P. Lather. Do you want them to save you from your emancipatory intentions?

Patti: Well, again that goes back to the larger questions that are huge on the ethics end of it and on the politics end of it. Sometimes I say, why do empirical work at all? What does it mean to use other people's lives as data?

Mary: Who is your audience?

Patti: We are going to mess these questions over with them. What kind of writing should come out of this practice: a monograph that is quick to pull together? They want to see whatever we write come out pretty soon so they can give it to doctors, nurses, families as a legacy; they want a book—

PJ: So a variety of writing will come out of this?

Patti: Yes.

PJ: So what is your piece in this?

Patti: I will do most of the writing, mostly as a conduit for their stories.

Liz: What might it do to the questions you are raising here to think of yourself not only as researcher or maybe not as researcher at all, but as teacher?

Patti: Who am I teaching?

Liz: Well I wonder what it might be like to conceptualize this as a pedagogical intervention in dominant discourses about AIDS. How does that shift you vis a vis them? Why approach it as a researcher?

Patti: Why do I want them to be data, rather than my teachers?

Liz: That turns it for me. In thinking about them being their own ethnographers in the sense that you teach them how to tell their stories in a way that acknowledges that they know how to tell them to each other, but there is something more to telling them beyond that support group, to a larger audience and in a public forum.

Patti: Part of my resistance is that I want to claim research as a place that is not necessarily so power imbalanced. What does it mean to make people data for our books? That is a big question for me. I don't want to give up research. I'm interested in how to do research in ways that are mutual. What kind of practices can be set up? "Getting our voices heard" is what they want the title to be.

Liz: So what is the mutual need?

Janet: That is one of their needs as they perceive. You either have to trash that, validate that, or ignore that. Like can that co-exist with your need to do all kinds of different things? Like it can't be one or the other.

Patti: No, it is a relation. How do they construct themselves in the face of being HIV+?

Mary: We started this by my seeing women talking on a TV talk show, and they all had AIDS. They were so astounding, they were articulate, they were focused, they had a point, and they wouldn't let the audience construct them in the way the audience wanted to construct them.

Liz: Which was how?

Mary: Immoral, the audience wanted to know their story, and if those women were bad women then they were going to be able to make certain sorts of judgments and they wanted that no matter that these women kept saying "it doesn't matter how I got it, you too, this could be you, we are not some 'they.' "

Patti: At the retreat they never talked about where they got it. By and large that question was not a very interesting question to them. And I think it is part of a self-conscious political intervention in the way that AIDS is being constructed. That was Mary's point.

Liz: There is a whole movement that they draw from. What those women were saying does not come out of nowhere.

Mary: So, how do they construct their own meaning, refuse being positioned? They didn't care about origins, where the disease came from. They were actually resentful that the audience wanted to talk about it. Their mission was to warn that no woman is safe. The black women were especially insistent on getting that message across. A lot of these women have kids. Many are concerned about their children. And there is not much anger about biology trapping us once again and how much easier it is to be a man.

Janet: Have any of the women asked to see your writing?

Patti: No.

Janet: They are taking your co-researcher's word that you will get things out?

Patti: They did ask me, well how do we know that this is going to get published?

Janet: That is an incredible amount of trust at a time when there isn't a whole lot of trust in their lives.

Liz: I think what you might be right about is a reading of their self-conscious political intervention into discourse about themselves. I don't know if I would agree that you are right about reading off of those performances, off the Donahue show, for example, the reality of their lives, the truth of their lives. And so I think all of us present ourselves different in different contexts. So to make one singular reading of them, like this, or they are becoming angels, makes me really nervous. I guess I really want to contextualize your conclusions about the meanings that you are drawing.

Mary: You may be right, my characterization of the HIV+ women on this talk show might be romanticizing and also might be the result of performance on the part of those women. They had rehearsed segments. Part of this visceral feeling that I had about the program, this was a performance. So I think we have to recognize that performance thing in order to keep it away from exoticization or romanticism or canonization.

Liz: All of us function on different levels, and I would imagine that I would present myself as a woman with AIDS very differently on Oprah than with my support group or my lover, or with my mother—

Janet: And there are lots of other women watching who might be angry, maybe they feel that they are worthless because they got it, I mean there are so many different—

Patti: This project brings me face to face with the limits of the ways that I work in the world. There is something so powerful going on that I have to somehow wrestle with that, and I better figure out how to get over some of that stuff or I am going to fall flat on my face—I won't be worthy of the task.

Mimi: And that sounds very much like the way that Western men have been using the Other, which is like to figure out who I am and to bring me face to face with myself. So to hear you say that echoes that in my ear again. It is like, white men say I want to study you so I learn what my limitations are. I learn who I am by studying you. You have to be very careful.

Liz: And the other thing too that I would add is that HIV+ people are living out some of the most profound, wild, ambiguous, contradictory moments, and so to be surprised that these people have this incredibly complicated analysis is like—is there an embedded assumption that only academics have this kind of like really complex, contradictory way of looking at our lives, and we are so surprised that someone who hasn't studied postmodern theory and—the situation is so fucked up, there are so many things that don't add up to shit. And to live that out day to day gives a variety of perspectives.

Patti: I just feel so fortunate that this dropped into my life, because it brings me face to face with things that it is easy to walk over. At least I want to begin the book, right now, with their stories about themselves. The first move is to let them talk. And then the second thing—I call it "Standing with Angels" and it is my story of telling their stories. In terms of the research design and the interview questions, I am not real attached to them. They are just floating around. Part of me thinks it is important to start with their questions. We want to do member checks; we want to do something with writing where they write reactions to what we write.

Janet: Has your co-researcher angelized these women?

Patti: She is interested in what it means to be a feminist and how AIDS has made these women more female-identified. They wouldn't call themselves feminists, but through their experiences with the support groups, they are making community with women.

Janet: It is interesting that you are identifying her as the co-researcher and not the women. You are still positioning them as the researched. So when you say they will have some degree of editorial control—

Patti: I think I want to do something honest about what it means to negotiate that space. I think there is a lot of bad faith, talk going on in the name of collaboration. What does it mean to negotiate that space more honestly, about who owns what, who cares about what, who is invested in what? It is almost like a division of labor at some point, so what does it mean to negotiate research space in a way that is outside that romantic idea?

Janet: There are specific situations. Your negotiations with these women would be different from my negotiation with teachers. So your particular situation will yield different situations.

Mimi: How does that all get back to—they are trusting you with something?

Patti: That is really interesting because it was elaborately set up in the beginning and as it proceeded—the thing I kept saying that happened at the retreat is that at some level this research project doesn't matter to them nearly as much as it does to me. They got a lot of other things going, and they are willing for some very interesting reasons to give me some time.

Janet: Well what else is happening? What competing things are going on in their lives?

Patti: Work, health, social lives. To me it is such a compelling opportunity to be forced to think about what it means to be an academic researcher who pokes around in other peoples lives, in particular ways, for particular reasons, almost always clothed in the rhetoric of doing good. What does that mean in this context? I've never been a part of something like this before, I've never before been invited into a research project.

Liz: To be of use, to be of use to whom is the primary question. What are your boundaries about being of use to them? What are theirs about being of use to you?

Janet: Research is never just clean. It becomes part of our lives. What are the boundaries?

PJ: I had a major piece of research blow up due to a so-called collaborative process. It became very scary to me, about what I am doing. You can frame all of these things in ways that violate the people you are working with. What you are about to step into, there are going to be some things that you can't even count on. And when you are done, you will probably say that you will never do research like that again.

Liz: I think that it is great to be debugging your own research approach, to the extent that you can. Your assumption that they are becoming like angels, it may be just because no one was looking at it, that AIDS didn't bring it out, it was there, and now because they got AIDS, somebody is seeing.

Patti: Liz, you keep saying, but you are bringing it back to yourself. What else can I do?

Liz: I wasn't saying so much yourself, as in the autobiographical moment, but these women in this geographical location, in this support group and you, in your institutional location, your life situation. Bring yourself back to the situation so that you constantly frame these questions out of that situated context, not as the big philosophical questions. But rather, how do I operate in this context, with these women? And then what do I learn about research by trying to be of use in this context? Not how can I be of use to all HIV+ women as researcher with a capital "r".

Janet: I am arguing that the autobiographical is implicit in everything said. And then a choice of writing and how you want to present all of that could include, I would argue, strongly, that I would want it to include explicit grappling with all of this.

Patti: One of the things that I appreciate about Agee's book, he wrestles so much with what it means to tell the stories of others and what it means to be on a spying mission. He constructs himself in that book as very awkward. What is underneath this caution you keep giving me about keeping it located in the particular situation, to not spin off into meta? How can I do meta talk? I don't want to give up meta talk.

Liz: Don't we live that? I mean where is our question from? Isn't this like meta everything and concrete too and always both and neither? How can we not do it?

Janet: How can we write it is one question, but we certainly live it. I mean, say two words in this room and we shoot from meta to concrete or whatever frame that we want to put on that in a split second. We live in the concrete, we live in details; we think in abstractions, but we live our lives in particulars.

Liz: For me the caution comes from keeping from bumping it up to an abstraction that is in fact an oppressive category. Like going from these women with AIDS in this support system to capital WOMEN—also, the postmodern breakthrough is the refusal of universals; there are no universals. So what is meta then if it is not seeking universals? Well, I think it is trying to understand the moment in ways that allow a connection with intersections with many moments; it's to network—

Mary: As a historian I would say we come to the moment with universals, with stuff we have lived by. We come to here and we understand this moment by that stuff.

Liz: But we also have the knowledge of how those universals don't work, the gaps, the omission, the unsayables. There are power relations running through what we learned and what we didn't learn. You learned one set and you another, because of how power is played out. It's the particulars that keep us honest. We can't not build theories. We have an experience and we build a theory about how the world is based on our experiences, and so it is those particulars that keep coming at us, that rub up against those theories about the way things are that keep us living our lives more honestly.

And it is not the theories that are the problem, it's not the universals, it's not the symbols, it's not the language. It's the power that gets attached to them that becomes the problem. So yes, we are always talking meta, always bumping things up, always talking abstractness at some level and coming up with theories. We have to do that. But then it is like how power gets connected and that's the enemy. And the problem is that historically research has been used in such oppressive ways that it has almost become synonymous with power-over—with abuse of power. It's a particularly problematic practice, one of the ways that abstractions become abusive is by making other ways of knowing invisible. That is like one of the major mechanisms of power. At some level that is the oppressiveness that we do in the academy in the name of research.

Janet: I come back to the question, what motivates these women to say yes to you?

Patti: My feeling is that it is much more casual than we in the academy often think. Part of what I am interested in is what we as scientists give import to and they don't.

Janet: Particular intentions direct the research. Your intentions, as well as these women's intentions toward the research, in fact frame and direct the intention of the research. It's part of the particular. And what are your intentions? What motivated you to a category like angels, at least the general category? They will all be doing it for different reasons. And some of them may not be angelic in the way we would want to think. They may think, this just gets me out of the house—

Patti: Who knows, but when we talk about situatedness and the particulars of this—and in a way I haven't begun to probe, I think this angels metaphor is really important. Who knows what is going to happen to it over the life of this project, but it is a real vivid metaphor for what my investments are.

Liz: I think you need to own that metaphor; it's yours. And that's okay. But in terms of a caution, to impose it on them may or may not work for them.

Mimi: It's almost like excessive, it's so excessive that you—it raises all these red flags.

Chapter 3

Double(d) Science, Mourning, and Hauntology

Scientism, Scientificity, and Feminist Methodology

This cloudy distribution.—Scientism.—Old scientism: Of objectivism.—
New scientism: What happened to philosophy?—Scientificity.—
Foucauldian scientificity: Undoing Positivity.—From scientism to a
more capacious scientificity.—Implications for (post)feminist methodology.—Ends, Continued.

Learning to live with ghosts means learning to understand what has been
lost in the self and what has been lost in the social.

Britzman, 2000

This chapter plunges into old and difficult questions regarding the scientificity
of science as a set of protocols of choice, decision, and calculation where the
policy, economy, and practice of science shift across historical times and
places. Redner (1987), for example, tracks across ancient and classical science to what he terms world science (p. 5) where hegemonic practices
include "arithmomorphic science, reductive science, Big Science and techno-
logical applied science serving military and industrial ends" (p. 287). As
Redner notes in his history of the policy and economy of science, within the
critical sciences, while there is a lot of talk about scientific revolutions and
paradigm shifts, there are few examples of new scientific approaches.

   Of interest in recent permutations of a long-running feminist interest in
science is a shift in the debate away from rather tired epistemological contests

and toward what Wilson (1998) terms a "deconstruction-empiricism" (p. 23) that recognizes our debt to scientific tradition while trying to twist it away from patriarchal presumption and toward a "faithful transgression" (p. 36). "What kinds of feminist projects remain unthinkable," she asks (p. 17) as she urges a break from "the increasingly restrictive parameters of our own critical methodologies" (p. 5) in a way that puts the nature of scientificity on the feminist agenda. In Wilson's case, this involves attention to neuroscience against the "curiously abiological at the center of feminist thinking" (p. 15), but the key is that the "equivocation over scientificity" (p. 71) is constitutive of the new scientific approaches both called for and contributed to by feminists over several decades.

This chapter uses such feminist work to flesh out what Foucault termed a counterscience, by which he meant a science that takes values and power seriously. In this task, my reading of Nietzsche suggests that all the disguised theologisms of our modern secular faith in science begin to announce themselves as ghosts we thought we had been rid of. If science, too, can be seen as a piety, what comes after the necessary nihilism that accompanies the breakdown of Enlightenment rationality at the end of modernity and its belief in perfectability and progress and anthropomorphism? Between the impossible dream of certainty and an interminable deconstruction, what might this less ascetic science look like? In search of practices that demolish great illusions, a contrary-wise praxis that enables the working through that allows one to go on, what would practices look like that hold the limits of our knowing as a good thing?

Addressing the science possible after the questioning of the grounds of science, I explore how the ghost of scientism might be used as a resource in formulating a double(d) science. My central move is to use this ghost, and the mourning it evokes, as energy toward a refusal to concede science to scientism. Situated against the "repositivization" at work in global neoliberalism, I conclude the chapter with a look at the implications for feminist methodology of a more capacious sense of scientificity.

This Cloudy Distribution

> My work? . . . There is beneath that which science knows of itself something that it does not know . . . I have tried to extricate . . . the unconscious of knowledge.
>
> —Foucault, in Davidson, 1997

In *The Order of Things*, Foucault (1970) advises that, rather than looking for a coherent definitional field, we attend to the overlapping, contradictory, and conflictual definitional forces that constitute our pursuit of a counter-science. Rather than the "physics envy" that characterizes the parade of behaviorism, cognitivism, structuralism, and neopositivism, he posits a social science that runs counter to received notions of science as value-free.[1] Against the objectivist strands with their failure to successfully study human activity in a way modeled after the assumedly cumulative, predictive, and stable natural or "exact" sciences, Foucault locates the human sciences in the interstices of the mathematizable and the philosophical. "This cloudy distribution" (p. 347) is both their privilege and their precariousness. "Dangerous intermediaries in the space of knowledge," essentially unstable, uncertain as sciences, "the complexity of the epistemological configuration in which they find themselves" (p. 348) is their particular positivity.[2]

As what Nietzsche (1974) terms the "unnatural sciences" (p. 301), Foucault's notion of the social sciences as counter-sciences is opposed to the "great certainty" of the natural sciences by their address to language, meaning, the limits of consciousness, and the role of representations: the stuff of human seeking to know. Rather than lacking in exactitude and rigor, the human sciences are more a " 'meta-epistemological' position" in being about "finitude, relativity, and perspective" (Foucault, 1970, p. 355). Here, their very "haziness, inexactitude and imprecision" (ibid.) is the surface effect of the forms of positivity proper to the human sciences: "blurred, intermediary and composite disciplines multiply[ing] endlessly" (p. 358). Across the biological (Comte) and economic (Marx) models of earlier centuries, we arrive via the linguistic/interpretive turn (Freud) to a focus on the need for a "reflexive form of knowledge" where there is "always something still to be thought" (p. 372). The "primacy of representation" is "the very field upon which the human sciences occur" (pp. 362–63). "Unveil[ing] to consciousness the conditions of its forms and contents" (p. 364) is its task.

Whether this is "truly scientific" or not is a "wearisome" discussion (Foucault, 1970, p. 365). The human sciences do not answer to criteria of objectivity and systematicity, the formal criteria of a scientific form of knowledge, but they are within the positive domain of knowledge as much as any other part of the modern episteme. There is no internal deficiency here; they are not "stranded across the threshold of scientific forms" (p. 366). They are not "false" sciences; "they are not sciences at all" (ibid.). They assume the title in order to "receive the transference of models borrowed from the sciences" (ibid.).

Trying for some years now to understand what Foucault meant by this, I found some help in Tiottama Rajan's (2002) book on deconstruction and the remainders of phenomenology, which uses Foucault to look at the human sciences. Working this section of *The Order of Things* very closely in relation to Husserl, Rajan unpacks Foucault to mean that the human sciences are necessarily situated between "positivity and reflexiveness," "'surreptitiously'" demathematizing in ways that have a "deterritorializing effect . . . in the cartography of knowledge [that] is entirely unintentional." Unable to achieve "the transcendence that Husserl sought through geometry," unable to be their own foundation, they "mimic the sciences." This marks both themselves and the natural sciences as "doubling" sorts of practices and situates the human sciences as mirror to the constitutive void that effaces positivity (pp. 194–95).

Enacting "a perpetual principle of dissatisfaction, of calling into question, of criticism and contestation" (Foucault, 1970, p. 373), such knowledges are tied to a praxis of the representations we give to ourselves of ourselves, a "counter-science" (p. 379) that "unmakes" us as it "traverse[s], animate[s], and disturb[s] the whole constituted field of the human sciences . . . threatening the very thing that made it possible for man to be known" (p. 381). Here is where we learn to think again, "in the process of disappearing" (p. 385), opening ourselves to a future thought of the knowledge of things and their order.

In short, by "counter-science," Foucault is referring to those knowledges that " 'unmake' that very man who is creating and re-creating his positivity in the human sciences" (1970, p. 379). Elsewhere, Foucault situates science as a discursive event where the "inexact knowledges" become "a *field of strategic possibilities*" (1998, p. 320, emphasis in original). Noting how his own work is tied to "that strange and quite problematic configuration of human sciences" (1998, p. 311), Foucault's interest is in "undoing and recomposing" the very ground he stands on. Here, demarcation issues are refused, distinctions are seen as uncertain, and "the play of immediacies" becomes the point of analysis (p. 306).

The "privilege accorded to . . . 'the sciences of man' " is based on the "political arithmetic" (1998, p. 323) that makes particular kinds of discourse both possible and necessary. This is not so much about concepts on their way to formation or even the price paid for scientific pretensions, but rather about understanding claims to scientificity as discursive events. Such an understanding of the human sciences is more about "the play of its differences, its interstices, its distances—in some sense its blanks rather than its full surfaces" (p. 321) than it is about foundational epistemological claims, "unfold[ing] as broadly as possible" the historical space in which it has come to rest (p. 327).

Against a narrow scientificity, a social science that approaches what Bourdieu terms " 'fieldwork in philosophy' " (quoted in Flyvbjerg, 2001, p. 167) articulates Foucault's point that real change comes from changing our selves, our bodies, our souls, our ways of knowing (1991). To make difficult what we take for granted as the good, to see, in fact, what Nietzsche saw: that perhaps "there has never been a more dangerous ideology . . . than this will to good" (Flyvbjerg, 2001, p. 95), this is the first step in becoming moral, this realization that, in Foucauldian terms, ". . . everything is dangerous, which is not exactly the same as bad. If everything is dangerous, then we always have something to do" (Foucault, 1983, p. 343).

Foucault is most useful in seeing how, in the continuation of the science wars, the line between a narrowly defined scientism and a more capacious scientificy of disciplined inquiry remains very much at issue. In terms of the desirability of degrees of formalization, mathematized, generic procedures, and rigorous differentiations, there is virtually no agreement among scientists, philosophers, and historians as to what constitutes science except, increasingly, the view that science is a cultural practice and practice of culture. What are the possibilities and limits of scientificity in such a place? In what follows, I do a sort of archaeology of the term "scientism" as a way to clear the ground for a look at the less used but arguably more important term of scientificity.

Scientism

> Nobody espouses scientism; it is just detected in the writings of others.
>
> —*The Oxford Companion to Philosophy*, 2005

The problem of scientism runs through the field of science and is enjoying a resurgence, in spite of its aura of disrepute. While it may be true that no field of inquiry is unable to benefit from the methods of the natural sciences, it is quite another thing to hold up as the "gold standard" a very narrow idea of scientific method.[3] This is, it is important to note, as true for the natural or "exact" sciences as it is for the social or "conjectural" sciences, to use Lacan's terms (Leupin, 1991, p. 4), as both have a wide array of methods in use.[4]

Many logically distinct positions can be called scientism.[5] As noted in an edited collection from a conference on the "proper ambition of science" (Stone and Wolff, 2000), the questions shift from whether the laws and theories of physics can in principle subsume everything to whether everything should be studied by the methods of the physical sciences. My tack here is to focus on how what we call "science" relates to the nature and scope of philosophy, particularly the inadequacies of naturalist orthodoxy where philosophical rigor is modeled on problematic ideas of scientific work (De Caro and Macarthur, 2004). Hence, my critique is, interestingly, directed more toward philosophy of science than it is toward science itself. In this, I am, of course, in the company of Thomas Kuhn, about whom a recent book (Sharrock and Read, 2002) argues that this distinction is important in any effort to reduce the vitriol of the science wars and get us back to working across the "hard' and "soft" (or "wet" and "dry") divides toward the science possible after our disappointments in the science so structured by "a patriarchal symbolic" (Butler, 2004, p. 208).

In the science wars, an anti-science position on the part of critics is too often assumed, whereas the real target is a traditional philosophy of science with its received categories of rationality, progress, and the growth and accumulation of knowledge. This "ahistorical and mostly formalistic" (Sharrock and Read, 2002, p. 12) philosophy of science reduces scientificity to a methodological imperative and a quantitative one at that. In what follows, I divide scientism into "old" and "new" forms in the hope of saying something fresh about such well-trod ground.

Old Scientism: Of Objectivism

In a "classical argument against scientism" (Uebel, 2000, p. 151), the noted economist Friedrich August Hayek warned of the efforts to force upon the social sciences the methods of the natural sciences. First published in the early 1940s in *Economica* and then collected under the title *The Counter-Revolution of Science: Studies in the Abuse of Reason* in 1952, Hayek's polemic ranges across scientism and science, society and collectivism, subjectivism and objectivism, as well as theories of history.[6] With "the unwarranted and unfortunate extension of the habits of thought" of the physical sciences to the study of society, this narrow definition has led to confusion, discreditation, and what Hayek terms the "'scientistic'" prejudice involving "the mechanical and uncritical application of habits of thought to fields different from those in which they have been formed" (pp. 15–16). This "trespass of scientism" is "injurious" to the progress of the social sciences (p. 270). Just as science had to fight the religious prejudice, now it has to fight a scientistic prejudice, which Hayek terms a "decidedly unscientific" attitude.

Hayek became a Cold War figurehead for his "deep agenda" of worries about how scientism bred socialism (Uebel, 2000, p. 159), and he has played a major role in the articulation of neoliberal economics (Lawson, 1997). Indeed, Baez (2005) suggests that Hayek may be of more use than Dewey in helping progressive thinkers in education locate their work under conditions of neoliberal governmentality.[7] But my interest here is in his production of "one of two most famous of twentieth century polemics in philosophy of science" (Uebel, 2000, Popper being the other) that both captures and effects the beginning of the loss of authority of a tradition in a way that is prescient of later postmodern critiques (Burczack, 1994).

The loss of authority of a science reduced to scientism was further exacerbated with the work of Habermas in the 1960s. According to Habermas, scientism is part of the dominance of instrumental reason; his particular concern was the scientization of politics (Outhwaite, 1994). *Knowledge and Human*

Interests, "a systematic critique of scientism" (Critchley, 2001, p. 112), argued in 1972 that it is not obligatory to science to exclude ideas of critique and emancipation. Tapping into the long-running discussions in Germany about the differences between the human sciences and the sciences of nature, Habermas argued that the social sciences are necessarily hermeneutic and require history and sensitivity to situation-specific understandings of meaning.

Habermas's great contribution was articulating alternative methodological orientations for the social sciences. His insistence on the interplay of the philosophical and the empirical and his focused concern with scientism laid the groundwork for filling out what a critical social science might look like (e.g., Fay, 1987). Salvaging a concept of scientific truth has remained a stickier point, given his cognitive-interest model of science that collapses science into politics and power. Epistemology becomes social theory where the self-reflection of the knowing subject is central in the development of a critical science that refuses the positivism that seduced Marx.

I return to this issue of rescuing a concept of scientific truth in the renewed focus on "the thing" and the critique of radical constructivism, but Habermas was key in demonstrating how, in the history of the way positivism has exercised its grip upon the social sciences, scientistic ideas are at the root of instrumental reason. They direct us toward technocratic ideals, and "in this respect a critique of scientism also acquires political consequences" (Outhwaite, 1994, p. 12) as it makes room to develop the social sciences in the direction of orienting action rather than serving the demands of economic and political powers (Flyvbjerg, 2001).

While Kuhn was not very interested in the social sciences, his work as well created space for the development of the historical-hermeneutic or cultural sciences with their different methodological procedures where the purpose is forms of mutual understanding for the possibility of orienting action. Kuhnian postpositivism interrupted the idea of a law-like world of predictability leading to technical control. Through contact with practical life, a critical social science became intelligible with its intentions of bringing about changes in the unreflected consciousness of social agents that work toward the abolition of present institutions (Teigas, 1995).

What is produced by the "old scientism" of objectivism that has been so excoriated since the work of Hayek in the 1940s? Under methodological scientism, things become outside of history and structure, decontextualized but measurable, what Hayek termed " 'of the same logical type as Plato's determination that a just ruler is 729 times as happy as an unjust one' " (1952, p. 51). Naïve realisms of various sorts are supported along with what Whitehead termed "fallacies of misplaced concreteness" (Hayek, 1952, p. 54). All sorts of pseudo-problems arise when, in spite of much rhetoric to the contrary, it is NOT the nature of the problems that guides the choice of methods in the social sciences but, rather, a scientism where unacknowledged objectivism is the water in which the fish swim.

In the present frenzy for accountability, scientism threatens to engulf us all. As an ideology about science, scientism functions as "a type of scholarly trespassing of pseudo-exactitude, embracing incongruous models of scientific method" (Stenmark, 2001, p. 2n1).[8] Driven by the hope that other areas will share in the success of the natural sciences, yet widely refuted in even analytical philosophical arguments these days (Morris, 1992), what is this "new scientism" that is so much with us in the present moment? To what extent is it a reaction formation against interdisciplinary moves into the social context of justification, and what happens to philosophy in such moves?

New Scientism: What Happened to Philosophy?

> Current philosophy makes the hypothetico-deductive style of reasoning the essence of science . . . Not all the historicizing of Kuhn and Lakatos has dislodged this opinion one whit . . . [but there is] a changing style of reasoning . . . [where I have] learned much from *The Order of Things*.
>
> —Hacking, 2002

Sorell (1991) coined the term "new scientism" to distinguish it from an older scientism that was an "occupational hazard in philosophy" in its insistence on not only philosophy, but all of culture being led by science. The resurgence continues with striking assertions about the capacity of science to improve the everyday. In assessing the politics of the resurgence, it is important to remember Dewey, who looked forward to the extension of science into ethical and social domains (Sorell, 1991, p. 11) and the socialism of the Vienna Circle. Given such roots, the "new scientism," in short, is both more and different than a vast neoliberal conspiracy (Jewett, 2003).

If Critchley (2001) is right that scientism equates with what Husserl called objectivism (p. 115), then the values at stake in doubting the objectivity of science are crucial to the self-image of philosophy (p. 25). From Hilary Putnam (1978) to Peter Winch (1990), the cozy relation of analytical philosophy to science has been held to task for the road to nihilism that accompanies a scientism that holds that the model of the natural sciences should hold for philosophy. Since Descartes, the search for certain foundations of knowledge is part of the way epistemological justifications have been articulated. A post-Habermasian move into the social context of justification is now challenged by a resurgent scientism on the one hand and a "return of the thing" on the other (Latour, 1999, 2004; Wylie, 2002; Brown, 2001).

Jewett (2003) traces how the "ongoing struggle over the meaning of modern science for American democracy" (p. 64) sets the stage for the science wars.

In the old scientism, Dewey's value-laden take on science as a way of thinking about social, ethical, and moral questions is front and center in the shifting fortunes of the naturalist argument for the unification of science and its capacity for leadership in the development of social values. In the new scientism, such arguments are mobilized toward the same effect, but with a twist away from Dewey's focus on science as builder of participatory democracy and toward what science offers by way of management for purposes of governmentality. It is my argument that what is displaced in this move is philosophy.

This displacement maps on to an earlier displacement of philosophy by the post-Habermasian shift from epistemological to social context justification that so opens up the question of the legitimacy of an engaged social science. This shift, I posit, is both the producer and effect of the loss of the authority of philosophy, or at least the kind of philosophy that excludes from science the political, institutional, and rhetorical contexts of knowledge production and reception (Dosse, 1999). This is the philosophy that tried to transform itself into a natural science by holding that truth is only accessible through scientific method.

In Judith Butler's (2004) *Undoing Gender*, her final chapter is entitled "Can the 'Other' of Philosophy Speak?" Her interest is in a philosophy that has lost control in patrolling what is philosophy, a philosophy that has found itself doubled, outside itself, "lost" in the other, face to face with the philosophical value of not being so sure of itself (p. 234). With continental philosophy largely performed outside the boundaries of philosophy departments, literary critics, cultural critics, and social scientists have created an interdisciplinary "theory/philosophy conflation" (p. 247) that makes "the very notion of philosophy a stranger to itself" (p. 250). Here, Butler argues, philosophy proper becomes "a loner, territorial, protective, increasingly hermetic" (p. 246).

Critchley (2001) argues that obscurantism is the ghost that haunts continental philosophy and scientism is that which haunts analytic philosophy. My argument is that the issue is larger: the displacement of philosophy itself by social theory.[9] To explore this possibility, I turn to the concept of scientificity.

Scientificity

Whichever way you cut the cake, it looks like scientificity just ain't in the institutions (alone) . . . You cannot actually move from a pre-paradigmatic state to one of normal science by trying to force a particular fantasized normal science on your colleagues, even if you have the institutional muscle.

—Sharrock and Read, 2002

I first ran across this term in my reading of Foucault and have since found that scientificity has long been at the heart of the demarcation debates. But one example is the "scientificity of psychoanalysis," the seemingly endless adjudications over the scientificity of Freud (Leupin, 1991). Also of note here would be the desperate quest across various fields for scientificity, from economists (Cullenberg, Amariglio, & Fuccio, 2001) to the Institute of Educational Sciences and its determination to counter the "explosive growth of qualitative research studies" by funding only those studies that adhere to its "methodological orthodoxy" of experimental design (Bryant, 2004, p. 5). From Popperian falsifiability to Lakatosian research programmes, from criteria of testability and prediction to more recent pronouncements on reliability and generalizability (National Research Council, 2002), scientificity is about the constitution of science as science. While the recognition that science is evolving, social, and historical is oftentimes spotty, even in philosophy of science where one might expect better, the criteria of scientificity are much debated.

Historically, scientificity in the social sciences has been based on measurability, the degree to which an area resembled inquiry in physics (Rorty, 2001). Two generations of post-Kuhnian work has "done its best to fuzz up the logic-rhetoric and hard-soft distinctions" (ibid.). While what Nancy Cartwright (1999) terms "scientific fundamentalists" still hold to the task of demarcation, focus has shifted to the general structure of scientificity with openness to specific disciplinarity. Here, scientificity is continuously adapted to new contingencies. Isabelle Stengers (1997), for example, argues that scientificity is a productive constraint. Getting access to the singularity of scientific activity in the drive to address what makes a science a science, the pre-existent, neopositivist criteria are but one form in "the criteria of scientificity that are currently on the market" (p. 81). Conditions of scientificity can be mutilating; they can construct object and question in a unilateral way, drawing on social power, eliminating a priori anything that does not appear to guarantee an objective approach (p. 146). Most importantly to Stengers, it is "trivial" to solve the problem of what science is by defining science "through its objectivity" (1997, p. 81).

Foucauldian Scientificity: Undoing Positivity

In mapping such territory, Foucault describes the thresholds of positivity, epistemologization, scientificity, and formalization in his *Archeology of Knowledge* (1972, p. 186). His interest is in discourses that have the status of scientificity or pretentions to it, and those that present the formal criteria of a science in how they function as an element of knowledge (p. 184). What he does here is localize science in the framework of more general knowledge. He looks at how a science structures certain of its objects, systematizes parts of it, formalizes, underwrites strategies: here science finds its place (p. 185) where it functions among other practices; here is its ideological function (ibid.). "Ideology is not exclusive of scientificity," Foucault writes (p. 186), and the role of ideology does not diminish as rigor increases and error is dissipated. For those who know their Althusser, this is quite another cup of tea than the science/ideology distinctions that formerly reigned in the Marxist claim to scientificity. To tackle the ideological functioning of a science is to take on the "system of formation of its objects, its types of enunciation, its concepts, its theoretical choices. It is to treat it as one practice among others" (p. 186).[10] Foucault's question is "what is it for that science to be a science?" (p. 192). His answer is that to focus on demarcation criteria is to miss how "all the density of the disconnections, the dispersion of the ruptures, the shifts in their effects, the play of the interdependence are reduced to the monotonous act of an endlessly repeated foundation" (p. 188).

What Foucault helps us see is how the methodological reductionism that has radically flattened the methods into a single model is being displaced by a sort of situated scientificity that neither constricts "science" to one or two privileged models nor allows an anything goes arbitrary concept of science. While a general attitude of and emphasis on rigor and objectivity are part of a "plurality of models and types of scientificity suitable for the requirements of diverse fields," different but compatible models of scientificity are elaborated across disciplinary sites while working to avoid methodological fragmentation. In addition, recent exhortations to scientificity are more rhetorically sophisticated in urging adherence to scientific norms.[11] Here, scientificity becomes a performance—for example, the textual display of the absence of the author and/or the veneer of scientificity accomplished by the use of mathematics.[12] Bourdieu (1990) writes of this as "to simulate scientific rigor" (p. 37), "imitat[ing] the advanced sciences" (p. 39) in his argument against positivist orthodoxy and its "false rigors" (p. 40).

In this context of proliferating, situated, rhetorically-inflected scientificities, the judgment criteria for scientificity enacts an ongoing crisis. In sum, scientificity is an arena of struggle in broadening the definition of science. Given that the human sciences work with a vague concept of data, traditional notions of rigor are thwarted, especially epistemological definitions of objectivity. Sociocultural context matters here, unavoidably. Focus shifts to the proper characterization of the object, not control of the subjectivity of the knower. A science defines its own scientificity by elaboration of the conditions that determine the objects of a science and data about them. These are methodologically built objects located between radical constructivism and objectivism, both found and made, always caught in flux, in-the-making.

From Scientism to a More Capacious Scientificity

What I am endorsing here is a sort of post-methodology that bespeaks an end of grand narratives about research. Fuller (1997) refers to this as the "secularization of science." While methodology remains key to demonstrating scientific credentials, the ground would shift to foregrounding disagreements, ambiguities, uncertainties, contradictions, and incoherencies. Political, social, ontological, and personal concerns have now invaded what before was thought to be a technical arena. This is the "post" of post-methodology. Rather than essential features of science offered as a benchmark for assessing scientificity as movement toward "real science," the move is toward a scientificity defined as how a discipline works toward creating new phenomena (Hacking, 1983; Bachelard, 1949).

Osborne and Rose (1999) give an example of this in their project on the history of empirical social thought where they look at public opinion research. Embracing a scientificity that is not just exactitude, epistemology, and methodology, but involves material and technical factors as well, they look at how stable methods and instruments enhance consensus around a sense of objectivity of what has been discovered. In the social sciences characterized by no agreed-on research front, that are more about lineages and recycling back to earlier framings, recurrent commentaries, endemic disagreement, no substantial consensus, and questionable applicability, the use of statistics toward exactitude and calculability is not enough (Hacking, 1991). The central question of discovery is far more interesting than the demarcation debate.

Osborne and Rose argue that the social sciences have brought a great deal into discovery, not only public opinion and the consequent "scientization of politics" that so concerned Habermas, but also juvenile delinquency, midlife crisis, stages of moral development, self-esteem.[13] This is quite Foucauldian, of course, but it is also quite Latourian.

Latour has been a leader in this shift from epistemological, philosophical questions of demarcation to sociological questions of laboratory life and a focus on how truths and phenomena are constructed. His interest is phenomena-creation and consensus-generation processes. The world is full of facts, he argues. They are the outcome of micro practices that put them into circulation. A reality effect is produced once controversy settles through processes other than simple reference. In short, objectivity is conferred so that research on it can proceed. Candidate facts abound about a phenomena, some get "reality effect" and some don't. This is where it gets interesting, the "contingent historicity of truth" where some things become true rather than others (Latour, 1999).

What gets in the way of the social science creation of phenomena is "the illusion that the essence of scientificity lies in the formal properties of their representational systems, their theories" (Latour, 1999, p. 12). In a Foucauldian vein, the social sciences have been quite successful if we look at how they have reshaped the ways humans think about themselves, how capacity and possibility are activated.

Yet scientificity is destroyed if all the sciences are looked at only so-cially. The thingness of the thing has to be taken into account. This, Latour says, is the critique of the social studies of science. To recognize the resis-tance of natural objects to social explanations is to call for a new respect for the adequacy of objects where "Things have become Things again" (Latour, 2004, p. 236), something more and different than mere projections onto an empty screen.[14] "The old tired theme of social construction" (Stengers, 1997) means the demise of society as an adequate source of explanation. Another type of scientificity is needed for the social sciences, a postpositivist, inter-pretive scientificity that takes into account the ability of the object to object to what is told about it. Here objectivity renders objects capable of resisting social explanation.

Imitating the natural sciences won't get us to such a reinscription of objectivity, a postscientistic sort of objectivity. Latour (2000) calls for studies where objects are rendered as recalcitrant as possible, "as disobedient as possible to the protocol" (p. 6). This is a postintentional sort of objectivity that backgrounds the consciousness and reflexivity that have been front and center in efforts toward a different science. But it is also a sort of post the "post-modern eulogy of networks, fluids and fragments" that abandons the quest for a common world. Things have neither the unity of the modernists nor the multiplicity of postmodernists, Latour argues. The social is only one voice in this.

At the least, such arguments lead one to recognize that there are many kinds of objectivities. They include Haraway's formulation of the promise of objectivity where scientificity becomes partial connection and ontological relationism (1991, p. 193). They include Latour (1999) who distinguishes between "the polemical kind of objectivity" versus the objectivity created by science in action (p. 20). Perhaps explanations "resorting automatically to power, society, discourse had outlived their usefulness," Latour (2004) sug-gests (p. 229). Urging a "second empiricism," he tracks how many partici-pants are gathered in making a thing a thing. Objects are a gathering, and critique needs to move not away from but toward the gathering of the "Thing," mediating, assembling, gathering many more folds (p. 246).

One example of this approach is *The Body Multiple* (2002) by Annemarie Mol, a Dutch professor of political theory, who does social studies of medical knowledge practices. Moll documents how context-specific medical interven-tions are in a study of athrosclerosis. Moving beyond perspectivalism and constructivism, she foregrounds materialities and events in practice in order to explore how social order is possible. To give an object a complex present (p. 43) is to move beyond the "turtles all the way down" that has dominated interpretive work. "Something complicated is happening here" (p. 67), she argues, spreading the activity of knowing widely, beyond knowing subjects and objects to be known. In her work that combines ethnography and reflection on the literature in a split-text format, a sense of acute situatedness is the key in enacting how ontologies are brought about in practice. Maybe something else is happening, she argues, a sort of coherence in tension where incoherence is not a lack of scientificity. In her work, an ontology of variants in tension contributes to the "rich, adaptable, and yet tenacious character" of good practice (p. 115). The object becomes a conjunction with various distributions where ongoing incompatibilities co-exist.

This is a kind of thinking from matter and a speaking to/learning from relationality that has been pioneered by feminist science studies (Haraway, 1991; Wylie, 2002). Now linked to a critique of strong constructivism, a sort of postrealism is aborne, a new materiality that refuses the ideal/material split. This is a new objectivity about neither results nor detached knowledge, but rather what art historian Steven Melville (1996) terms "objectivity in deconstruction" where the nostalgia for transparent presence is put in tension with a respect for the object's capacity to surprise and exceed us in a way that foregrounds the inadequacy of thought to its object. Moving back closer to the object via our failed engagement with it, Melville asserts that the Kantian object argued an irreducible phenomenological status to the object that exceeded interpretation. While Kantian foundationalism caught the object in static frames, it did foreground the object's excess that resisted containment without remainder by any sense-making machine. To recover meaning is to understand the ways of grasping an object, our being struck by it. This banishes both universalism and subjectivism. A postmodern materialism, then, is about the evasion of presence. But it is also about that upon which deconstruction does its work, that which survives deconstruction by being that upon which it depends.

Kathleen Stewart (1996) enacts this in the context of ethnography where she writes of home and "how it gives rise to the desire to chronicle, to remember, how it insists on the materiality of things that matter" (p. 42). And, later, after calling on James Agee, Stewart writes of moments of inquiry that

insist on the situated and contingent and demand an interpretive space in which people can make something of things through mimesis, remembrance, and desire . . . At once concrete and ephemeral . . . accidents and derailments, watching to see what happens when things collide or de-compose. It encounters things, takes to things, piles things up, soothes, and has to get out and go. It digs itself in and grows vigilant. It claims a place for itself only through the constant experimental activity of foolin' with thangs, and so finds itself vulnerable to things frightening and sublime, uncanny and disastrous. (pp. 205–206)

In sum, the search for a normative philosophy of science has been a wrong road on both epistemological and ontological counts. A philosophy of science that abstracts from practices rather than prescribing them would include the political, institutional, constructive, and rhetorical features and contexts as well as the conditions of production and reception. The dream of the social sciences of short-cutting politics via social engineering has led to an "extravagant scientism" that thwarts efforts toward problem solving. In contrast, feminist work has long been about increasing the legitimacy of an engaged methodology that explores how a complexified social science enriched with contextual factors can be of use. I turn now to how an articulation of an interpretive scientificity might make a space for feminist empirical work to flourish in such a moment of the culture wars/science wars. Such an effort is part of what Foucault (1991) terms "the absolute optimism" of "a thousand things to do" where our constant task is to struggle against the very rules of reason and practice inscribed in the effects of power of the social sciences (p. 174).

Implications for (Post)Feminist Methodology

The proposal here is not that of giving up on knowing. To the contrary, what is at stake is the political objective to confront the postcolonial condition of love and knowledge simultaneously by cultivating a feminist ability of engaging with (not knowing) that which is constituted in part by its own effacement and limits.

—Davis, 2002

Judith Butler has recently written that "feminism is a mess" (2004, p. 175) given the meltdown of its central terms, now situated, in best practice, as historical and performative in their continued rearticulation out of engaged political practices. As such, the feminism[15] to which I am committed demonstrates how putting one's necessary categories in crisis can help us see how such categories work across time and what they exclude. Here, rearticulating begins when "the excluded speak to and from such a category . . . opening up the category to a different future" by contesting the power that works in and through it (Butler, 2004, p. 13). This is a kind of double(d) movement that uses and troubles a category simultaneously, operationalizing the classic move of deconstruction: under erasure. This reinscribed feminism is, then, again in Butler's words, "to assert an entitlement to conditions of life that affirm the constitutive role of gender and sexuality in political life while also subjecting our categories to scrutiny for their exclusions" (p. 37). This is a sort of loss, a disorientation where openness and unknowingness are part of the process, a self-reflexive, nondogmatic feminism that relishes conflicting interpretations without domesticating them, a permanent unsettlement in what might be termed a postfoundational feminism. Here, feminism is both freed from the demand to be one thing in its task of challenging how knowledge is constrained by a patriarchal symbolic and lost, "ruined by the improper use of its proper name" (Butler, p. 233, speaking of philosophy), a self-loss that is the beginning of a postidealist community. To turn, then, to scientism and scientificity in the context of a feminist effort toward a double(d) science is to address the science possible outside of the constraints of the patriarchal symbolic that Butler speaks to and against so powerfully (2004, p. 208).

Since at least Judith Stacey's 1988 "Can There Be a Feminist Ethnography," there has been a reflexive turn in feminist work. This turn has produced a plethora of internal debates, critiques, and reflections on the meaning and scope of feminist methodology. First, in their 1991 edited collection, and fourteen years later in a special issue of *Signs* devoted to feminist methodology, Fonow and Cook provided a window into these debates. Guiding principles in their earlier work consisted of reflexivity in attending to gender asymmetry, ideology critique or consciousness-raising as ways of seeing, challenges to objectivity, attention to the ethics of knowing and being known, and the empowerment of women toward the transformation of patriarchy as the ends of feminist research. Their recent survey of "newer trends and debates" (2005, p. 2215) includes: an epistemic and ontological turn toward the body, the limits of reflexivity, the deepening of the crisis of representation where we can't "get the real right" (p. 2222), and a turn to social policy, including a new emphasis on quantitative methods, as part of a continued focus on social action.

To probe this survey more deeply, I enfold an earlier articulation of feminist methodology within a nascent fold where a fold is distributed and parallel rather than sequential and linear (Martin, 2001, p. 375).[16] Hence, my point is not that feminist research is so much smarter now, but rather that the logic-in-use (Kaplan, 1964) has shifted from an earlier emphasis on countering objectivism, developing "women's ways of knowing" (Belenky et al., 1986), and debating "essentialism/constructivism" to addressing the unintended consequences of such efforts and "respect[ing] the demand for complexity" (McCall, 2005, p. 1786). The latter particularly refers to a stance toward "categorical complexity" (p. 1774) spurred by both the critique of feminism by women of color and the varied "post" movements that have so troubled Western philosophy, history, and language.[17]

As captured by Cook and Fonow (1991), the feminist methodology of the 1980s and early '90s trafficked in such terms as situated knowledges, positionalities, intersectionalities, egalitarian and empowering, praxis and reflexivity.[18] While feminist theory has always had a meta-theoretical moment in thinking about how we think (Hanssen, 2001, p. 73), more recent articulations raise troubling questions about how we think about how we think and learning to learn differently where "giving voice," "dialogue," "telling and testifying," and "empowerment" have lost their innocence. At least since Wendy Brown's 1995 "Wounded Attachments," resentment politics and the exclusionary work that identity categories do in feminist work have been much critiqued. Rosi Braidotti (2005) notes how the theoretical agenda has been reset in what she refers to as "post-post" times toward embodied materialisms, situated epistemologies, scattered hegemonies, and disseminated hybridities. The task is to do justice to the complexity and instability of all of this in addition to the dislocated identities of posthumanism that challenge oppositions of language/material and culture/nature.

The result is what Braidotti terms a sort of "post-secular" ethics (2005, p. 178) at "the end of postmodernity" (p. 171) or "late postmodernity" (p. 175) where feminist post-postmodernism faces a resurgently conservative, neoliberal timespace. Here, dialectics is inadequate in coming to grips with our time and what it might mean to try to make a difference in it. In a Deleuzean vein, her advice for strategy and hope is the "becoming minoritarian of Europe" where "the centre has to deconstruct its powers and let them lie, while the margins are the motor of active processes of becoming" (p. 174).

What this might look like begins to take shape in the displacements that abound across a broad array of trends and movements in the field of feminist methodology: "the ability of not knowing" (Davis, 2002); holding open a space for treating the "*not known*" creatively (Martin, 2001, p. 378); "a challenge to *learn*, and not to *know*" (Probyn, 2000, p. 54); the limits of empathy, voice, and authenticity (Lather, 2000); and "to persistently not know something important" (Kostkowska, 2004). Much of this echoes what Gayatri Spivak has been saying for years in terms of learning to learn from below. Alongside unlearning our privilege as a loss, more recently, Spivak (2000a) urges that we move toward "claiming transformation" and standing together as subjects of globalization as we acknowledge complicity in order to act in less dangerous ways in a "non-Euro-US world."[19] Justyna Kostkowska (2004) captures such moves well in her essay on the work of Nobel Prize-winning poet Wislawa Szmborska's privileging of uncertainty and doubt where we are fortunate to not know precisely: "This is not a will *not* to know, as the condition of ignorance, but an ability to engage with what escapes propositions and representation" (p. 199).

This move is captured in Kesby's (2005) work with HIV/AIDS in Zimbabwe where he urges a transvaluation of participatory action research that both takes poststructural concerns into account and recognizes that "some things are more dangerous than others" (p. 2043). Participation can be tyranny, yes. The World Bank's "global neoliberal strategy" (p. 2059n14) accommodates it well. But it is also a "valuable resource on which women and men can draw in order to challenge the status quo" (p. 2050). Empowerment, too, has its uses as well as abuses. Reconceptualizing rather than abandoning such discourse/practices as "contestable, incomplete work in progress" (p. 2052) can both strengthen theory and improve practice. Up against the limits of deconstruction, the task becomes to "live with its not knowing in the face of the Other" (Butler, 2001, p. 17). To not want to not know is a violence to the Other, a violence that obliterates how categories and norms both constrain AND enable. "We must follow a double path in politics," Butler (2001, p. 23) urges, using familiar terms and categories but also "yielding our most fundamental categories" to what they rend unknown. This is the double(d) science I am calling for, a double task that works the necessary tensions that structure feminist methodology as fertile ground for the production of new practices.

Given the impossibilities attendant upon complex systems, the twentieth century crisis of word and meaning defines modernity. The postmodern, then, from Nietzsche on, constructs a different relation to the exhaustion of science as certain knowledge, a subsided shock, a negativity that is outside Hegelian logic, a more heterogeneous logic, both culmination and negation of the completion of the crisis of modernism. Here, the death of god or any master signifier and the end of "the West and the rest" sort of thinking are revalenced as hardly news. The task is to reanimate via that which is still alive in a minimally normative way that does not reinscribe mastery. By creating new spaces on the edge of the intelligible, projects are put at risk rather than set up for accomodational inclusion or positioned to claim a "better" vantage point. Work is situated as ruined from the start, a symptomatic site of the limits of our knowing.

Here, feminist methodology begins to elude its capture in Hegelian terms of the dialectic and the universal, "the 'pompous march of historical necessity' " (Benhabib, quoted in Alcoff, 2000, p. 849) where big bang theories of social change have not served women well. Here, something begins to take shape, perhaps some new "line of flight" (Deleuze and Guattari, 1987) where we are not so sure of ourselves and where we see this not knowing as our best chance for a different sort of doing in the name of feminist methodology.

Ends, Continued

> End of story; end of a certain kind of story. Perhaps more precisely, end of a certain kind of writing; end of a certain kind of thinking; end of a certain notion of end(s).

> —Nealon, 1993a

In this chapter, I have made an effort toward an alteration of the science wars by engaging in a critique of philosophy of science more than of science itself. Urging a healthy respect for the adequacy of the object, I have reinscribed objectivity and articulated an interpretive scientificity that is grounded in the need for an applied social science that can cope with the multiplicity of the world. Situated in the times and places in which it is given to us to write, such work searches for the sort of doubled practices that "let the story continue," as Britzman (2000) refers to the work of representation. Caught within the incomplete rupture with philosophies of the subject and consciousness that undergird the continued dream of doing history's work, my interest is in the science possible after the questioning of the ground of science, perhaps a less ascetic, pious science, some sort of "blurred genre" or "leaky narrative" that seems monstrous to our ears at this time and place, ears still attuned to the quest for certainty and foundations.

Believing strongly that every historical era offers a new chance for knowledge, my reading of Nietzsche has convinced me that we are still recovering from the lie about the possibilities of the naked truth. Perhaps what I am advocating, then, is attention to the paradoxes that structure our work. Such attention to the collision of humanist and posthumanist assumptions in efforts to voice and make visible can help us move toward the sort of doubled practices that prompt a rethinking of the research imaginary. What I am endorsing is not the skepticism that so worries those invested in a resurgence of traditional warrants of science (e.g., Phillips and Burbules, 2000), but the yes of responsibility within possibility as well as the necessity of history and what remains to be done.

If We Held a Reunion, Would Anyone Come?

Chris Smithies, Ph.D.

When *Troubling the Angels* was published in 1997, Patti and I had not fore-seen that the book would become a historical chronicle. With the miraculous impact of the antiretrovirals that effectively managed HIV/AIDS for those with access, our work was changed forever. It became a documentation of the "first phase" of the AIDS crisis as experienced and told by 25 Ohio women. What a stunning surprise ending: the final chapter was no longer illness and then death, but the opportunity to reclaim the uncertainty of living life with a restored future.

The new millennium brought hope and demanded new direction in the lives of those who had been united and focused on surviving a virus. There was cautious exuberance, confusion, even depression as so many faced the restoration of life and with it, responsibility and the need for new identities. Would these women have spouses or partners or would loneliness be the price for living with a quieted but omnipresent infection? Would it be possible to return to school or former jobs? One woman asked "how do I face my credit card debt now that I am going to live?" Off to credit counseling for her.

The new space in so many lives created a dramatic shift in relationships that once seemed cemented together by the mission of survivorship. By 1998, our Columbus support group had become a social group that met several

79

times a year. We still ate great food and talked about the changes in everyone's lives. There were several marriages, a healthy baby, relocations, new jobs, and eventually a Ph.D. Some relationships continued as solid friendships, gifts of the AIDS crisis. But eventually, we just stopped meeting, a phenomenon, not a decision.

This phenomenon was perfectly timed for me. It allowed a graceful exit from a mission that had defined and absorbed me for more than a decade. HIV/AIDS was undoubtedly the most meaningful, rewarding, and challenging work of my professional life. I also maintained a thriving but demanding clinical practice as a psychologist. By 2000, I was burning out, an experience painfully familiar to most providers of mental health and social services. I watched the clock during counseling sessions and I was tired of struggling with managed care companies to make a living. It was difficult to read or listen to anything about AIDS. I was relieved that *Troubling the Angels* was finally published and the support group was finished. Worst of all, I saw no attractive professional opportunities. How would I redefine my self?

My personal life was a consuming and healthy distraction. In *Troubling the Angels*, I credited my AIDS work with Ohio women for inspiring me to follow the dream of becoming a mother. Elena was born in 1994, in Paraguay, and my partner and I adopted her when she was three months old. In *Troubling the Angels*, I also shared the joy I experienced when our infant daughter was passed lovingly from one HIV+ woman to another; those women graced her with their love, affection, and optimism. Elena has developed into a preteen who lives without fear or judgment of AIDS or other differences. Her outlook on life has been only positive. Her moms have become deeply proud that she has developed into a loving, thoughtful, accepting, and insightful young person. So far, so good.

When it was time for Elena to start kindergarten, we chose an outstanding private school, Columbus School for Girls. This environment nurtured our daughter's spirit as well as her intellect. Friends teased that I would do school all over again, uniform and all, if I had the chance. In 2003, that chance arrived when I applied for the position of Middle School Counselor. I would work with sixth-, seventh-, and eighth-grade girls and their families. I had no professional experience in school environments and I had not applied for a job in 15 years. I was nervous but gleeful when I was hired—big challenge, new environment, colleagues, regular paycheck, and plenty of female energy!

The first year at Columbus School for Girls was tough. Working collaboratively with Patti was one thing, but now I was in an institutional environment where "team work" and collaboration were the hallmarks of daily life. I had to learn "school culture," "girl culture," and earn the respect of my colleagues. Slowly, I became a counselor, guide, consultant, resource, advocate, and humorist to 150 girls and 25 faculty members. The vitality and intellectual life of the community were contagious; I soon cherished the opportunity to work with young and healthy girls in a feminist environment. As these students have struggled with identity formation, friendship issues, and family problems, my small contribution has been to empower them to stay healthy and to grow toward their potential. I have envisioned amplifying the voices of these remarkable young women with a qualitative and collaborative research effort that will likely mirror *Troubling the Angels* in process, function, and form.

Such a project would require a co-researcher, a co-author, a relationship as genuinely collaborative as the one I experienced with Patti. I only see Patti two or three times a year now, another effect of a project and era completed, but the respect and friendship have been abiding in both our lives. We have discussed our "marriage of purpose" and have agreed that years of feminism, whether academic or activist, prepared us for our collaboration. We agreed on the big picture, a book that would pipeline the voices of HIV-affected women to the world. Our own strong wills and independent minds were yoked by the urgency and fascination of this task, by the backwash of AIDS survival. As Linda B. reminded us when things were going slowly: "Some of us are on deadline, you know."

That's how it was then for the Ohio women. Now with more than 40 million people worldwide infected with the HIV virus, it is still the common story for those without access to treatment.

In *Troubling the Angels*, I wondered what the world would hold for Elena's generation with regard to sexuality and HIV/AIDS. When Elena was a precognitive infant, I practiced talking to her about adoption and sexuality. We have since managed to be very open about both topics. Soon the time will come to show her a condom, an event that would alarm many parents in our seemingly safe world of private education and unmitigated opportunity. Parents have hoped that their daughters would postpone full sexual activity until they have achieved emotional maturity. How easily we have forgotten our own early experiences! In reality, many teens have experimented and made poor choices. Parents must shield daughters and sons with knowledge, self-esteem, and yes, condoms, so our children might emotionally and physically survive the demands of a media-driven and sexualized culture.

For more than a decade, HIV/AIDS was daily news in the United States. Our Ohio women were brave, open, sisterly, and humorous. *Troubling the Angels* connected their stories to women all over the world. Our model of research was quite secondary to their purpose and needs, though many "got it" as our work progressed toward publication. We never expected that our work would be a snapshot of an era before medical science transformed devastation to survivorship to full lives. Today, the surviving Ohio women have become wives, partners, mothers, farmers, teachers, nurses, social workers,

students, workers, retirees, and undoubtedly they continue to be strong, ram-
bunctious, and caring.

If we had a reunion, would anyone come? Yes, because there was a
significant life experience shared by these women, similar to veterans who
survived a war. The love, affection, and support were sustaining and sometimes the only available medicine. No, because it would be too painful to
revisit the fear of the era, the grief of missing friends because they died of
AIDS. Life has moved on for all of us.

I am hopeful that we will have a reunion because I will bring Elena. I
want her to know these women not only from the pages of a book, but as real
women who graced our lives with their courage, fortitude, and humor.

Chapter 4

Textuality as Praxis

With Ears to Hear the Monstrous Text

Troubling clarity.—To pose the problem of the text.—Refusing to produce the tidy text.—With ears to hear: Response data.—The work of theory: Scattered speculations on the question of values.

"Nothing more subtle than the advice to be clear in order at least to appear true," wrote Walter Benjamin (1989, p. 6). Such words trouble the call for plain speaking that is often assumed to be the innocent other to "elitist" and "difficult" writing. By "trouble," I mean to interrogate a commonsense meaning by mobilizing the forces of deconstruction in order to unsettle the presumed innocence of transparent theories of language that assume a mirroring relationship between the word and the world. I ground my remarks in Chris and my effort to write a multivoiced text that speaks to a broad audience about the experiences of women living with HIV/AIDS (Lather and Smithies, 1997).

There is no small amount of debate within feminism on such issues. "Accessibility" is seen as "essential to the feminist message" on the part of a major feminist journal editor who insists on moving against complex language to interrupt corruption by the academy (Joeres, 1992, pp. 702, 703). Against such either/or framings of the accessibility/inaccessibility issue, Diane Elam (1994) argues that challenging disciplinary boundaries and interrupting disciplinary procedures is political work that has to be both within and against disciplinary standards of discourse, especially renegotiating the limits of philosophy.

I am not uninterested in how academic work can enter common parlance and contribute to the struggle for social justice. My goal is not a "for

or against" widespread cultural dissemination of ideas, but rather an exploration of possibilities in the face of limit questions. Limit questions are both
insistent and indeterminable, such as the theory/practice relationship, which
is always both urgent and unanswerable in any context-free way. My objective, then, is to enact a double reading, to think opposites together in some
way that is outside any Hegelian reconciliation that neutralizes differences. In
order to enact such a double reading of the insistent and interminable question of accessible language in academic writing, I proceed according to
deconstructive moves. First, I perform an oppositional reading within the
confines of a binary system, by reversing the binary accessible/inaccessible.[1]
Second, I perform a reflexive reading that questions the inclusions/exclusions,
orderings/disorderings, and valuations/revaluations of the first move of reversal,
as an effort to reframe the either/or logic that is typical of thinking about the
issue at hand. It is here that I delineate Chris and my textual and interpretive
moves in *Troubling the Angels* in the paradox of writing that is both accessible
to a broad audience and troubling of the uses of transparent language. Using
what Gayatri Spivak (1987) has termed scattered speculations on the question
of value, I conclude with some thoughts on the work of theory in thinking the
multiple (im)possibilities for thought outside the normalized, routinized,
commodified structures of taken-for-granted intelligibility.

The Reversal: Troubling Clarity

In an essay on "responsibility," Gayatri Spivak writes "as a practical academic" about Derrida's use of "a language that must be learned" as a "teaching language" that "may be accessible to a reading that is responsible to the
text" (1994, p. 27).[2] Hortense Spillers (1994), writing from an African-
American subject position, argues that intellectuals cannot be embarrassed
out of the advantage of being able to probe the contribution that theory can
make to exposing and illuminating oppression. This is what she calls "the
question for theory" (p. 107), as she writes against outcries that scholars of
color must always write so as to be readable by some general public. Wahemma
Lubiano (1991) concurs as she urges marginalized intellectuals to "elbow"
themselves into the site of postmodernism in order to "figure out what happens when the idea of metanarratives is up for grabs" (p. 152). Using Catherine
Belsey to argue that realism is about "a world we already seem to know" that
"offers itself as transparent" (p. 165), Lubiano urges the use of other practices
of representation that decenter traditional realistic narrative forms. Such urgings
are about the relationship of theory and practice, language and power, and the
need for new languages to create new spaces for resistance and the
(re)construction of knowledge/power relations.

Patrick McGee (1992), in *Telling the Other*, writes that to aim at transparent meaning in ethnographic practice is to inscribe one's ideas within the
immediate understanding that resides in the register of the real. Against this,
he quotes Lacan to posit a writing that "is not to be understood . . . Reading
does not oblige us to understand anything. It is necessary to read first" (p.
69). Reading without understanding is required if we are to go beyond the
imaginary "real" of history. Truth is what cannot be said, what can be only
half said: "truth is what our speech seeks beyond meaning" (p. 71). Refusing
to substitute one semblance for another, with various people contending for
positions as the police of truth, McGee uses Lacan to argue that what is
speakable is coded and overcoded. As disruptive excess, the unspeakable
cannot be reduced to the easily understood. To speak so as to be understood
immediately is to speak through the production of the transparent signifier,
that which maps easily onto taken-for-granted regimes of meaning. This runs
a risk that endorses, legitimates, and reinforces the very structure of symbolic
value that must be overthrown. Hence, for Lacan, not being understood is an
ethical imperative.[3]

This is not to deny that the mystifying effects of academic language
support the illusion that those institutionally situated are "in the know" and
that "those who cannot understand have been legitimately excluded from
understanding" (McGee, 1992, p. 121). But neither is the transparent use of
language innocent. Clear speech is part of a discursive system, a network of
power that has material effects.[4] Premised on incorporating a particular form
of everydayness into public statements as tools of circulation and naturaliza-
tion, charges of "not in the real world" or "too academic" (Miller, 1993, p.
164) have particular kinds of effects. For example, the easy to read is positioned against the unreadable by a "get-real press" rife with journalistic in-
tolerance for deconstruction in the face of information overload and a "get to
the point impatience" (Nealon, 1993a, quoting Stephens, p. 176).

Such calls for clear speech from the "real world" charge that academic
"big talk" about "high theory" is a masturbatory activity aimed at a privileged
few (Spivak, interviewed in Winant, 1990, pp. 90–91).[5] Against such calls, the
example of Sigmund Freud serves to illustrate how a clinician's turn to theory
can safeguard the practitioner against the immediacy of the demands of clinical practice. Freud gave a weight to client utterances that carried the charge
of questions posed to theory and, as a result, brought practice and theory to
productive crisis. Hence, psychoanalytic theory works in the clinical encounter as a need for rigorous questioning, not as an avoidance of the call of
suffering, but as an attempt "to allow it the time of another hearing"
(Shamdasani, 1994, p. xiv). This revaluation work of folding back on practice
of another hearing outside the safe assurance of a pregiven interpretation is

far closer to the demands of practice than is first supposed. In Freud's work, theory and practice interpenetrate one another into a discontinuity where each calls the other into question. Theory itself becomes pragmatic, even as the pragmatic action of therapy becomes theory.

Sometimes we need a density that fits the thoughts being expressed. In such places, clear and concise plain prose would be a sort of cheat not untied to the anti-intellectualism rife in American society (Giroux, 1992). Hence, "the politics of clarity," to use Giroux's title, is a central issue in the debate over the relationship of theory and practice. Positioning language as productive of new spaces, practices, and values, what might come of encouraging a plurality of theoretical discourses and forms and levels of writing in a way that refuses the binary between "plain speaking" and what Judith Butler refers to as the "values of difficulty" (2003)? What are the issues involved in assumptions of clear language as a mobilizing strategy? What are the responsibilities of a reader in the face of correspondence theories of truth and transparent theories of language?[6] What is the violence of clarity, its noninnocence?

In a talk at Ohio State's Wexner Center for the Arts,[7] Steven Melville (1986) spoke of Stanley Cavell's (1976) questions: What is the problem in "not getting it"? Who is on trial: the receiver? the sender? The dilemma can't be solved, Melville argued; there is no referee, but the dilemma can be insisted on. Just as the photograph is particularly dangerous for its purported realism and painting less so, Melville delineated practices that juxtapose traditional and uncanny forms. The uncanniness is due to attention to the act of appearing, to the layers and filters that are the conceptual frames that are the conditions of an object's appearing. What is the claim of the mirror, he asked. Is it a false promise of verisimilitude where the "real" message is that the appearance of the same is not the same? What is the political bite of such practices of layers of wandering, gestures toward styles, practices that cancel themselves to work against the emergence of directedness, that run the risk of knowledge in texts that work over and through themselves, within "the dream of doing history's work"?

Building on Melville's questions, in the face of pressing problems around language, knowledge, and power, across multiple publics and diverse levels of intelligibility, how might we expand the possibilities for different ways of writing, reading, speaking, listening, and hearing?

The Reflexive Move: Troubling the Angels

What follows is a sort of "autotranslation," a textual self-speculation that is both necessary and impossible about Chris and my book on women living with HIV/AIDS. My move assumes that to stage the problem of the text is to think philosophically, given that philosophy is about always trying to comprehend its own thought and practice (McDonald, 1985).

In *Troubling the Angels*, my co-researcher and I attempted practices that move across different registers into a sort of hypertext that invites multiple ways of reading. Our task from the beginning was to produce what the participants in our study called a K-Mart book, a book widely available to HIV+ women like themselves and their families and friends. Combining this with my gnomic and abstruse ways of knowing was a source of both energy and paralysis. The result is a book shaped by the doubled charge of creating a text that would do the work the women wanted while taking into account the crisis of representation.

Decisions about the textual format grew out of many factors: my interest in nonlinear, many-layered textuality, the practical need for a format that would allow Chris and myself to write separately and then combine parts, our desire to include whatever the women themselves wanted to contribute in the way of writing, and, finally, my interest in the angel as a means of addressing what Rilke (1989) terms the "Too Big" or "too great, too vast" (p. 317) in a way accessible to a broad-based audience.

By refusing to produce a "tidy" text that maps easily onto our usual ways of making sense, Chris and I reach toward a generally accessible public horizon while moving from a "realist" to an "interrogative" text. Rather than seemingly unmediated recounting of participant narratives or unobtrusive chronicling of events as they occur, we "both get out of the way and in the way" (Lather and Smithies, 1997, p. xiv) in a manner that draws attention to the problematics of telling stories that belong to others. Ruminating on Nietzsche's textual style in terms of the question of audience provides a kind of sense of what Chris and I have done in the name of creating a multiply-coded text on women, AIDS, and angels.

In *Nietzsche's Philosophy of Science*, Babette Babich (1994) argues that the key to Nietzsche's style of philosophy is a resolute provisionality that moves from skepticism to affirmative experimentation with illusion via a style that is multivalent, heterogeneous, and multivoiced, even choral. Challenging even the credibility of its doubt (p. 21), the Nietzschean text works "to spur what would be the best reader, whether or not this reader could ever exist" (p. 23). Via a kind of "oblique search for the right reader," the text disrupts what in itself is available to the general reader in order to spur the "right reader" (ibid.). Quoting Nietzsche in his "slow search for those related to me" (ibid.), Babich delineates how Nietzsche puts into play the hermeneutic polyphony and ambivalence of reception. Knowing the power of the reader to make the text, Nietzsche's practice was to affect, forearm, and disarm the reader. Putting the author's style up against the reader's style, the Nietzschean text issues a kind of "herald call" that challenges any easy reading via shifting styles/masks, "seeking the reader who would be caught in this way" (p. 24). "Lured by the shifting of such a multifarious text," the engaged reader "is the reader conceived as a thinker" (ibid.).

This reminds me of a woman who approached me at a conference to urge me to keep the angels in the book, to not eliminate them in the name of not imposing what is, unarguably, my own investment in the work of the angels in the text. Telling a story of being a woman outside of formal education, hungry to feed her mind but not knowing where to turn except the book racks at grocery stores and K-Marts, she troubles any easy notions of a reader "willing to confront and answer the challenge of philosophic thought" (Babich, 1994, p. 24). What is on the inside/outside of accessibility and how can we tap this and evoke in readers a complicity toward troubling the taken-for-granted? Babich asks what audience is there for a kind of "skewed hermeneutic nexus of romance and rapture, conflict and accession [which] transcends critique? . . . Who can have ears for such an author?" (1994, p. 25).

Situating the text as a kind of doubled gauntlet, both a challenge to read and a course to be run, the Nietzschean text "draws and then evades . . . seducing the reader with 'ears to hear'—that is, the reader who can think—by means of the mutable allure of a shifting text" (Babich, 1994, p. 27). Creating a text, then diverting it in a way that returns the question from reader to author, undercutting both authority and tradition and the reader and the author, Nietzschean textuality effects a multiregister movement, "interior to the discourse that is not only self-reflexive but self-subverting" (ibid.). This is a writing for the reader able to understand, but it is also an active filter aimed at eliciting differing capacities for understanding.

Within Nietzsche's textual practice, reading becomes rumination and fosters brooding, a way of reading that produces a reading and then, "within the reflective memory of the first reading, read[s] again" (Babich, 1994, p. 28). This is Nietzsche's signature: advance and demurral, deliberate inscription and covert subversion (ibid.), a double valencing that constructs both a broad appeal and a kind of "renewedly new" reading with each reading. This concept of "coded coding" that has it both ways (p. 33) helps me to locate myself in the problematic of a text that works toward a practice that erases itself at the same time as it produces itself. Like Rilke's *Duino Elegies*, in a text that accumulates meaning as it progresses, a reader must move across the different registers of a text that has become a series of reflections and retractions, propositions and rejections, models and deflation of models, backtracking to issues that can't be settled for long, ruminations that dramatize the construction of a poetics as well as an ontology, canceling the distance between subject and object, reader and writer and written about (Komar, 1987). Here, the text turns back on itself, putting the authority of its own affirmations in doubt, an undercutting that causes a doubling of meanings that adds to a sense of multivalence and fluidities. Such a practice makes space for returns, silence, interruptions, and self-criticism and points to its own incapacity. Such a practice gestures beyond the word via a textuality that works at multiple levels to construct an audience with ears to hear.

Enacting the tensions between broad accessibility and the complicated and complicating moves of Nietzschean textuality, *Troubling the Angels* is a hypertextual pastiche that is a "warping of comfort texts" (Meiners, 1994), aimed at opening up possibilities for displaying complexities. Given the critical practices at work in this text that requires more of readers, why couldn't *Troubling the Angels* have been a "simple" text, a "realist tale" (Van Maanen, 1988)? Such a tale would tell the stories that the women want to tell and would not risk displacing their bodies and their stories with high theory. Why did I feel I had to read Nietzsche in order to proceed? How do I reconcile myself to palpable costs in terms of time and the ethics involved in using the site of this inquiry to wrestle with what it means to move toward a less comfortable social science? As one of the women in the study wrote, "When are you guys going to publish? Some of us are on deadline, you know!" And as Simon Watney notes, much writing on AIDS in the social sciences is "taking the scenic route through an emergency" (1994, p. 221).

Such questions and cautions push my own motives and form the basis for this second reading of the politics of accessible language, a reading that reflexively addresses what was absent in the first move of reversal of the accessibility/inaccessibility binary. That reversal troubled calls for clarity in academic writing in order to denaturalize such calls, to situate them as noninnocent. This second reading explores possibilities in the face of limit questions about the kinds of knowledge and reading practices that reinscribe the relation between accessibility/inaccessibility so as to change not only the terms, but the ordering structure of relations.

With Ears to Hear: The Monstrous Text

Let's say I was trying to produce texts that produce other ears, in a certain way—ears that I don't see or hear myself, things that don't come down to me or come back to me. A text, I believe, does not come back.

—Derrida, in McDonald, 1985

Derrida writes of "the text [that] produces a language of its own, in itself, which while continuing to work through tradition emerges at a given moment as a *monster*, a monstrous mutation without tradition or normative precedent" (in Kearney, 1984, p. 123). While *Troubling the Angels* has precedent,[8] it is an effort to "perform what it announces" through its textuality. What helps me to navigate the (necessarily) troubled waters of this inquiry designed "to be of use" (Piercy, 1973) is a movement between, with, and across academic "high" theory and the reactions of various readers of the book. In what follows, these reactions are presented within an argument that an ending commensurate with the complications of such a study is enriched by the "fold" (Deleuze, 1993) of this sort of "response data" (St. Pierre, 1997a), where "the audience teaches you something," perhaps particularly that "we need other people to help us think."[9]

Fold 1: Graduate Students

One fold is from student writing from a 1994 summer course I taught at the University of British Columbia. Their comments were written in reaction to my paper "The Validity of Angels" (Lather, 1995). On the one hand, there was resistance to the seduction into angelizing and concerns about latent New Age triggers, the dangers of seeming to point to a way out, the deflection of the "main" task, and the reinforcing of binaries and romanticizing in a way that elides material contexts.

> The discussion of how to 'do' science differently raises important ques-
> tions, but not with women who are dying . . . the philosophy of the
> research has overtaken the bodies of the women with HIV/AIDS . . . I
> am so overwhelmed with questions about ethnography and the contra-
> dictions of Social Science . . . I am excited about the philosophy and
> am seduced by its radical freedoms; I am skeptical of its abrogations
> and its recklessness at the same time. More than before I am thinking
> about responsibility—as a writer, a researcher, and as a woman in the
> institution (Diane Hodges).[10]

On the other hand, my insisting (on) angels in this study was read as a de-demonizing discourse that worked to decenter the "main" topic in a way that parallels the lack of an epicenter in the pandemic itself. "Here, conventional stories of science and praxis won't do" (Cliff Falk). Working toward some different concept of (dis)ease, the economy of troubling angels posits "in-your-face" angels who are about the lack of social resources and workable spirituality and the lack of control over death that so troubles a society used to controlling through science. One student wrote:

> As a First-Nations person . . . I am familiar with the notion of the un-
> knowable or uncontrollable . . . I like your use of troubling angels be-
> cause it troubles the space between life and death, the material and the
> un-material (Elaine Herbert).

Another student wrote a more conflicted response:

> The angel [works] as a means of writing the unwritable. I do like the
> idea of not creating a 'simple' story, whatever that may be. These women

are not living a single story although we have, as a society, constantly attempted to write one for them and for us around the issue of AIDS. And the angel, as you have presented, holds the possibility of the telling in excess of our frames of reference. Be that as it may, the angel is still a troubling choice . . . The redemption angel is so present in our culture, especially right now . . . The kind of angel you are attempting to evoke seems a metaphor for AIDS and how it brings us up against so much of what we attempt to avoid in this society: death, our lack of control over death and our struggle to make sense of that which does not make sense. The angel as a critical gesture is very powerful if somehow you, and the reader, can generate an angel such as Benjamin's in the context of these women's stories (Robin Cox).

Fold 2: Undergraduate Students

A second fold of response data is a collage from student writing from an undergraduate anthropology course on AIDS where the desktop-published book was previewed.[11] Alternating fonts indicate a different student voice.

I couldn't follow along regarding the women's identities . . . divided pages . . . and angels . . . unsettling . . . I wanted to find out about the women, but I felt like there was always something in my way: either random boxes, lines across the page, or angels floating by. *All most people expect is a kind of voyeurism into lives usually unseen . . . book kept my attention. I did struggle with the format, but it was survivable. I found myself pondering the points made in the angel intertexts . . . It may be that I am not being sufficiently post-modern when I see the need to connect the layers of meaning. If struggling with the text is the entire point, point taken!* frustrated . . . angry, at the structure and some of the content of the book . . . I had tried to actually KNOW who each of the women is . . . However this aspiration to understand who each woman is was perhaps stifled . . . Maybe we aren't supposed to form attachments to the individual women, to imply that they are merely representatives of the thousands of women living with HIV/AIDS, but I don't find this as effective as portraying them as whole and real people. *I did not at all understand the significance of the angels . . . they really were in no way related to most of the book. Sadly enough, the angel chapters seemed to resemble commercials. I started to flip the pages as one would flip the channel . . . The work was supposed to be on women speaking their minds in support groups, but before you know it, we're introduced to the personal lives of the authors and sit in on conversations during car rides.* The poignant and richly informative [stories in the book are] about women and AIDS for women with AIDS, [but the text] violated my traditional reading patterns. The layers of meaning and detail were simultaneously literal and metaphorical . . . intentionally simultaneous . . . esoteric but at the same time wildly interesting . . . [where] I found myself getting lost in those levels of discourse all too often. *Like any other college student, [I] read it all the night before we were to discuss it in class. And while this reading style would have worked for any other book, it was difficult to do for this book. The difficulty arose in part due to the fragmentary style of the book, but mostly from the trouble I had trying to refrain from stopping and thinking about what I had just read.* I felt lost . . . I actually feel this is a disservice to all the women who participated in this book . . . intellectualized and theorized . . . I had many expectations that were not met and were actually contradicted.

How am I to hear such commentary? Refusing textual innocence and an untroubled realism, I have moved to what Deborah Britzman (1995) terms ethnography as "a site of doubt" where the focus is on how poststructuralism fashions interpretive efforts, "the disagreements, the embarrassments, the unsaid, and the odd moments of uncertainty in contexts overburdened with certain imperatives" (p. 236). Here, the task becomes to operate from a textual rather than a referential notion of representation, from persuading to producing the unconscious as the work of the text (Lather, 1996). Such a move troubles the sort of reflexive confession that becomes a narcissistic wound that will not heal and eats up the world by monumentalizing loss. My interest is, rather, in Derrida's ethos of lack when lack becomes an enabling condition, a limit used (Butler, 1993b).

Maybe it is a matter of something like Maurice Blanchot's "This work is beyond me" (1982, p. 126). Maybe the book is not respectful of its sources, putting style ahead of ethics and substance. Perhaps it falls over the edge of "vanity ethnography" (Van Maanen, 1988) in not avoiding the self-indulgence that "goes too far" in efforts to bring the researcher into the narrative as an embodied knower (Mykhalovskiy, 1996). And what of the problems with the translator as betrayer, intercepting rather than relaying the women's stories? In our desire to address what it means to know more than we are able to know and to write toward what we do not understand, how do we deal with what Renato Rosaldo (1993) terms "the vexed problem of representing other lives" (p. 117)?

"Easy to spot the problem hard to supply the ethic!" Serres writes, in addressing a code of practice for messengers (1995a, p. 101). His answer is quite useful here in all its density: that the task of the translator is to fade out behind the message, once the incomprehensibility of the message is communicated, once philosophy herself appears, in the flesh. Becoming visible as an intermediary, the task of the translator becomes to empty out the channel while still foregrounding the productive and distorting effects of the channel, a kind of presence, and absence, and presence again (p. 104). The only way to break free from this is to invent new channels, which will soon become blocked again as we derive importance from the channels we create, but the goal is to disappear in delivering the word of the something else which the word signals and gestures toward.

Serres helps me situate myself and follow the relations between, with, and across a text that layers the women's stories of living with HIV/AIDS, researcher interpretive moves, and "factoid" boxes, all juxtaposed with angel intertexts that bring moments of sociology, history, poetry, popular culture, and "determined policy talk" into a network of levels and orders. Deleuze and Guattari (1983) have termed such an assemblage a rhizome, an open trajectory of loose and resonating aggregates as a way to trace how the space of knowledge has changed its contours. Such practices of writing call out an audience with ears to hear. It is here that the response data is of use to me in forming resources for thought in what it means to pose the problem of the text.

Reception, of course, takes on a momentum of its own and moments of failure are particularly important in tracing the kind of work that something does. It is this that draws me in the response data, particularly the references to how *Troubling the Angels* defies "our narrative urge to make sense of, to impose order on the discontinuity and otherness of historical experience" (Hansen, 1996, p. 298). In a space where untroubled witnessing will not do, the text undercuts any immediate or total grasp via layers of point-of-view patterns. Working toward a broad public horizon to present traumas that cannot be approached directly, a sort of resolute materialism is performed via a "flood" or "blizzard" of too much too fast, data flows of trauma and shock, and asides of angel breathers, breaking down the taxonomic principles we bring to reading (Ellison, 1996, p. 358), renogiating the limits of philosophy in staging the problems of representation.

Hybrid ethnographic texts are nothing new; neither is the effort to popularize and reach a broader audience. Ruth Behar (1995a) points this out in her introduction to *Women Writing Culture*, calling on the work of Zora Neale Hurston. "Writing hurts," Behar goes on to say, telling the story of Esperanza, her informant in *Translated Woman*, who refused to take a copy of the book that Behar had traveled to Mexico to give to her. "Please, take this back, too. We can't read it, anyway" (Behar, 1995b, p. 77).[12]

Such tensions have moved me to produce a book written out of a kind of rigorous confusion where representation is practiced as a way to intervene, even while one's confidence is troubled. The task becomes to work the ruins of a confident social science as the very ground from which new practices of research might take shape. In this move, I have come to think of the book as an unauthorized protocol developed in the face of our unbearable historicity, a sort of stammering relation to what it studies that exceeds the subjectivity and identity of all concerned. Here, we all get lost: the women, the researchers, the readers, the angels, precipitating an "onto-epistemological panic" (Derrida, 1994) aimed at opening up present frames of knowing to the possibilities of thinking differently.

In this account of strategies risked, perhaps the angel is the sort of writing out of failure that Blanchot (1986) speaks of in *The Writing of Disaster*. "Falling beneath Disastrous necessity," (p. 11) writing "In failure's intensity . . . when history takes fire and meaning is swallowed up," (p. 47) Blanchot separates himself from that which is mastery and power as he strives toward a language "where the unrepresentable is present in the representation which it exceeds" (p. 111).

In a context where AIDS is overburdened with representations (Treichler, 1988), here is yet another. Circulating among many questions, sharpening problems, making insufficiencies pressing, and clarifying the limits of any easy resolutions, the angel works to make the text say more and other about something as absurd and complicated as dying in the prime of life of a disease of global proportions. Via a path of detours and delays, in an alchemy beyond conscious intentionality, the angel gains a new and unsettling valence. Here, Chris and I settle for ". . . something other than to entertain in the key of sentimental optimism . . . some fusion of kitsch and death that is adequate to the topic it engages" in a form that defies our need to understand what can be said and known about the lives of others and the meaning of history (Hansen, 1996, p. 298).

Even as we are suspicious of "the mystifying ends to which enchantment can be put" (Cohen, 1993, p. 259), the angel functions in a space-time of turbulence and passages of relational bodies "where the most fragile bring the new and have to do with the future" (Serres, 1995b, p. 123). Working to reject sentimentality, the angels provide a resonant spectacle in the crucible of lives lived in historical time. Hence, the very dangers of angels may signal their usefulness in Chris and my search for a multiply-layered way of telling stories that are not ours.

In using the response data to locate myself in this text of responsibility, I am paradoxically attracted to wandering and getting lost as methodological stances. Trying "to stay lost, bewildered, suspended, and in flight" (Serres, 1995a, p. 264), I am simultaneously stuck against the humanist romance of knowledge as cure within a philosophy of consciousness, while turning toward textual innovations that disrupt humanist notions of agency, will, and liberation. In this doubled space, trying to elicit differing capacities for understanding, Chris and I send out possibilities for a different kind of thinking about representation. The nonarrival of such messages is part of the play of the network (Nealon, 1993b, p. 233). Working out of the place and necessity of represen-tation, Derrida advises "knowing how not to be there and how to be strong for not being there right away. Knowing how not to deliver on command, how to wait and to make wait . . ." (Derrida, quoted in Nealon, 1993b, p. 234).

Enacting a rhizomatic thinking in a text that peforms what philosophy has become in the postmodern, Chris and I cannot reconcile the contradic-tions that traverse this book about bodies of knowledge and knowledge of bodies. Rather than resolution, our task is to live out the ambivalent limits of research as we move toward something more productive of an enabling violation of its disciplining effects. Inhabiting the practices of its rearticulation, "citing, twisting, queering," to use Judith Butler's words (1993b, p. 237), we occupy the very space opened up by the (im)possibilities of ethnographic representation.

The Work of Theory: Scattered Speculations on the Question of Value

[Efforts toward practicing a representation responsible to a different way of thinking] go beyond understanding in some way, they go past the usual understanding . . . indeed, they just don't quite go. It is a question, in truth, of the impossible itself. And that is why I took the risk of speaking a moment ago of aporia. It would have to fail in order to succeed. In order to succeed, it would have to *fail*, to fail *well* . . . And while it is always promised, it will never be assured . . . a work that would have to work at failure.

—Derrida, 1996a

To conclude, I return to the work of theory in thinking the multiple (im)possibilities for thought outside taken-for-granted structures of intelligi-bility. In reinscribing the parameters of responsible practices of academic writing, I find Spivak's (1993) thoughts on the politics of representation particularly useful. Thinking her way out of the philosophy of consciousness of humanism, Spivak probes the kinds of narratives that are of use in a postfoundational era. Spivak's interest is in "the responsible study of culture [that] can help us chart the production of versions of reality . . . the respon-sibility of playing with or working with fire [that does not] pretend that what gives light and warmth does not also destroy" (Spivak, 1993, pp. 282–83).

Hence, this chapter is an account of staging the problems of represen-tation within a posthumanist frame (Spanos, 1993). Like Spivak, my invest-ment is in negotiating with an enabling violence attentive to frame narratives that works against the terrain of controllable knowledge. Stubbornly holding on to the rhythms of the unfoldings of a book that as much wrote me as the other way around, I turn to the theory that helps articulate the investments and effectivities of what Chris and I have wrought. Here, I read the affirmations and critiques of our effort as troubling thought about what it means for a book to interrogate, through its particularity, transparent theories of language and, consequently, the status of ethnography.

In sum, working from, with, and for women living with HIV/AIDS, like Fiske (1996) in his juxtaposition of black voices and Foucault as a white theoretical discourse in regards to the differential spread of AIDS, I am unsure as to whether the book is symptom, index, or intervention. It is a risky business, this mining of discursive resources toward a kind of knowledge that jolts us out of our familiar habits of mimesis, referentiality, and action (Cohen, 1996). My reach has exceeded my grasp and that's just fine, this awkwardness, given that much of the book is about what Rilke (1989) termed the Too Big. As Derrida (1979) says about Nietzsche, I might well be "a little lost in the web of [my] text . . . unequal to the web [I have] spun" (p. 101). My sense of responsibility is not to seduce or persuade some audience as much as it is to implicate by setting up the obligation to see how we see. Such a text is doubled in imposing radical complications that enact the desire for interpretive mastery while surrendering the claim to simplicity of presence.

The danger, as Fiske notes, is to steal knowledge from others, particularly those who have little else and use it for the interests of power. This is so even when the intended goal is to extend the reach of the very counter-knowledge upon which the book is based, the stories entrusted to those "who enter such alliances from the side of privilege" in order to transform the ubiquitous injustices of history into a readable place (Fiske, 1996). Here, the work of theory is to help us think through our enabling aporias as we move toward responsible practices of academic writing.

Interlude

E-mail Updates (Excerpted)

Linda B, 2004–2005

Linda B is the participant in *Troubling the Angels* with whom I have kept in most touch over the years. This is largely, I think, because we had established an e-mail correspondence while still working on the book, thereby making it easier to continue the connection.

February 24, 2004

I don't know how to get a hold of Chris. I'm anxious to know how you two are doing.

For me, I guess you might want an update huh?

Well, in 1999, I decided it was time to see what the real world of HIV as a heterosexual, single woman may hold for me.

I bought a computer as you remember. I started attending as many heterosexual HIV events that time and money would allow. Yes, I'm still raising hell for the rights of gays and HIV/AIDS.

I had lost about 75 pounds because my thyroid had gone overactive from running ten miles a week. I was a mess. I've gained about 20 back, but my legs and arms are still skinny. I have a vascular necrosis in both hips and am not allowed to run because of bursitis in the right hip.

I dated a law student in Topeka, Kansas for a while. Too much for me. Then an aviotics man in Houston. Naaa, too young. Too much for me. I did have a ball though.

Then, in 1999, I met this man who is 15 years younger than me. We realized real soon that we had so many things in common in the way of interests it was uncanny. We traveled together all over the U.S. and Mexico.

We are now living on a 54-acre farm that is about 45 acres of woods.

As I sit here looking at my copy of *Troubling the Angels*, I fully realize there are few of us still living. Those who went before me left a legacy. I've been blessed to continue to build a legacy. One of life, love, and the pursuit of happiness in spite of HIV and AIDS.

I now have 4 grandsons. 11, 10, 5, 4. I also have a great granddaughter who just turned one, by my granddaughter who is now 22.

Please let me know how you and Chris are doing. Let me hear from you. I see 'stories' in your future.

Love and hugs and blessing all around,

February 25, 2004

Gee Patti, sounds like *Troubling the Angels* may have lost its purpose as many of us women had envisioned. For most of us, we wanted an audience that would see us as women with HIV/AIDS. To understand how this cross section of many different classes, races, and economic backgrounds coped with the same disease.

For me, to have my words in print was a form of therapy. Whether they agreed with the content, the layout of the book or the manner in which it came to be, we still got to tell our story.

I often think of the women in those pages. Who is still among the living? Who has gone on to the other side? When CR died, I sort of dropped out of the whole HIV/AIDS scene. The only reminder of the disease was when 'happy fun pill time' came twice or three times a day. Having lost my best friend, I remained lost for about a year. One day just melted into the next. At some point, I had to pull myself up by my bootstraps and carry on.

It wasn't easy being a heterosexual woman with HIV in a city that had yet to show me one heterosexually infected man. The HIV women had melted into the mainstream of sorts, leaving me wondering if I could completely deny my status. Of course, I couldn't. My conscience won't let me go that far.

My friends had either married, died or moved to another city. I was truly alone in the big city. The response for me was to start traveling. As a result, I feel I was able to grow even more and understand that life really is what you make it.

Please do ask questions you may want to include in your book. I'd be very happy to give you some insight on what it's like to be 'the sole survivor.'

I have 3 years 10 months and 6 days to retire.

M and I talk about writing a book. I've yet to figure out how you find the time to sit and spit out these books one after another. Maybe when I retire, I can compile all of these diary notes, scribbles on paper, and memories into some form of a book.

Throw HIV/AIDS in there and we'd really have something to talk about. Hardly mainstream.

Keep in touch. I'd love to read these books. Where do I get them?
Hugs and prayers,
Linda B

July 23, 2005
Patti,

Let me tell you another story about *Troubling the Angels*. I got into a pen pal program at Central Florida University that is attached to an HIV/AIDS class taught by a grand lady we call Teach.

I guess I'm on my 10th pen pal by now. We are just finishing a semester. It's a type of therapy like no other.

I was writing to a young lady named K last Christmas. Such a sweet little child of Hindu descent. I talked to her on the phone, wrote to her, traded pictures, and still write to her. One night she told me that she had read a book and that there was a person in the book that reminded her of me. Well, it was me. She had read *Troubling the Angels*. I nearly fell out of my chair!!

I guess the book is touching those we hoped it would touch. I'm happy. It is still telling the stories we wanted told. Whether the reader knows these women are among the living is not relevant. Those were the days when we didn't want to hear any loud noises because we were afraid it was the 'other shoe.'

As for what is going on here now. We planted, stripped, and sold our first tobacco crop last December in time for our birthdays. We have our second crop in the ground now and look forward to doing it all over again.

We also put out a quarter of an acre of garden. Duh . . . what were we thinking? Neither one of us can get around too well. Neuropathy has really gotten to us. I'm still working and driving 80+ miles one way to work. I've yet to get tired of it. Meditation while driving isn't too bad.

I have two years to go to retire. We are trying to finish up the little things that need to be done around here. There was a day when retirement was something 'normal' people dreamed of. Does this mean I'm normal?

I miss those ladies that helped me through those days I thought my life had turned into a sewer. Nancy B., CR, Janie, Lori. All of them. The guys, too—all of those who are gone. I don't miss those days at all. They were hard. The 'normal' life that I yearned for is sitting beside me. But, that doesn't mean I don't miss those warm bodies that made life worth living back in the 'dying years.'

I'm still gaining weight. I'm so sick of the side effects of these life-saving drugs. I've gone from a 36C to a 40DD. I'm still not even close to being as heavy as I was at one time, but the lypodystrophy sucks. I still don't have a butt and there's no such thing as a pair of size 14 pants with a size

10 butt. I'm walking a mile a day and riding my stationary bike that I keep in the barn so I can watch nature as I ride. But, this doesn't seem to help.

Gosh, Patti, do tell when are you going to put this book to bed? Remember when I told you two that you needed to get crackin' because some of us are on a deadline? We're all on a deadline, honey. We just don't know when the Great Publisher is going to ask for the Papers.

Write soon. Need anything, just holler.

Love ya,

Linda B, now known as Mrs. W.

These e-mails have been edited for length and to protect identities.

Chapter 5

Applied Derrida

(Mis)Reading the Work of Mourning in Social Research

Reception of the "post."—Nihilism/nothing outside the text.—
Conflating ideology critique and deconstruction.—Applied post.—
Praxis under erasure.—Caught between an ungraspable call and
a setting-to-work.—The work of mourning.

This chapter began as part of a symposium on Marxism today within the
context of educational research.[1] It moves through a necessarily guilty reading of the reception of the "post" in that field[2] and then turns to its primary
interest, the uses of deconstruction in reinscribing praxis under conditions of
postmodernity. While its examples come from education, the reception story
of the post in educational research is not that much different than in other
social science fields where efforts to accommodate/incorporate the "post"
have not been easy.

In the pages of the *Educational Researcher* alone, McLaren and
Farahmandpur (2000) warn against "the decline of class politics," textualism,
"toothless liberalism and airbrushed insurgency," nihilism, localism, and relativism, all wrapped up in "a facile form of culturalism" that paralyzes progressive politics. Constas (1998) offers a typology of the postmodern
noteworthy for its use of the very logic that the "post" sets out to undo (St.
Pierre, 2000; Pillow, 2000). Howe (1998) contrasts "postmodernists" and
"tranformationists" and worries about "paradigm cliques" (p. 20).

Of use in trying to understand the reception of the "post" in academic circles is Harold Bloom's (1975) famous argument that all readings are misreadings, given the weight of perspective on what we see and how we see it. I adapt Bloom's thesis in my reading of the space of the range of discussion concerning the "post" in educational research as symptomatic of the anxieties attendant upon the collapse of foundations and the end of triumphalist versions of science. In order to make the project doable, I concentrate on the reception of Derrida as a "part-for-whole" or synecdoche for the heterogeneous "post" of postmodernism, including deconstruction.

At the risk of a proper reading, my interest is in three gestures of thought at work in the reception of the "post" in much of educational research in what might be said to lead to a mistaken identity. The three gestures of thought are: 1) charges of nihilism/textualism, 2) conflating ideology critique and deconstruction, and 3) compelling understanding too quickly in terms of the uses of deconstruction. I conclude with an example of "applied Derrida" that troubles the concept of praxis in the context of writing a book about women living with HIV/AIDS (Lather and Smithies, 1997).

Nihilism/Nothing Outside the Text

Derrida's "there is nothing outside the text" from *Of Grammatology* (1976, pp. 226–27) is, according to John Caputo, "one of the most thoroughly misrepresented utterances in contemporary philosophy" (1997a, p. 78). Rather than some scandal of "linguisticism" (Derrida, in Caputo 1997a, p. 104), Derrida means by this that there are no cultural practices that are not defined by frameworks that are "caught up in conflicting networks of power, violence, and domination" (Baker, 1995, p. 129). Derrida says "I never cease to be surprised by critics who see my work as a declaration that there is nothing beyond language . . . it is, in fact, saying the exact opposite. The critique of logocentrism is above all else the search for the 'other' and the 'other of language' . . . If deconstruction *really* consisted in saying that everything happens in books, it wouldn't deserve *five* minutes of anybody's attention" (quoted in Baker, 1995, p. 16).

Rather than an occlusion of "the real," the deconstructive claim is that there is nothing that is not caught in a network of differences and references that give a textual structure to what we can know of the world. There is a "thereness" that includes the frames, horizons of intelligibility, and sociopolitical presuppositions of the necessary, irreducible, and inescapable epistemic and archival violence that constitute Derridean textuality. This is about the loss of transcendental signifiers and the situating of reference within the differential systems from which making meaning is possible. To quote Derrida, "Deconstruction starts with the deconstruction of logocentrism, and thus to want to confine it to linguistic phenomena is the most suspect of operations" (in Brunette and Wills, 1994, p. 15).

Working the failure of the oppositions that assure concepts, deconstruction remains in excess of traditional political agendas. The speculative force of this excess works toward establishing new relational structures with "a greater emphasis on ethics and its relationship to the political" (Spivak, 1999, p. 426). "One needs another language besides that of political liberation," Derrida says (in Kearney, 1984, p. 122). In deconstruction, the terms of political struggle shift from class as a subject of history to the cultural constitution of subjectivity via the workings of disciplinary power. Here, the complexity of subject formation includes how various axes of power are mutually constitutive, productive of different local regimes of power and knowledge that locate subjects and require complex negotiations of relations, including the interruption of coherence and complete subordination to the demands of regulatory regimes.[3] Engaging the real is not what it used to be. Different ideas about materiality, reality, representations, and truth distinguish different epistemological orientations where reality does not precede representation but is constituted by it. Such a shift from the sociological to the cultural brings textuality, discourse, and representation to the fore. The means of production are less the struggle than "the nature of social representations" (Foster, quoted in Altieri, 1990, p. 457) with its questions concerning the psyche, subjectivity, and the self as sites for the production of social categories. Calls for "resistance postmodernism" or "left deconstruction" à la Tony Bennett and Terry Eagleton, among others, offer a "reductively oppositional" (Altieri, 1990, p. 475) reading of the post that reinscribes it back into modernist categories of political struggle (e.g., Kincheloe and McLaren, 1994; Gabardi, 2000). Fekete (1995) terms this a recuperation of postmodernism into a politically intelligible place "in the frame of the already established purposes of the day" (p. 208).

Derrida (1994) is clear that we "cannot not be" the heirs of Marx's break with myth, religion, and nationalism as ways to think the world and our place in it (p. 91). Derrida's "turn or return to Marx" breaks his silence on Marx in the face of proclamations of "the end of Marxism" (p. 32). He seeks the Marx outside of "the dogma machine" (p. 13) where the place for justice is "the infinite asymmetry of the relation to the other" (p. 22) as our way into a better future. Against charges of the nihilism of deconstruction, Derrida speaks of "a certain configurativity" where "the coming of the other" produces a democracy to come (Sprinkler, 1993, p. 231). In a present marked not by crisis so much as by *structural incompetence*, a "wearing down beyond wear" of the "conceptual phantasms" that have guided us through modernity (Derrida, 1994, p. 80), Derrida sees a moment of contestatory possibilities where more is at stake than philosophy when philosophy is at stake.

Spivak terms this a place for justice, a problematic of a responsibility, "caught between an ungraspable call and a setting-to-work" (1994, p. 23). Other to "inspirational academic heroics" (p. 26), a problematic of responsibility is premised on "the something that must of necessity not go through" (p. 20). Rather than a task of uncovering hidden forces and material structures and a textual(rhetorical)/real(material) binary and oppositional (dialectical) contradictions, this is about working the ruins of Marxism toward an other logic. As delineated in *Specters of Marx*, this different logic works against the leveling processes of the dialectic and for the excess, the nonrecuperable remainder, the different, the other/outside of the logic of noncontradiction.

Worries about privileging text over people and narrative over life elide how "the real is no longer real" in a digitalized era that interrupts the easy real (Poster, 1989). How discourse enframes and words the world becomes the issue, as opposed to searching for the "beyond" of ideology of "real" social forces and material structures. Instead of the nihilism so frequently evoked by the academic left in its efforts to make sense of the post, this is the yes of the setting-to-work mode of deconstruction that faces unanswerable questions, "the necessary experience of the impossible" in responding to the call of the wholly other (Spivak, 1999, p. 428).[4]

Conflating Ideology Critique and Deconstruction

Understanding the social and historical meanings of representational practices has encountered much resistance from traditional positivist knowledge approaches, but this is a shared project of Marxism and the post. There are, however, key differences between ideology critique and deconstruction.

Ideology critique is about uncovering hidden forces and material structures in a discursive field organized by concerns for "truth." It endorses a binary of textual/material in its calls for grounding knowledge in "the crucial facticity of determinant brute economic reality" (Leslie, 2000, p. 33). An Enlightenment project, ideology critique offers a material real in contrast to the ontological uncertainty of deconstruction. "If such a thing exists," Derrida writes, over and over again, marking that indeterminacy that is the "originary complication" of a deconstruction that is not an unmasking but a keeping open, alive, loose, on guard against itself.

The critique of ideology was the "essence of structuralist cultural studies" in a way that moved from interpreting reality as determined by some assumedly knowable empirical and historical presence to attending to the unconscious, imaginary relations and the construction of subjectivity (Van Loon, 2001, p. 275). Experience became an effect of structure in an early version of the decentering of the subject that prepared the way for the linguistic turn that followed Althusserean structuralist Marxism. From early semiology through discourse analysis to an increasing attention to deconstruction, troubling language as a transparent medium has undercut universal categories and a romanticized, universalized subject.

Deconstructive destabilization works otherwise. Its interest is in complicit practices and excessive differences rather than unveiling structures and illuminating the forces and relations of production. Purposefully doubled in its necessary implications in what it seeks to trouble, deconstruction works against the critical righteousness of ideology critique where "the materialist critic has an educative role that involves the propagandistic task of eliciting correct consciousness" (Leslie, 2000, 3). In reading the subject, modes of investment are no longer based on traditional notions of categorical thinking such as false consciousness, on the one hand, or the more idealized model of intentional agency of reason and will. Indeterminacy and paradox become conditions of affirmative power by undoing fixities and mapping new possibilities for playing out relations between identity and difference, margins and centers. Ways of knowing become "an archive of windows," a study of the histories of enframing that focuses on the staging of truthfulness. Particularly interested in that which works to efface the frame effect, the deconstructive shift is from the real to the production of the reality effect. In this shift, practices dedicated to the disappearance of anything easily identifiable as "the real" are claimed as political work.

Practices of respectful twisting open up to difference and get things moving as practical or praxiological engagements that say yes to turning forms against themselves. This is an immanent critique, a critical intimacy of intervention from within. Quite other to the masterful, totalizing critical distance of ideology critique with its assumptions of an outside, this is Derrida's thesis of necessary complicity, the necessity of participating in what is being reinscribed in a way that responds to the call of the wholly other. Perplexed by design, doubled in implication, the practical politics of putting deconstruction to work entail a sort of getting lost as an ethical relationality of nonauthoritarian authority to what we know and how we know it.

Applied Post: Misreading the Work of Mourning

The century of "Marxism" will have been that of the techno-scientific and effective decentering of the earth, of geopolitics, of the *anthropos* in its onto-theological identity or its genetic properties, of the *ego cogito*— and of the very concept of narcissism whose aporias are . . . the explicit themes of deconstruction. This trauma is endlessly denied by the very movement through which one tries to cushion it, to assimilate it, to interiorize and incorporate it. In this mourning work in process, in this interminable task, the ghost remains that which gives one the most to think about—and to do. Let us insist and spell things out: to do and to make come about, as well as to let come (about).

—Derrida, 1994

In an interview for the 1995 conference, "Appying: To Derrida," Derrida says, "Deconstruction cannot be applied and cannot not be applied. So we have to deal with this aporia, and this is what deconstruction is about" (1996c, p. 218). In order to invent the impossible, application is much more about dissemination and proliferation under conditions of responsibility within indeterminacy, "a moment of non-knowledge, a moment beyond the programme" (p. 223) than it is about something technical and neutral, programmable and predictable.[5]

Calls to attend to the real world, "a mobilization of a sense of urgency—an urgency to act, to declare, to represent, to render an account" are situated in the history of the fraught relationship between French and continental philosophy and Anglo-Saxon sociohistorical empiricism (Van Loon, 2001, p. 280). Against the "fiddling while Rome burns" characterizations of deconstruction, deconstruction is aimed at provoking fields into new moves and spaces where they hardly recognize themselves in becoming otherwise, the unforseeable that they are already becoming. Demand that it serve an immediate and evidently useful purpose belies its "exorbitant method" that is loyal to a tradition by keeping it alive while transgressing the horizon of legitimation, a performative within/against where it is what it does in an undecidability that is never over and done with (Caputo, 1997a).

Here is where the case of educational research can be of interest across an academy struggling with changing expectations in terms of the relationship between research and policy. One could talk of a "public or perish" governing mentality of educational research of late, the increased demand for its usefulness in the context of policy and practice (Willinsky, 2001). It is tempting to revert to the quick and narrow scientism of the past (e.g., Ladwig, 1996). But the game has changed. Accounting for complexity and contingency without predictability is what now shapes our conversations and expands our idea of science as cultural practice and practice of culture. My argument is that the educational research of most use will be produced out of and because of the paradoxes of projects that develop a better language to describe a more complicated understanding of what knowledge means and does than by reinscribing the idealized natural science model.[6]

Make something new, Derrida says, that is how deconstruction happens. In the final section of this chapter, I use the efforts of my co-researcher, Chris Smithies, and myself to tell the stories of women living with HIV/AIDS to ask what it means to put deconstruction to work in the telling of other people's stories. I will draw on this work not so much to give flesh and blood to abstractions as to evoke what Derrida terms a "ghost effect" of spectral movement where ontology can only be a conjuration, a more demanding ontology of an other logic calling for other concepts.

In *Specters of Marx*, exploring a logic of mourning and haunting, Derrida enacts an in-between logic, between presence and absence, in order to unlock thinking and help us otherwise. What I have discovered in my reading of this book is that my mourning in relation to Marxism is for a certain praxis characterized by salvation narratives, consciousness-raising, and a romance of the humanist subject and agency. In spite of poststructural critiques of the doctrine of eventual salvation, voluntaristic philosophies of consciousness, and vanguard theories of "emancipating" some others implicit in Marxism, I am unable to do without the concept of praxis. It seems to be the space, for me, of the "experience of the promise" of Marxism.

In the distinctions Krell (2000) draws between Freud and Derrida, it is impossible mourning, unsuccessful mourning that is, in Derrida, the very promise of affirmation. As opposed to Freud's theorized "hyperbolic identifications and narcissistic or anaclitic [libidinal] object choices in the first place" (p. 15), Krell sees the undecidability of Derrida's mourning as facing that "there never was any *there* there for us" (p. 18). Remaining true to the memory of the other is not about withdrawing affirmation but about being "always a bit lost" (p. 20) to one another, a loss of presence at the heart of being, as opposed to the "too solidly *taken over*" of the orthodox "legitimation by way of Marx" (Derrida, 1994, p. 92).

Mourning work always follows a trauma. Philosophically, the work of mourning is about ontologizing what remains after the rigor of troubling or problematizing a concept. My work in this final section is to use my continued post-Marxist haunting by the ghost of praxis to reinscribe praxis in a way that mourns its remainders and irremediable losses. To be post-Marxist is not so much to be out of date or surpassed as confronted with undecidability, incompleteness, and dispersion rather than the comforts of transformation and closure. This calls for a praxis "after the trial of undecidability," a praxis of aporia: "as tentative, contextual, appropriative, interventionist, and unfinished effort to shift the terrain" (Rooney, 1995, p. 195).[7]

Such a move is in, with, for, and against the privileging of containment over excess, thought over affect, structure over speed, linear causality over complexity, and intention over aggregative capacities (Levinson, 1995). Ontological changes and category slippages mark the exhaustion of received categories of mind/body, nature/culture, organism/machine (Haraway, 1997). The goal is to shape our practice to a future that must remain to come, in excess of our codes but, still, always already: forces already active in the present. Perhaps a transvaluation of praxis means to find ways to participate in the struggle of these forces as we move toward a future that is unforseeable from the perspective of what is given or even conceivable within our present conceptual frameworks.

Praxis under Erasure: Between Concepts

My present reach is toward a praxis thought against the humanist figure of a consciously choosing subject, what Judith Butler refers to as "a fiction of the ego as master of circumstances" (1993b, p. 124). In this move, I reach toward what William Spanos (1993) writes of as the "postmodern theoretical demystification of the discourse of deliverance" (p. 187) that positions narratives of salvage and redemptive agendas as ever deeper places for privilege to hide. Much of this is prefigured in feminist concerns with emancipatory agendas as under suspicion for their coercion, rationalism, and universalism, but deconstruction adds a twist with its central thesis of complicity, its refusal of an innocent position "outside" power networks. Spivak, for example, claims that "deconstruction does not aim at praxis or theoretical practice but lives in the persistent crisis or unease of the moment of techne or crafting . . . It is a negotiation and an acknowledgement of complicity" (1993, p. 121). Rather than trying to legitimate, a deconstructive problematic tries to trouble, to look for dangers, normalizing tendencies, tendencies toward dominance in spite of liberatory intentions (Sawiki, 1988, p. 166).

What does this mean for the concept of praxis? Has what Gramsci (1971) termed "the philosophy of praxis" disappeared, or is "the disappeared" the consolations of humanism given the proliferation of differences that signals the radical impossibility of social totalities? To address these questions, I explore the parameters of a praxis under erasure, keeping the term as both limit and resource, opening it up to its margins.

Literary critic Wlad Godzich postulates that post-Hegelian praxis is about gaps, remains, radical alterities (1994, p. 26), the philosophy of the cry versus the Hegelian philosophy of the concept. Beyond absorption into present frames of intelligibility, such praxis is excessive, diffuse, an exacerbation of the tensions native to concepts that reveal their undecidability, their constitutive exclusions. This sort of category shake-down is evident in Bill Haver's (1996) proposal that the question of how to intervene be grounded in a shift from totalities to noncontainment, a principle of excess and infinite proliferation where a rigorous praxis refuses much in an effort to "stop thinking straight." Arguing the limits of our frames of intelligibility which render the world thinkable and knowable, Haver moves toward practices that are in excess of subjects presumed to know about objects presumed to be knowable.

Hence, what I am trying to think here is a praxis of the trial of undecidability. In excess of binary or dialectical logic, I seek a form of praxis that disrupts the horizon of an already-prescribed intelligibility to address Derrida's question: "What must now be thought and thought otherwise"? (1994, p. 59). The logic of negation as a trial to go through before restoration of some lost unity breaks down in the face of the challenges of social changes that collapse our categories. Derrida (1994) begins a list: labor, production, unemployment, free market, foreign debt, arms industry, interethnic wars, mafia, and drug cartels. All present concepts outdated in their very axiomatics by tele-technic dis-location, rhizomatic spreading and acceleration, and new experiences of frontier and identity. In short, the organization of knowledge ruled by the Hegelian inheritance is radically insufficient in the face of a new set of givens that disrupts the conceptual oppositions that structure traditional thinking.

In the post-Enlightenment stirrings and strivings of contemporary theory, the philosophy of the subject, reflection, and praxis are being rethought. Levinson (1995), for example, formulates a "post-dialectical praxis" that is quite different from a Kantian or Hegelian analytic. The modernist metaphysics of presence, assured interiority, and subject-centered agency, the valorizing of transformative interest in the object, Hegel's affirmative negativity and dialectical overcoming: all are at risk, refused in a way that attempts to signal the size and complexity of the changes involved. Such a praxis is about ontological stammering, concepts with a lower ontological weight, a praxis without guaranteed subjects or objects, oriented toward the as yet incompletely thinkable conditions and potentials of given arrangements (Levinson, 1995). This is a sort of "praxis under erasure." To explore such a concept of praxis, I turn to Chris and my textual practices in *Troubling the Angels: Women Living With HIV/AIDS*.

Caught between an Ungraspable Call and a Setting-to-Work: Praxis as a Living On

> One makes oneself accountable by an engagement that selects, interprets, and orients. In a practical and performative manner, and by a decision that begins by getting caught up, like a responsibility, in the snares of an injunction that is already multiple, heterogeneous, contradictory, divided.
>
> —Derrida, 1994

While Marx questioned the concept, Derrida's (1994) interest is "the concept of the concept" (p. 147), a thinking of excess and dissemination against the limiting fixity of conceptualization. To think praxis as a concept of living on where "one must work—practically, actually" (p. 131) while simultaneously dislocating the self-presence of the concept as a sort of redemption: this is the logic I am trying to enact. Situating praxis as a ruin made habitable by a fold of the between of presence and absence (p. 187), Chris and my practices in *Troubling the Angels* are both more and other than an example. As a topology for new tasks toward other places of thinking and putting to work, I wrestle with what I have learned from our construction of this text of responsibility. My interest is a praxis that attends to poststructuralist suspicions of rationality, philosophies of presence, and universalizing projects, a praxis that "does not put itself in place of theory; it would be theory itself becoming practical—the opposite of pragmatism" (Tiedemann, 1989, p. 202). In terms of *Troubling the Angels*, what did Chris and I do to make (and let) come about in terms of a thinking that does its knowing from its doing?

Any research is concrete and complex, a knotted and undecidable situation. Invited in to do the job of getting into general circulation the women's stories of living with HIV/AIDS, Chris and I stumbled into a hypertextual pastiche of split text, angel interchapters, and the juxtaposition of various presentations of information, from graphs and charts of demographic variables to participant narratives. Getting lost was one of my methodological goals in my desire to interrupt the reductiveness of restricted economies of representation. Hence, *Troubling the Angels* is organized around and courting of complexities and undecidables.

In making textual decisions, Walter Benjamin served as "an indispensable point of departure" (Holland, 1993, p. 3) in moving toward mosaic, multileveled forms of representation. Via a community of quotations, didactics, reflections, and images, we intended some clustering that sets up resonances to move readers toward thinking about meaning in history within the crisis of representation. Attempting practices that foster a grasp of the everchanging logic of the time in which we find ourselves, in this case, of AIDS as a "massive readability" (Derrida, 1993), our effort was toward reading out traces of not only the history of AIDS, but also of history itself, of how history happens. Following Benjamin's textual practice of an assemblage of fragments, a methodical, continuous experiment of conjunction, we jammed ideas, texts, traditions, and procedures together. Moving among different levels, our practice condenses and juxtaposes "different dimensions, of different registers of space and time, of different levels of existence and experience" (Felman and Laub, 1992, p. 262) of a testimony we might prefer not to hear. Facing our own avoidance, we move toward a vacillation between knowing and not knowing where our questions become, "What does it mean to inhabit history as crime, as the space of the annihilation of the Other?" (p. 189). What does it mean to be wretched away from received categories of thought, to acknowledge one's intellectual bewilderment, one's noninnocence in the face of the failure of representation? How can articulating the very inarticulateness of history as a limit experience performatively create in us the power of a call, "the chance, of our response-ability" (p. 203)?

The Epilogue of *Troubling the Angels* presents the women's reactions to our writing of their lives and it seems we managed, unevenly, to satisfy their desire to have their stories out and available to a reading public well beyond the academy. Key here was positioning the women not as objects of exchange and spectacle, voyeurs or eavesdroppers on a conversation not meant for them, but rather as interlocutors of our storying of their lives. Chris called them our editorial board. This destabilized our authorial position and disturbed us by situating them not so much as "ours" in some possessive prerogative as us "theirs," those to whom we were accountable, "my personal psychologist," as CR referred to Chris, capable of getting "so much smarter," as Amber referred to me.

Where it gets interesting, however, is where, whatever our authorial intentions, we were, as writers, also a registering apparatus, a kind of seismograph, an ensemble, an aggregate of registrations (Holland, 1993, p. 260). Here, quite open to chance, connections, many of which align or resonate with one another, are made under contingent circumstances. "What matters is the registration of historical process, and questions as to the degree of consciousness or unconsciousness of an author simply do not arise" (p. 262). Judith Butler (1993b), too, speaks of a writing "which precedes and mobilizes the one who writes, connecting the one who writes with a language which 'writes' the one" (p. 266). Chris and I both knew and did not know what we were doing, both intentional agents and vessels of history writing us in ways we did not and do not always understand.

In sum, given that praxis is a concept I cannot seem to do without, the praxis that I want to salvage from Marxism is a praxis with less ontological content, an immanent praxis of conjunction that calls out aggregative capacities from within the play of the forces of history. In the case of *Troubling the Angels*, to argue for textuality as praxis is a refusal of a textual/material binary toward a practice of living on. This is a nonreductive praxis that calls out a promise, not of a new concept but of practice on a shifting ground that foregrounds the limits of the fixing, locating, defining, and confining that is the work of the concept. This is a praxis that can survive the critique of Marxism, a praxis immanent in practices that helps us think not only *with* but *in* our actions.

Conclusion: The Work of Mourning

—Can one ever accept working for His Highness Mourning?
—How can one not accept it? That is what mourning is, the history of its refusal, the narrative of your revolution, our rebellion, my angel.

—Derrida, 1991

In this chapter, I have risked a "proper reading" of Derrida as endlessly open, enacting a principle of multiplication and dispersion that is neither straightforward continuity nor radical rupture (Bennington, 2000, p. 184). In this, I have echoed Derrida's (1994) claim that deconstruction only ever made sense to him as a radicalization of Marx (p. 92).

The ghost of Marx, the work of mourning, the debt to be paid: perhaps in the interminable task of mourning work in process, the ghost that gives us much to think about and to do is the "will have been" of the century of

Marxism. In the decentering of the *anthropos*, the onto-theological, and the *ego cogito* and its narcissism, Derrida offers a "difficult knowledge" (Pitt and Britzman, 2003) to those of us who insist on the worldly engagement of deconstruction. Running with concepts that destroy their own names, we seek an unsuccessful and hence possibly faithful mourning for that which we think we cannot think without. This is mourning not as consolation but as a tracing of loss that doubly affirms: both the loss and the still yet of the yes. This is "affirmation with no ax to grind, affirmation without mastery or mockery, without outcome or end, affirmation without issue ... affirmation without exit" (Krell, 2000, pp. 209, 212).

Interlude

Déjà Vu All Over Again

Feminism, Postmodernism, and the Educational Left

February 17, 1993
To: Afterwords, *Educational Theory*
From: Patti Lather and Mary Leach
    Regarding: Lanny Beyer and Daniel Liston, "Discourse or Moral Action: A Critique of Postmodernism" (*Educational Theory*, 1992, 42(4), 371–393).

    As feminists, reading the article, it was "déjà vu all over again." Beyer and Liston's worries recall for us the "serious reservations," "the concerns," and "moral disapprovals/disavowals" that were directed toward early feminist positions. As feminism began to be heard by the mainstream/malestream, it evoked worries about divisiveness, separatism, and loss of connectedness. What we see happening now, 20 years later, is a similar move, but this time the sin is the postmodern turn. We are confused.

    As feminists, what we find most confusing is Beyer and Liston's unremarked displacement of our political grounding in feminist struggles. Feminism's persistent demands for social justice mandate radical praxis, foundations or no. The erasure of feminism in Beyer and Liston's use of our work, its conflation onto a singular scene of postmodernism, recalls for us similar reservations that arose with earlier feminist challenges to Left male hegemony. Hence, under the guise of raising theoretical reservations about postmodernism, it seems to us that they are simply raising these older concerns all over again.

    As feminists, engaging with Beyer and Liston, we read their desire to be an unproblematized reinscription of authenticity, community, and moral

113

and epistemological imperatives that transcend the local. Concomitantly, we read their worries about the postmodern turn regarding textuality, aestheticism, partiality, situatedness, multiple voices, ambiguity, and the loss of general principles as an inscription of the frequently rehearsed objections to postmodernism on the part of the Left.

We read the Left's inability to deal with the continued recycling of these problems as symptomatic of the exhaustion of abstract, decontextualized, universalist approaches to metanarrative and vanguard politics. Feminists have been problematizing these approaches for over 20 years. Beyer and Liston have put their finger on the cost to the male Left in education of eliding feminist problematics. In our reading of their concerns, postmodernism has become the scapegoat for the failed practice of the Left, just as feminism was positioned 20 years ago.

As feminists, our interest is in how postmodernism can be an important critical force. As feminists, we position postmodernism as a stage for the complexities and contradictions of contemporary theoretical debates. As feminists, we want to use postmodernism to resist pitting modernism, postmodernism, and feminism against one another and to instead use this juxtaposition of incommensurable discourses to recoup multiple bases for radical action. Worrying that the center will not hold, Beyer and Liston try to oppose postmodernism from some position entirely outside it. We read their concerns about the politics of difference, "diminished capacity," and the need for some moral grounding for action that is outside of discourse as a desire for some regime of unproblematized transcendent generality that can serve as a refuge for weary travelers of the postmodern.

Our interest is in those feminists who want to use postmodernism to open up spaces of contestation in which no position is by nature correct, all positions are subject to critical investigation, and every position must be argued for, with no one position automatically at the center. As feminists, we believe that the meanings of human rights, liberation, community, and social justice cannot be assumed unproblematically anymore. As feminists, our project is not to shun engagement with ideas, but to carry out that engagement in a space women can inhabit without becoming commodities in dominant masculine economies, be they liberal or Marxist. For example, we have little interest in the economy of rivalry between "good" (antitextual) and "bad" ("hostile to 'community' ") feminists.

As feminists, there are ways in which our project is not so unlike Beyer and Liston's, and there are ways in which it is crucially different. We agree that "to deny the interconnections and tensions among people, ideas and social practices and systems" (p. 377) is to entrap us in sterile and fruitless debates. But the Hegelian reconciliation that underscores the Habermasian male leftist thought so rife in education has lost its purchase. The otherness of the other is not recuperable in the moment in which we must live. Given this, the task of rethinking democracy in the face of global change will not be aided by an unnecessary polarization between critical theory and postmodernism.

If our reading of the continuing saga of the unhappy marriage of Marxism and feminism is salient, the "we" of us on the Left must figure out how to negotiate the crisis of difference and turn it into opportunity. This is about thinking and doing difference differently, outside of binaries and "win-lose" scenarios. It is about difference without opposition and hierarchy; it is about community without elision of difference; it is about seeing ambivalence and difference not as obstacles, but as the very richness of meaning-making and the hope of whatever justice we might work toward. It is about the difficulties of situating emancipatory work in a postfoundational time.

Chapter 6

Fertile Obsession

Validity after Poststructuralism

Validity as an incitement to discourse.—The masks of methodology.—
Transgressive validity.—Counter-practices of authority: simulacra/
ironic validity, Lyotardian paralogy/neopragmatic validity, Derridean
rigor/rhizomatic validity, voluptuous/situated validity.—Transgressive
validity check-list: A simulacrum.

Validity As an Incitement to Discourse

Poised at the turn of the new century, the human sciences are in search of a
discourse to help chart the journey from the present to the future. Confer-
ences are held to explore the End of Science;[1] others argue for science as
rhetoric, narrative, and/or social practice. Regardless of terms, each is part of
some move "to grow up in our attitudes toward science" in an antifoundational
era characterized by the loss of certainties and absolute frames of reference
(Fine, 1986).

This chapter comes out of such ferment and is written against "the
merely deconstructive and the endlessly prefatory" (Borgmann, 1992, p. 2).
Believing that "science is a performance" (Fine, 1986, p. 148), my effort is
to anticipate a generative methodology that registers a possibility and marks
a provisional space in which a different science might take form. Seeking
answers to such a project in inquiry as it is lived, this chapter works at the
edges of what is currently available in moving toward a science with more to
answer to in terms of the complexities of language and the world.

In pursuit of a less comfortable social science, I continue my seeming obsession with the topic of validity: the conditions of the legitimation of knowledge in contemporary postpositivism. Over the last 20 years or so of postpositivism, the boundaries surrounding the issue of research legitimation have been constructed from many angles: naturalistic and constructivist, discourse theory, ethnographic authority, poststructuralism, forms of validity appropriate to an emancipatory interest. Long interested in how the core but changing concept of validity is shaped across the proliferation of paradigms that so characterizes postpositivism (Lather, 1992), my thoughts on validity are on the move again. While extending my earlier work toward counter-practices of authority that are adequate to emancipatory interests (Lather, 1986a,b), my primary desire here is to rethink validity in light of post-foundational discourse theory. Rather than jettisoning "validity" as the term of choice, I retain the term in order to both circulate and break with the signs that code it. What I mean by the term, then, is all of the baggage that it carries plus, in a doubled movement, what it means to rupture validity as a regime of truth.

"Where, after the metanarratives, can legitimacy reside?" Lyotard asks (1984, p. xxv). This chapter addresses Lyotard's question via a dispersion, circulation, and proliferation of counter-practices of authority that take the crisis of representation into account. What are the postfoundational possibilities outside the limits of the normative framings of validity in the human sciences? What might open-ended and context-sensitive validity criteria look like? Why is validity the site of such attraction? How much of this obsession with legitimation/validity issues in research methodology is part of the disciplinary nature of our society of confession and conscience? This chapter is situated at the nexus of such doubled questions. Fragmenting and colliding both hegemonic and oppositional codes, my goal is to reinscribe validity in a way that uses the antifoundational problematic to loosen the master code of positivism that continues to so shape even postpositivism (Scheurich, 1996). My task is to do so in a way that refuses oversimplified answers to intractable questions.

The Masks of Methodology

> Now the rhetorically minded seem prescient . . . for the masks of methodology are wearing thin.
>
> —Nelson et al., 1987

In terms of the distinction between viewing ethnographic stories as about "found" versus "constructed" worlds (Simon and Dippo, 1986), the effacement of the referent in postmodern culture has made "the real" contested territory. To shift our sense of the real to "discourses of the real" (Britzman, 1991) is to fore-ground how discourse words the world. Whether this is an opening for liberatory politics or the end of politics/history is much debated (e.g., Hartsock, 1987; Harvey, 1989; Hutcheon, 1989; Alcoff, 1989; Nicholson, 1990; Spivak, 1991, 1992). Whether to celebrate or lament the felt loss of found worlds depends on how one reads the political possibilities that open up when "truth" is positioned as made by humans via very specific material practices.

Postfoundationalists argue that the thing itself, in its absence, cannot be witness to a representative validity. In poststructuralist terms, the "crisis of representation" is not the end of representation, but the end of pure presence. Derrida's point regarding "the inescapability of representation" (Arac, quoted in McGowan 1991, p. 26) shifts responsibility from representing things in themselves to representing the web of "structure, sign and play" of social relations (Derrida, 1978). It is not a matter of looking harder or more closely, but of seeing what frames our seeing—spaces of constructed visibility and incitements to see which constitute power/knowledge.

Rather than epistemological guarantees, such concerns reframe validity as multiple, partial, endlessly deferred. They construct a site of development for a *validity of transgression* that runs counter to the standard *validity of correspondence*: a nonreferential validity interested in how discourse does its work, where transgression is defined as "the game of limits . . . at the border of disciplines, and across the line of taboo" (Pefanis, 1991, p. 85; see also, Foucault, 1977).

In the discourses of the social sciences, validity has always been the problem, not the solution (Cronbach and Meehl, 1955; Kvale, 1989). Across such qualitative practices as member checks and peer debriefing (Lincoln and Guba, 1985), triangulation, (Denzin, 1989), and catalytic validity (Lather, 1986b), various postpositivist efforts have been made to resolve the problem without exhausting it, constantly providing answers to and freeing itself from the problem, but always partially, temporarily. More attuned to discourse theory, Mishler's (1990) reformulation traces the irrelevance of standard ap-proaches to validity through various postpositivist efforts to rearticulate it. Reframing validity as "problematic in a deep theoretical sense, rather than as a technical problem" (p. 417), Mishler surveys some "candidate exemplars" for generating new practices of validation that do not rely on a correspon-dence model of truth or assumptions of transparent narration. To not revert to the dominant foundational, formulaic, and readily available codes of validity requires the invention of counter-discourse/practices of legitimation.

Like Woolgar (1988), my own position is that the most useful stories about science are those that interrogate representation, "a reflexive explora-tion of our own practices of representation" (98). This entails taking a posi-tion regarding the contested bodies of thought and practice that shape inquiry in the human sciences, negotiating the complex heterogeneity of discourses and practices. This ability to establish and maintain an acceptable dialogue with readers about the construction of reality involves making decisions about which discursive policy to follow, which "regime of truth" to locate one's work within, which mask of methodology to assume. What follows is, in effect, a call for a kind of validity after poststructuralism in which legitimation depends on a researcher's ability to explore the resources of different contemporary inquiry problematics and, perhaps, even contribute to "an 'unjamming' effect in relation to the closed truths of the past, thereby freeing up the present for new forms of thought and practice" (Bennett, 1990, p. 277).

Transgressive Validity

In addressing what one does with validity once you've met poststructuralism, I proceed via what Deleuze and Guattari (1983) term "activating by invention" in order to move from "yesterday's institutions" to some other place of social inquiry. In this move, I position validity as a space of constructed visibility of the practices of methodology and "a space of the *incitement* to see" (Rajchman, 1991, p. 85), an apparatus for observing the staging of the poses of methodology, a site that "gives to be seen" the unthought in our thought. In what follows, I present four "framings" of validity that take postfoundational discourse theory into account. Within each, I present an exemplar[2] of empirical work that moves discussion from the epistemological criteria of validity as a relation of correspondence between thought and its object to the generation of counter-practices of authority grounded in the crisis of representation. I conclude with a "Transgressive Validity Checklist" intended to both sum up the counter-practices of authority that I have delineated and disrupt any effort toward their standardization.

Counter-Practices of Authority

The following is a dispersion, circulation, and proliferation of counter-practices of authority that take the crisis of representation into account. In creating a nomadic and dispersed validity, I employ a strategy of excess and categorical scandal in the hope of both imploding ideas of policing social science and working against the inscription of another "regime of truth." Rather than the usual couching of validity in terms of disciplinary maintenance, my goal is to open new lines of discussion about changed conditions and possibilities for a critical social science (Fay, 1987) and the discourse theories that so problematize that project. Rather than prescriptions for establishing validity in postpositivist empirical work, like Walter Benjamin, I offer "a forthrightly personal and deliberately ephemeral antithesis"

(Werkmeister, 1982, p. 114) to more conventional and prescriptive discourse-practices of validity.

Frame 1: Simulacra/Ironic Validity

Simulacra are copies without originals. The Baudrillardian (1983) argument is that we have shifted from a culture of representations to one of simulacra. Simulacra function to mask the absence of referential finalities. Using simulacra to resist the hold of the real and to foreground radical unknowability, poststructuralism "breaks all adequation between copy and model, appearance and essence, event and Idea" (Young, 1990, p. 82). This disruptive move foregrounds the production of meaning-effects.

Contrary to dominant validity practices where the rhetorical nature of scientific claims is masked with methodological assurances, a strategy of ironic validity proliferates forms, recognizing that they are rhetorical and without foundation, postepistemic, lacking in epistemological support. The text is resituated as a representation of its "failure to represent what it points toward but can never reach" (Hayles, 1990, p. 261), an ironic representation of neither the thing itself nor a representation of the thing, but a simulacrum. This move into the hyper-real implodes copies via an operation of displacement rather than representation where the distinction between the copy and the real ceases to have meaning.

James Agee and Walker Evan's (1988) *Let Us Now Praise Famous Men*, originally published in 1941 and recently claimed as a postmodern text (Rabinowitz, 1992; Quinby, 1991), illustrates what I mean by ironic validity. Documenting the devastation of rural America by the economic disasters of the 1930s through the study of three white tenant farm families, the text is prefaced by Evans's uncaptioned photographs which set the stage for the focus on the politics of knowing and being known. Agee's text, which serves somewhat as one long caption for the photographs, foregrounds the insufficiencies of language via prose that is meandering, incantational, and deeply inscribed by musical forms. Beginning with three vignettes and concluding with multiple endings, Agee presents his awkwardness and hesitancies where his anxiety about "his relationship to his subjects becomes an anxiety about the form of the book" (Rabinowitz, 1990, p. 160). Both seeking and refusing a center, he combines documentary and autobiography to describe with "words which are 'not words' " (p. 161) as he moves from representations of the tenant families to the disclosure of his own subjectivity. Agee's "self-indulgent, confessional narrative of middle-class seeing" is both redeemed and problematized by Evan's photographs which resist narrative, sentimentality, and sensationalism while still "reveal[ing] the ways differences can be organized and contained" (p. 163).

As such, the book both reinscribes familiar regimes of truth and narrative and anticipates a much less comfortable social science in its embodiment of the anxiety of voyeurism. Disrupting their intelligence mission, the authors resist both "the claims of disciplinary power to represent objective reality" and obscene prying into the lives of others in the name of science, "the commodification of one set of human beings for the consumption of another" (Quinby, 1991, pp. 104–105). Deferring any final saying, the text is an "excursion into the radical unreliability of meaning," the "rupture between language and the world" (pp. 108–109), the unrepresentable. Enacting a doubled movement, Agee both uses words and casts doubt on any transparency between the word and its object via a kind of genealogical specificity that is counter-espionage data well outside the conventions of social science discourse.

Endlessly shifting the location of the unknowable and ironically using researcher power to undercut practices of representation, Agee and Evans create a text that is dense with the absence of referential finalities. Foregrounding the production of meaning-effects, they nonetheless construct a text of such specificity that the human cost of economics run amuck is made "visible" in ways that are amplified in flesh.

Refusing closure and turning the analytical categories of the human sciences against themselves, Agee and Evans enact the struggle of an "I" to become an "eye" that both inscribes and interrupts normalizing power/knowledge (Quinby, 1991). Sixty plus years after its original publication, their self-scrutinizing, nonnormalizing production of knowledge is generative of research practices that, by taking the crisis of representation into account, create texts that are both double without being paralyzed and implode controlling codes.

Frame 2: Lyotardian Paralogy/Neopragmatic Validity

Displacing both the criterion of efficiency and the Habermasian drive for consensus, Lyotardian paralogy (1984, p. 60) is that which "refines our sensitivity to differences and reinforces our ability to tolerate the incommensurable" via "the constant search for new ideas and concepts that introduces dissensus into consensus" (Fritzman, 1990, pp. 371–72). Its goal is to foster differences and let contradictions remain in tension. Paralogy legitimates via fostering heterogeneity, refusing closure. It entails "knowledge of language games as such and the decision to assume responsibility for their rules and effects" (Lyotard, 1984, p. 66). It recognizes the multiplicity of language games and the "temporary contract" of any consensus. Its goal is something not entirely subordinated to a system's goals, yet not so abruptly destabilizing of a system that it is ignored or repressed.

A dissertation on African-American women and leadership positions in higher education gives some feel for the parameters of paralogic validity

(Woodbrooks, 1991). Woodbrooks's study was "designed to generate more interactive and contextual ways of knowing" (p. 93) with a particular focus on openness to counter-interpretations: "The overarching goal of the methodology is to present a series of fruitful interruptions that demonstrate the multiplicity of meaning-making and interpretation" (p. 94).

In analyzing interview data, Woodbrooks made extensive use of two familiar qualitative practices of validity, member checks and peer debriefing (Lincoln and Guba, 1985). Using both to purposefully locate herself in the contradictory borderland between feminist emancipatory and poststructural positions, she attempted to interrupt her role as the Great Interpreter, "to shake, disrupt, and shift" her feminist critical investments (Woodbrooks, 1991, p. 103). Peer debriefing and member checks, both coherent within present forms of intelligiblity, were used to critique her initial analysis of the data, her "perceptions of some broadly defined themes that emerged as I coded the transcripts" (p. 132). Reanalyzing the data and her original analysis, Woodbrooks then sent a second draft out to participants and phoned for responses. This resulted in a textual strategy that juxtaposed the voices of the white female researcher with those of the African-American female participants.

In her textual strategy, Woodbrooks first tells a realist tale which backgrounds the researcher's shaping influence and foregrounds participant voices. She interrupts this with a critical tale that foregrounds how her theoretical investments shaped her analysis of the data. Finally, in a third-person voice, she tells a deconstructive tale which draws on participant reactions to the critical tale. Here, she probes her own desire, "suspicious of . . . the hegemony [of] feminism" (p. 140) in her analysis which marginalized both African-American identity as a source of pride and strength (ascribing it totally to gender) and participant concerns with male/female relations. "This stragegy [of feminist consciousness-raising] perpetuates feminism as a white middle class project and trivializes the deep emotional ties that black women share with black men" (p. 200).

Holding up to scrutiny her own complicity, Woodbrooks creates a research design that moves her toward unlearning her own privilege and displacing the colonizing gaze. Foregrounding the availability of multiple discourses and how they can be used to decenter the researcher as the master of truth and justice, she enacts her knowledge of language games as she assumes responsibility for the rules and effects of her investments. Such a strategy refines our sensitivity to differences, introduces dissensus into consensus, and legitimates via fostering heterogeneity. Woodbrooks's expanded use of the familiar techniques of member checks and peer debriefing, a using of what is already available "rather than hoping for something else to come along or to create utopia from thin air" (Kulchyski, 1992, p. 192), results in a search for instabilities and a foregrounding of the multiplicity of language games.

Frame 3: Derridean Rigor/Rhizomatic Validity

Derridean rigor undermines stability, subverts and unsettles from within; it is a "vocation," a response to the call of the otherness of any system, its alterity. It is Derridean play in the face of the absence of the transcendental signified as it supplements and exceeds what order has tried to make stable and permanent. Most importantly, such rigor is about a "meticulous diffidence" in its refusal of some great transformation (McGowan, 1991, p. 109). Rather than presenting deconstruction as a counter-ontology, a method, a concept, or an origin, Derridean rigor is a nominalist counter-logic: it is what it does (p. 122) as it situates itself in the interstices of the no longer and the not yet.

The rhizome is a metaphor for such a reinscription of rigour. Deleuze and Guattari (1983) suggest the tree as the modernist model of knowledge with the rhizome as the model for postmodern knowledge. The Chomskyan tree of structural linguistics, for example, presents "a limited number of paths along which words can enter a relationship" (Lecercle, 1990, p. 132). Rhizomes are systems with underground stems and aerial roots, whose fruits are tubers and bulbs. To function rhizomatically is to act via relay, circuit, multiple openings, as " 'crabgrass' in the lawn of academic preconceptions" (Ulmer, 1989, p. 185). Rhizomatics are about the move from hierarchies to networks and the complexity of problematics where any concept, when pulled, is recognized as "connected to a mass of tangled ideas, uprooted, as it were, from the epistemological field" (Pefanis, 1991, p. 22). Rather than a linear progress, rhizomatics is a journey among intersections, nodes, and regionalizations through a multicentered complexity. As a metaphor, rhizomes work against the constraints of authority, regularity, and commonsense and open thought up to the creative constructions that arise out of social practices, creativity which marks the ability to transform, to break down present practices in favor of future ones (Deleuze, 1992, pp. 163–64).

To probe what rhizomatic validity might mean in the context of an empirical study, I draw from the dissertation work of Erica McWilliam. In a study of student needs talk in preservice teacher education, McWilliam (1992) developed a research design that involved 1) an initial reflexive phase where researcher theoretical and political investments were put under scrutiny by moving back and forth among various contestatory discourses in a way that resituated the researcher away from the "transformative intellectual" come to "save" the oppressed; 2) an empirical phase that focused on student-teacher constructions of teacher work; and 3) a final reciprocal phase designed as reflection in action and an extended co-theorizing process that contested and reconstructed the researcher's reading of the phase II data. Each stage paid particular attention to discrepant data, the facts unfit to fit categorical schemes in a way that both uses and collides with poststructuralism and feminist emancipatory discourses. Of note are McWilliam's learnings that research practices which interrupt researcher privilege must be more about constructing "an interrogative researcher text . . . a questioning text." Such a text overtly "signals tentativeness and partiality" in decentering expert authority and moving toward practices of co-theorizing (p. 271). Paying particular attention to the tendencies of much advocacy research toward inaccessible language and "bullying" of the researched, she attempts to create the conditions in which it becomes possible for both researcher and researched to rethink their attitudes and practices.

Ranging across rather standard attitudinal surveys, dialogic, reciprocally self-disclosive interviews, and sustained interaction, McWilliam works to decenter both her own expertise and the participants' commonsense about teaching practices. Her "double-edged analysis" breaches both "congealed critical discourse" and the dominant traditional discourses (p. 30). She remarks on the "untidiness" of "this straddling of agendas" (p. 91) and the "state of tension" (p. 257) that exists between feminism and those who unproblematically side with or against Enlightenment projects. As such, her work enacts what it means to let contradictions remain in tension, to unsettle from within, to dissolve interpretations by marking them as temporary, partial, and invested, including her paradoxical continuing investment in transformative praxis.

More interested in networks than hierarchies and research that gestures toward the problematics of representation, McWilliam fleshes out a rhizomatic journey among intersections, nodes, and regionalizations through a multi-centered complexity that is, like Woodbrooks's, particularly noteworthy for attending to the creation of interactive social relations in which the inquiry can proceed. Rather than focusing exclusively on textual strategies that disrupt illusory notions of found worlds, both Woodbrooks and McWilliam illustrate how a poststructural focus on textual strategies can go hand-in-hand with developing interactive social relations in inquiry.

Frame 4: Voluptuous/Situated Validity

My last "framing" of validity posits the fruitfulness of situating scientific epistemology as shaped by a male imaginary. It asks what the inclusion of a female imaginary would effect where the female is other to the male's Other. Irigaray (1985) terms this the maternal/feminine, the residue that exceeds the categories, a disruptive excess that reveals the limits of the hegemonic male imaginary. Her project is to create a space where women in their multiplicity can become—body, nature, maternal, material.

Serres (1982) writes:

It's the revolution of voluptuousness, the physics of Venus chosen over
that of Mars . . . The nature of Mars, of martial physics, is one of hard,
rigid, and rigorous bodies; the physics and nature of Venus are formed
in flows . . . It is difficult to think of a rigorous and exact science that
might have been conditioned by Venus and not by Mars, for peace and
not for destruction . . . since Western science has always followed the
weight of power. (pp. 101–106)

Irigaray argues that "the murder of the mother" is the founding act of
Western culture. Embodiment is relegated to the female, freeing the
phallocentric Idea to transcend the material, creating the deadly split between
epistemology and ethics (Whitford, 1991). The feminist debates over objectivity are situated in overcoming this split. Haraway (1988), for example,
argues that self-conscious partiality is a necessary condition of being heard
to make rational knowledge claims. This constructs a politics and epistemology of positionality versus universal/objective claims. The "view from everywhere" (which is the universalized "view from nowhere" of objectivism) is
contrasted with explicit incompleteness, tentativeness, the creation of space
for others to enter, the joining of partial voices. Authority then comes from
engagement and self-reflexivity, not distanced "objectivity."

Whether it is possible to produce the maternal/feminine and be heard
in the culture raises the issue of the politics of excess. The eruption of the
mother in feminist discourse was the unthought that was originally perceived
as unreadable. This exceeds Lyotardian paralogy in exploring "the potent
marginality" (Kristeva, 1978–79, p. 6) of feminist critique, a deliberate excessiveness, what Fraser (1989) terms "leaky" or "runaway": practices "which
have broken out of discursive enclaves . . . a species of excess . . ." (p. 169).
This sort of going too far "is always some variety of the marginalized, un-
willing to stay out of 'the center,' who transgresses . . . who behaves, in this
moment, as though she or he has a right to lay claim to a place in the
discursive spotlight" (Lubiano, 1991, p. 150). This "emergent but not yet
'readable' discourse of women" (Con Davis, 1990, p. 106) is some other to
Lyotardian neopragmatism, something more akin to "risky practice" in terms
of "the politics of uncertainty" that underlies feminist praxis in postfoundational
times (Sawicki, 1991, p. 103).

An example of "going too far" is Richardson's (1992) essay about her
larger interview study of unmarried mothers. "Consciously self-revelatory" in
probing the lived experience of the researcher (p. 125), Richardson cheekily
hopes that she has not "ventured beyond Improper" as she "breache[s] sociological writing expectations by writing sociology as poetry" (p. 126). First
presenting "a transcript masquerading as a poem/a poem masquerading as a
transcript" (p. 127), her primary goal is "to create a position for experiencing
the self as a sociological knower/constructor—not just talking about it, but

doing it" (p. 136). Speaking autobiographically in order to provide "an opportunity to rethink sociological representation" (p. 133), Richardson writes of her need to break out of the "dreary" writing of " 'straight' sociological prose" (p. 131). The part of her that had written poetry for eight years is called on to "provide a new strategy for resolving those horrid postmodernist writing dilemmas" (ibid.). Deliberately choosing a transcript from a woman quite different from herself in order to encounter the "postmodernist issues of 'authorship'/authority/appropriation," she works toward a text that is "bounded and unbounded, closed and open" (p. 132).

Richardson concludes with five consequences to herself of the experience of producing and disseminating the story-poem of "Louisa May." We hear about changed relations with children; spirituality; Richardson's integration of "[t]he suppressed 'poet' and the overactive 'sociologist' " (p. 135); her increased attunement to differences in others and herself, including more caution "about what 'doing research' means" (ibid.); and, finally, some disillusionment at "the hold of positivism on even those I consider my allies" as she has presented this work (ibid.). "I experience isolation, alienation, and freedom, exhileration. I want to record what they are saying; I want to do fieldwork on them. Science them" (p. 136).

Richardson exemplifies a disruptive excess which brings ethics and epistemology together in self-conscious partiality, an embodied positionality and a tentativeness which leaves space for others to enter, for the joining of partial voices. Authority comes from engagement and reflexivity in a way that exceedes Lyotardian paralogy via practices of textual representation that, by hegemonic standards, "go too far" with the politics of uncertainty. This effect is achieved by blurring the lines between the genres of poetry and social science reporting. Theorizing out of autobiography where her "leaky" practice collapses the private/public distinction, Richardson is mother, wife, scholar, and poet in her desire to move toward some way of doing science more in keeping with her feminist poststructuralism.

Offered as more problem than solution, my scandalous categories and the exemplars I have recruited as provocateurs of validity after poststructuralism are performances of a transgressive validity that works off spaces already in the making. Situated in the crisis of authority that has occurred across knowledge systems, my challenge has been to make productive use of the dilemma of being left to work from traditions of research legitimacy and discourses of validity that appear no longer adequate to the task. Between the no longer and the not yet lies the possibility of what was impossible under traditional regimes of truth in the social sciences: a deconstructive problematic that aims not to govern a practice but to theorize it, deprive it of its innocence, disrupt the ideological effects by which it reproduces itself, pose as a problem what has been offered as a solution (Rooney, 1989). Derrida terms this "a 'science of the possibility of science' . . . a nonlinear, multiple, and dissimulated space ... Thus we discover a science whose object is not 'truth,' but the constitution and annulment of its own text and the subject inscribed there" (Sollers, 1983, pp. 137, 179).

How might the scandalous categories of "transgressive validity" as set out thus far in this chapter be of use in efforts toward generative methodology? To continue the scandal, let us imagine a checklist:

Transgressive Validity Checklist: A Simulacrum

Ironic Validity

_____ foregrounds the insufficiencies of language and the production of meaning-effects, produces truth as a problem

_____ resists the hold of the real, gestures toward the problematics of representation, foregrounds a suggestive tension regarding the referent and its creation as an object of inquiry

_____ disperses, circulates, and proliferates forms, including the generation of research practices that take the crisis of representation into account

_____ creates analytic practices which are doubled without being paralyzed

Paralogical Validity

_____ fosters differences and heterogeneity via the search for "fruitful interruptions"

_____ implodes controlling codes, but still coherent within present forms of intelligibility

_____ anticipatory of a politics that desires both justice and the unknown, but refuses any grand transformation

_____ concerned with undecidables, limits, paradoxes, discontinuities, complexities

_____ searches for the oppositional in our daily practices, the territory we already occupy

Rhizomatic Validity

_____ unsettles from within, taps underground

_____ generates new locally-determined norms of understanding, proliferates open-ended and context-sensitive criteria, works against reinscription of some new regime, some new systematicity

_____ supplements and exceedes the stable and the permanent, Derridean play

_____ works against constraints of authority via relay, multiple openings, networks, complexities of problematics

_____ puts conventional discursive procedures under erasure, breaches congealed discourses, critical as well as dominant

Voluptuous Validity

_____ goes too far toward disruptive excess, leaky, runaway, risky practice

_____ embodies a situated, partial, positioned, explicit tentativeness

_____ constructs authority via practices of engagement and self-reflexivity

_____ creates a questioning text that is bounded and unbounded, closed and opened

_____ brings ethics and epistemology together

This checklist, which mimes checklists, enacts how my ephemeral practices of validity after poststructuralism are "an arrangement of desire and of enunciation" (Deleuze and Guattari, 1983, p. 107) rather than a general recipe.[3] My intent has been to forge from a scattered testimony a methodology that is not so much prescription as "curves of visibility and enunciation" (Deleuze, 1992, p. 160). As experiments "that baffle expectations, trace active lines of flight, seek out lines that are bunching, accelerating or decreasing in speed . . ." (Deleuze and Guattari, 1983, p. 111), my evocation is the "horizons toward which experiments work" (Ormiston, 1990, p. 239) as we try to understand what is at play in our practices of constructing a science "after truth."

Interlude

Dear Elliot

August 1996–November 1997

What follows are extracts from my correspondence via emails and letters with Elliot Mishler, Professor of Social Psychology, Harvard Medical School, to whom I had sent a copy of a publication on the validity of angels (Lather, 1995) and the desktop-published version of *Troubling the Angels*. His response to the book was "cranky and testy" and not at all sure if "productive dialogue" was possible given his "discomfort with the book." A single-spaced four plus page letter dated November 1, 1996 delineated this "negative response." I do not believe I ever sent the following letter, although Elliot and I met for coffee in Columbus a few years later and he continued to send me "angel clippings" as he "hadn't exactly sworn an oath not to."

Dear Elliot,

In reading your reading, I want to remain engaged with uncertainty, allowing no one reading to own the book. In a way that is very different than the self-criticism of modernism, I am trying to attend to how the book falls back into what it must refuse. So I thank you for your frank engagement.

It was the mawkish, banal, and self-indulgent I was trying to avoid— to not be afraid of stirring up big emotions, but to do so responsibly. My ambitions for the book were many-layered and I was very much up against my limits with a keen sense of the risks I ran with, for example, the angels. Perhaps I overreached, embarrassed myself, the field, whatever, with some leaky feminist thing, a going too far. Having just sent final revisions off (October, 1996), I am mostly into the failures of the text to accomplish its ambitious goals and at a sort of peace with this. "Ruined from the start" as

I have come to think through reading Walter Benjamin, it is what it is, "too much, too little, too soon, too late," to quote myself from the book.

You write that the book "presses readers to assent to its argument," full of "Ozhio" dimensions of "Chris and Patti skipping down the yellowbrick road to see the Wizard, with added angel wings." This is similar to dance critic, Arlene Croce (1994), regarding Bill T Jones's *Still Here*, where she writes of how a nonbeliever perspective is denied legitimacy regarding "oppression" art which positions a dissatisfied reader with no viable subject position.

You particularly found the theological rhetoric coercive. It is my most Catholic book for sure, but I interrupted that with "god as an available discourse" and "post-wiccan spiritual sensibility." And I was very much invested in using the angels to interrupt our "disguised theologisms": progress, secular salvation through "knowledge as cure," the science that takes the place of god, etc.

You see angels as a mark of "facile transcendentalism" (Bloom, 1996). I use Benjamin and Rilke to try to do something else, some defamiliarizing move based on Benjamin's love for the Paul Klee painting, *Angelus Novus*, which Benjamin described as facing backwards the catastrophe of the past, wanting to make whole what has been so broken, but caught up in the violence of the storm of progress that propels the angel into the future (Benjamin, 1968).

The key to Benjamin's angelology is what Paul de Man (1986) notes as Benjamin's tendency to both use familiar tropes and displace them in order to signal the all-too-human appeal that they make to us. He particularly used messianic appeals toward displacing our sense of what is human, destabilizing the original, translating beyond the original, keeping the text in circulation, decanonizing it by making us aware of certain disjunctions, disruptions, accomodations, weaknesses, cheatings, conventions (p. 97).

Like Harold Bloom (1996), you see a "millennial decade lousy with angels," but Bloom's point is not angels but what we do with them. I have wrestled with this use of religious and spiritual themes in exploring Benjamin's juxtaposition of theology and Marxism in his theory of language and materiality. To situate the angel as a fraud, a staging that allows transcendence its final word only as "an emblem of illusion" (Rosen, 1977, 38) is to foreground the unavoidable discrepancy between a visual sign and its image or meaning. In this, I am following Benjamin in his attempt to appropriate what was left of a moribund religious culture, especially the largely untouched mystical strains, giving them a secular form, making them once again available via translation of their ruins.

I found it so interesting that it was a research note in story series three that drew you in and on, what I saw as perhaps the most conventional scholarly move of the book, the "theorizing" of the lives of others, the "situating" them within a literature review, etc. By presenting fragments from the interview transcripts woven together into a fiction of shared space and "emergent themes," the snippets from interview transcripts produce a parody of unmediated text, a representation by imitation where we mime the forms of expert testimony, putting them under erasure, putting the gaze on display, making it accountable.

You raise concerns about not being able to follow the same person, a fragmentation where the women become anonymous, where we overwhelm their voices as "real" persons, the "press release" nature of their accounts. My effort here was to substitute a theory of deferral for one of essence, a complication of the language of presence. This is a terrible intellectual ambition that calls for a necessary indirectness, a detour and delay to interrupt the quest for presence. It is an imposition of radical complications for any story that promises to deliver a message to its proper receiver—surrendering the claim to the simplicity of presence.

My goal was a practice that exceeds both authorial intent and reader interpretive competence to produce nonmastery. Complex and ambitious, it is a place of ghosts and ruins versus consciousness. In this ambition, I worried about standards so exalted that work never actually gets made.

In assessing its effectivity, I presume we are delivered from certain loosely positivist questions. Making representations only to foreground their insufficiencies, my central message is how nothing can deliver us from our misrecognitions. In hearing readerly reactions, my goal is to be neither apologetic nor ironic in trying to map something of both the global and the body. Many risks were taken and embarrassments risked in the effort to enact interpretation's desire for mastery in the face of the recalcitrance of the object to be fully grasped by our interpretive machinery. Always feeling unable to do the subject justice, trying to block impulses to romanticize, I saw my central task as being purposefully not intelligible within standard frames in order to produce a stubborn book that rubs against the desire for interpretive mastery and implicates an audience rather than persuades or seduces.

I see myself as a willful presence in the book rather than an authoritative knower of what can be said and done. Risking something "like a glory or a crime" (Stanley Cavell quoted in Melville, 1996, p. 164), the stakes are a science constructed in a kind of materiality that recognizes the absence of things and the noninnocence of our efforts to know.

Patti Lather

Chapter 7

Postbook

Working the Ruins of Feminist Ethnography

The ambivalent tensions of Western feminist ethnography.—The ruins of
ethnographic realism and the limits of voice.—The masks of authorial presence.—A recalcitrant rhetoric: Against empathy.—Toward a
methodology of getting lost: Research theory politics.

Looking back over our study of women and HIV/AIDS—where we began,
what we encountered, and how we moved—Chris and I were "always already" situated in the ambivalent tensions of Western feminist ethnographic
traditions of giving voice to the voiceless (Visweswaran, 1994).[1] The question
I offer in this chapter is how our study can be used to grapple with the ethical
and political implications of doing feminist ethnography within the postmodern.
I am particularly interested in the concept of doubled practices. These are
practices that might be of use in negotiating the tensions between the political
imperative of feminism to make visible women's experiences and poststructural
critiques of representation (Juhasz, 1999; Piontek, 2000).

In what follows, I raise three issues from Chris and my "postbook"
location: the ruins of ethnographic realism, the masks of authorial presence,
and the work of a recalcitrant rhetoric. I conclude with some thoughts on a
"methodology of getting lost" by looking at the intersection of research,
theory, and politics. Working both within and against disciplinary conventions, my sense of task is to explore methodological economies of responsibility and possibility that engage our will to know through concrete efforts
both to produce different knowledge and to produce knowledge differently.

135

The Ruins of Ethnographic Realism and the Limits of Voice

Troubling the Angels is no seamless ethnographic realism. Working the ruins of an earlier moment of a feminist ethnography assumed "innocent" in its desire to give voice to the voiceless (Visweswaran, 1994), Chris and I have attempted a text that both reaches toward a generally accessible public horizon and yet denies the "comfort text" that maps easily onto our usual ways of making sense. The women wanted what they termed a "K-Mart" book. I wanted to create a "messy text" (Marcus, 1994) while still honoring Chris and my charge of producing a book that would do the work the women wanted. Using the ruins of feminist ethnography as the very site of possibility, the book reflects back at its readers the problems of inquiry at the same time an inquiry is conducted. Such a practice strikes the epistemological paradox of knowing through not knowing, knowing both too little and too much in its refusal of mimetic models of representation and the nostalgic desire for immediacy and transparency of reference. The effort is, instead, toward a "posthumanist materialism" that shifts from mimesis to something "altered and altering in its approach to language and history" (Cohen, 1996, p. 80).

In contemporary regimes of disciplinary truth-telling, the concept of voice is at the heart of claims to the "real" in ethnography. Indeed, in the new ethnography, the authority of voice is often privileged over other analyses. Confessional tales, authorial self-revelation, multivoicedness, and personal narrative are all contemporary practices of representation designed to move ethnography away from scientism and the appropriation of others.[2] At risk is a romance of the speaking subject and a metaphysics of presence complicated by the identity and experience claims of insider/outsider tensions. From the perspective of the turn to epistemological indeterminism, voice is a reinscription of some unproblematic real. This is a refusal of the sort of realism that is a reverent literalness based on assumptions of truth as an adequation of thought to its object and language as a transparent medium of reflection. The move is, rather, to endorse complexity, partial truths, and multiple subjectivities.

My attempt here is to defamiliarize common sentiments of voice in order to break the hegemonies of meaning and presence that recuperate and appropriate the lives of others into consumption, a too-easy, too-familiar eating of the other. Such a move is not so much about the real as it is about a horizon *in* insufficiency (Scott, 1996, p. 127). Against homogeneous spaces of collective consensus and communication, such work is emotive, figurative, inexact, dispersed, and deferred in its presentation of truth-telling toward responsibility within indeterminacy. But the demand for voice also has much to do with subjugated knowledges and multiple fractured subjectivities, the unheard/unhearable voices of Gayatri Spivak's "Can the Subaltern Speak?" (1988).

Hence, my move is not so much "against" voice as it is toward a double economy of the text, to move toward destabilizing practices of "telling the other" (McGee, 1992). What is displaced is the privileged fixed position from which the researcher interrogates and writes the researched (Robinson, 1994). Arguing that recuperating traditional realism is no answer to the aporias of the Left, I am positioned with those who try to use poststructural theory to think against the various nostalgias of leftist thought and practice. Such issues can be gestured toward via a process of layering complexity and foregrounding problems: thinking data differently, outside easy intelligibility and the seductions of the mimetic in order to work against consumption and voyeurism. By working the limits of intelligibility and foregrounding the inadequacy of thought to its object, a stuttering knowledge is constructed that elicits an experience of the object through its very failures of representation.

To sum up this first point on the disruption of ethnographic realism, in an economy so marked by loss as the place of AIDS, the text undercuts any immediate or total grasp through layers of point-of-view patterns. Refusing much in an effort to signal the size and complexity of the changes involved in the move away from modernist metaphysics of presence, assured interiority, and the valorization of transformative interest, *Troubling the Angels* is written out of a kind of "rigorous confusion." Such confusion displaces the heroic modernist imaginary in turning toward otherness, being responsible to it, listening in its shadow, confused by its complexities (Hebdige, 1996). Here "the participant witness" (Gordon, 1995, p. 383) tells and translates so that something might be seen regarding the registers in which we live out history in evoking an ethical force that is directed at the heart of the present.

The Masks of Authorial Presence

There is no absent author in *Troubling the Angels*. In Preface I to the book, Chris and I speak of "both getting out of the way and getting in the way," as we tell stories that belong to others (1997, p. xiv). In this, we risk both "vanity ethnography" (Van Maanen, 1988) and the romance of voice. Chris and I address these problems via such textual practices as a horizontally split text and angel intertexts. In the former, the women's words are on the top of the page in a bigger font, and researcher narratives are on the bottom in smaller font. As an intervention in the machinery of mimesis, most pages combine a top two-thirds that appears to be an unmediated interview transcript that foregrounds insider stories and a bottom underwriting that both decenters and constructs authorial "presence" through a kind of temporal disturbance. By forcing a reading in two directions, such a textual display is designed to break the realist frame. In a second interruptive textual practice, the angel intertexts serve as a site of deliberate imposition to signal the inevitable weight of researcher interpretation upon the story told. Wanting to probe these textual moves in order to address issues around both confessional writing and the romance of voice, I set the stage with some excerpts from the

Epilogue, which recounts the women's reactions to an early version of
the text.

Patti: Were there any parts of the book that you didn't like?

Barb: The format. I wanted to read it all from one end to the other, and
it was hard to do because I was reading two different things. I would
have liked to read one part or the other in sequence.

Patti: So the top/bottom split text was irritating. And it never got easier
while you were reading along?

Barb: No.

Lori: I've given the book to four people, and they all said they had a
problem with the layout. Some people won't see a movie with subtitles.

Rita: I liked that part where the bottom was a little story, alongside the
top part. It made it more interesting, very much more interesting, but
I had a hard time with the middle part about angels. It's just a little bit
above me, I think.

Lori: I'll be honest, I skipped a lot of the angel stuff. I didn't get why
it was in there and I was really into the stories about the women. I was
enraptured by the women's stories, and I didn't want to waste my time
at that point with the angels. Now that I've seen the play *Angels in
America*, I'm going back to read it cover to cover. But at the time, it
did not captivate me at all. You're getting into a whole big thing about
angels and in a selfish way, I think it takes away from our stories.

Sarah: The angelology part was really interesting. To me it was just
interesting to know about angels in our culture and different cultures,
and then to tie it in with the struggle with the disease and how we think
about it. I learned some things I hadn't heard before. For people who
aren't familiar with HIV, they'll be learning from what the women have
to say. But if you've got it, what the women say is confirming, but I felt
like I learned some things from the inter-texts. I hope that if you get it
published, they don't massacre it!

Heather: It has to have angels in it. That's the whole context. I usually
don't buy into such stuff, but as I do this AIDS work, it's a feeling.

Amber: I hope this takes off and they make a little mini-series about it.

Patti: You could be the consultant.

Sarah: I think she wants to be the star!

And from the subtext of the epilogue:

Patti: The earlier self-published version of this book was no first faint draft. While re-orderings, updates and additions have been made, this version is no radical departure from its earlier incarnation. This is not out of some sense of the great sufficiency of what we have done, but rather out of our puzzlement as to how to proceed differently. For example, in the case of our continued commitment to the split text format in the face of participant reservations, we encountered publishers who also wanted us to get rid of it in the name of appealing to a broader range of readers. We tried other options. We knew we didn't want our commentary to come before the women's stories as we wanted to give pride of place to their words. We knew we didn't want our words to come after their stories as that set us up as the "experts," saying what things "really meant." We tried the idea of "asides," where we would put our comments in sidebars. But all of these efforts renewed our commitment to the kind of "under-writing" that we had stumbled onto in our efforts to find a format that didn't smother the women's stories with our commentary and yet gestured toward the complicated layering of constantly changing information that characterizes the AIDS crisis. Trying to find a form that enacts that there is never a single story and that no story stands still, we practiced a kind of dispersal and forced mobility of attention by putting into play simultaneously multiple stories that fold in and back on one another, raising for readers questions about bodies, places and times, disrupting comfort spaces of thinking and knowing.

Our charge was simple: get the story out. The deliberately discontinuous mosaic that we have settled on may be a case of putting style ahead of story and, seemingly, we could have found a publisher more easily without this complicated and complicating format. But we risked this practice in order to bring to hearing matters not easy to make sense of in the usual ways. Forced to deal with two stories at once, the split text format puts the reader through a kind of "reading workout," a troubling exercise of reading. It stitches together discontinuous bits and multiples of the women's stories through seemingly disconnected narrative worlds, angelology, e-mail and journal entries, letters, poems, interview transcripts, academic talk about theory and method, and autobiography. Multilayered, it risks a choppiness designed to enact the complicated experiences of living with the disease, layers of happy and mournful, love and life and death, finances, legal issues, spirituality, health issues, housing, children, as people fight the disease, accept, reflect, live and die with and in it.

At this point, when I have read the preceding to academic audiences, I have been asked, "but did you cry?" Trying to make sense of this response, further queries of my audience evoke some statement about how distanced and disembodied all of it seems, how caught up in academese. So I continue to read from the subtext of the Epilogue:

> I would not let the angels go, even in the face of resistance to their presence in the book.
>
> Part of this was my very personal need to negotiate a relationship to loss. Over the course of this project, I broke down badly twice. Once was in transcribing Lisa's story of the death of her son, a late data story that we collected in this project. Recovering, I wrote in my research journal, "I have just broken down, crying. This is the first tape I've transcribed that I didn't know if I could get through it or not. It *is* cumulative; it does get worse with each death and, of course, a child, a child and a mother talking like this about her child's death." A second time was reading Chris' draft of the acknowledgments and seeing Rex's name, my long-time friend cut down by AIDS in the prime of a life well lived, a friend who gave me every encouragement in this project while still holding me to the fire of responsibility. Two bad cries in such a project testifies to the work the angels did for me, their cooling comfort that let me get on with the book.
>
> This past July, Chris called to tell me of Lori's impending death. "I need to talk to someone. This is going to be a hard one. I've known her and her family for seven years. Her husband was my first AIDS death." I listen. We talk of the protease inhibitors and how, for some, they are too late. The weight of luck and conjunction and timing and being caught in history's web asserts itself once again. I mention Tracy saying that she had read from the desktop version of the book at Danielle's funeral about Danielle's relationship with her father and we wonder how many more stories like that we'll hear or whether the new treatments will end this funeral parade. And I think, again, of my stubborn attachment to my "necessary angels."
>
> The poet Rilke wrote of how "necessary angels" help us negotiate being plunged into death like a stone into the sea. And Benjamin helped me see early on how the angel could function somewhere "between theory and embarrassment" (Ellison, 1996) in this study, an index that lets us see how history happens as we attend to the line between the limits of where we are and what is gathering beyond. Grounded in the stories of women living with HIV/AIDS, trying to think about and against our habits of mind in making sense of social crisis, I have put the angels to work in order to continue the dream of doing history's

work in a way that is responsible to what is arising out of both becoming and passing away.

My interlocutors have seemed much more satisfied with this, until I raise the question: why the need to know I cried? Finding an authorial voice that does not lend itself to melodrama has been no easy task in this project. Seeking some undramatized, largely effaced narrator versus the "oprah-ization" of this era of confessional talk has been complicated by the effort to both deny the tidy text and yet appeal to a broad public horizon. Autobiography seemed requisite in this. Hence, in trying to do justice to the women's stories, I sought an authorial presence that was both embodied and yet avoided the "nostalgia-provoking, emotional-yanking" sort of narrative move that is used to sell everything from empathy to hammers.[3] What I have come to call the "validity of tears" brings me great discomfort, a discomfort tied, I think, to what Deborah Britzman (1997) writes of as contemporary ethnographers "incited by the demand for voice and situatedness" (p. 31). As some effort toward "recovering from objectivity," Britzman argues that this incitement is much about the nostalgia for presence and ontological claims of identity.[4]

Friedrich Nietzsche serves well to interrupt such incitements. Nietzsche believed that the way to whatever "truth" was possible was via the unconscious and forgetting. "Every opinion is also a hiding place," he wrote, "every word also a mask" (quoted in Kofman, 1993, p. 91). For Nietzsche, "unmasking is not about removing from the text a cloak that veils the truth, but rather showing the clothing which an apparent 'nakedness' conceals" (p. 92). Nietzsche's big question is what does the will that wants the truth want (Kofman, 1993, p. 24). His counsel was self-estranging breaks, where one could hardly recognize oneself in past productions as anything other than a palimpsest where under each layer is another layer. There is a vertigo produced by such a practice that risks not so much not being understood as one writes outside traditional norms as being understood by those who want the naked truth.

A Recalcitrant Rhetoric: Against Empathy

Troubling the Angels denies the comfort text. Reading perhaps too much Gilles Deleuze these days in order to think my way into postfoundational possibilities, an audience, I posit, reads itself into becoming part of the assemblage that is the text.[5] To take the Deleuzean turn from persuading to producing the unconscious as the work of the text is to put into play the ambivalence of reception. In a book where writing is a place where philosophy is less argued than enacted as a practice of not-knowing, to focus on conventional rhetorical tactics of persuasion would be to assume an a priori audience of address. To the contrary, I am interested in provoking a reading that finds out something about itself via a writing at the limit of taking any particular sort of reader into account.[6]

This is not the place, I think, to get into what art critic Hal Foster (1996) refers to as "the return of the real," but I am, in this project, much more about confrontation with the weight and density of the HIV+ women who are the object of my knowing than with some audience who reads about them. Here, the meaning of what we study, its objectness, is its effect on our knowing, and writing is an affirmative experimentation that displaces skepticism and irony with respect for that objectness. This attention to "objectivity in deconstruction" (Melville, 1996) is in opposition to the "too easy to tell tale" (Britzman, 1998) that collapses the weight of the object in a focus on how knowledge projects are linguistically mediated and rhetorically staged. This more complicated and complicating sort of tale insists on the ways we are struck by an object, captured by it, and then attempt to grasp the limits and possibilities of our grasp. Facing the inadequacy of thought to its object, stuttering of and into language, the book is written within my desire for a "posthumanist materialism" that sees the problematic of language less as formalistic play than as an agent of cultural intervention against the seductions of mimetic views of representation (Cohen, 1996).

As Nancy Johnson (1997, p. 1) points out, "traditional rhetorical theory has privileged persuasion and agreement as the goals of rhetorical practice," in effect erasing difference. In moving "toward the normative" where "authority" is based on "superior knowledge and appealing character," this "anticipatory stance" in regard to audience assumes how a general type of audience will respond. Instead, my work addresses Johnson's question: "How can feminist writers begin to re-imagine the goals of writing and subvert 'persuasion' as an aim for political work?" (1997, p. 2) Rather than conventional tactics of persuasion, my interest is in what Kate Lenzo terms "more nuanced authorial constructions that call into question the construction of authority itself" (1995, p. 4). This produces "a disjunctive space that expands rather than reduces interpretive possibilities" (McCoy, 1997, p. 500). Hence, this writing shows what it is to be seen and assembles an audience in a way that resists the ground of traditional persuasion.

Doris Sommer (1994) terms this a "recalcitrant rather than a persuasive rhetoric" (p. 542) in her exploration of texts that resist empathic reading. Disrupting fantasies of mutuality, shared experience, and touristic invitations to intimacy, Sommer delineates "uncooperative texts" (particularly that of Rigoberta Menchu about the struggles of Guatemalan Indians), which refuse mimetic desires and reader entitlement to know. Menchu (1984) says, "I'm still keeping secret what I think no-one should know. Not even anthropologists or intellectuals, no matter how many books they have, can find out all our secrets" (p. 247). Such practices are double, Sommer argues, both epis-temological and ethical. Such empathy-resisting texts are about what we can know but also about what we, perhaps, ought not to assume we have the right to know. This questions Enlightenment assumptions about understanding and knowledge. Interrupting our desire to possess, know, and grasp, such defiant rhetorics teach unanticipated lessons about the limits of knowing.

Such a practice asks how a readership can betray a text that is con-structed as a sort of trap that has to be broken with in order to rethink the relationship of knower/known and reader/writer/written-about as constitutive and productive. Through a different organization of space and visibility, the usual identification and consumption of some other as what Derrida calls "the mourning object" is interrupted (1996a, p. 187). Gradually building up by partial pictures the idiom of our history, this is a fold versus a depth model. Designed to disrupt the conditioned response of the modernist reader, such a fold elicits an experience of the object through the very failures of its repre-sentation. Such a fold sets up a different economy of exchange in order to interrupt voyeurism and the empathy that Walter Benjamin termed an "indo-lence of the heart" that keeps intact history as triumphalist narrative, the victor's story (1968, p. 256).

Eschewing sentimentality, empathy, and subjectivism, Benjamin's his-torical and sociological impulses underwrote the efforts of Chris and myself to construct a book on women living with HIV/AIDS where the reader comes to know through discontinuous bits and multiples of the women's stories. Such textual dispersal works against easy categories of us and them, where "us" is the concerned and voyeuristic and "them" are the objects of our pity, fear, and fascination (Fuss, 1996). Refusing to deliver the women to the reader in a linear, tidy narrative, we intended to block and displace easy identifications and sentimentalizing empathy. Thus, the text works toward constructing a respectful distance between the reader and the subject of the research, producing a kind of gap between text and reader that is about inaccessible alterity, a lesson in modesty and respect, somewhere outside of the "murderous mutuality" presumed by empathy (Sommer, 1994, p. 547).

Incited by the demand for voice and situatedness, but perverting, invert-ing, redirecting that demand, the book attempts to complicate the question of ethnographic representation. Irreducible to the terms of the real, its insistent move is from voice to inscription, from notions of the intrinsic to ideas of the frame. Here, the task becomes to operate from a textual rather than a refer-ential notion of representation in working the ruins of a confident social science. This is deconstruction "after the turn," in what Spivak calls its " 'set-ting-to-work' mode," which carries a greater emphasis on ethics and politics (1999, p. 429).

Toward a Methodology of Getting Lost:
Research Theory Politics

The critical desire—which is also the philosophical desire—can only, as
such, attempt to regain . . . lost mastery.

—Derrida, 1981

In this final section, we arrive at where we have, perhaps, been moving all
along: the political and ethical implications of the sort of stammering relation
to what it studies of a book intended to attest to the possibilities of its time
yet, in the very telling, register the limits of itself as a vehicle for claiming
truth. In what follows, I delineate the political point of the interpretive and
textual practices of the book, destabilize my own investment in those practices, and probe the possibilities of a "responsible deconstruction."

The Political Point: *Troubling the Angels* refuses much in an effort to
tell the story of others in a way that takes testimony seriously enough to not
tame its interruptive force into a philosophy of presence and a romance of the
speaking subject (Derrida, 1976). Chris and I risked this format in order to
bring to hearing the unspoken and unspeakable that is present when people
attempt to tell the truth about their lives. No longer feeling confident of the
"ability/warrant to tell such stories in uncomplicated, non-messy ways" (Lather
and Smithies, 1997, p. xvi), the straightforward story has become impossible.
"Innocent" ethnographic realism is displaced by practices of representation
where authors both get in and out of the way in an effort to honor the voices
of the women while not eliding the inevitable power researchers yield as
interpreters and writers. Deepened in encounter with such complicating of
testimony as Maurice Blanchot's *The Writing of the Disaster* (1986), Shoshana
Felman and Dori Laub's *Testimony* (1992), and the controversy around *I
Rigoberta Menchu*, Chris and I refuse to play the expert and explain the
women's lives. Avoiding the position of the grand theorist and master interpreter, we grant weight to lived experience and practical consciousness by
situating both researcher and researched as bearers of knowledge while simultaneously attending to the "price" we pay for speaking out of discourses
of truth, forms of rationality, effects of knowledge, and relations of power
(Foucault, 1998). To mark such complications, *Troubling the Angels* uses a
variety of devices, from shifting countervoices and subtextual underwriting to
dialogic openness and variability of meaning. Intended to rupture the narrative and force reading in two directions, such devices undercut the authors as
"the ones who know" by employing partiality, chunkiness, and deferral. Rather
than depiction through claims to "wholeness" and presence, representation is
presented as irreducible to the terms of the real, and closure is interrupted in

order to work against ending on the sort of recuperative note typical of "the religious left" (Gilbert-Rolfe, 1995, p. 56).

Such deauthorizing devices are evident in the book's final two pages where we both challenge the researcher's right to know and interpret and yet "get in the way" of any claim to an innocent ethnographic realism of voices speaking for themselves. Registering discomfort with the religious construction of AIDS as a "journey to God," I listen to one of the women read a poem at her final meeting with the support group. I write of God as, to me, "an available discourse. . . . For Holley, God is the Father she is ready to come home to" (Lather and Smithies, 1997, pp. 251–52). And then Holley's poem has its stage, the final page of the book, the final box of a book full of boxed knowledges, unexpected juxtapositions, mimetic ruptures, and changes of register from ethnographic voice to researcher confessionals to the latest demographics of AIDS. Situating our textual moves within and against the historical and normative status of the new ethnography, we try not to position ourselves as knowing more about these women than they know about themselves. Placing their voices above ours on the split pages and their poems in boxes seemingly out of the control of authorial judgment, our aim is not so much verisimilitude as a troubling of authority in the telling of the lives of others. Searching for ways to stage the aporias involved in telling other people's stories, the book works the ruins of feminist ethnography as the very ground from which new practices of ethnographic representation might take shape.[7]

The Aporia of Exemplarity: To risk applying methodological considerations to an example illustrates "the aporia of exemplarity" (Spivak, 1999, p. 430) where something can be "produced as truth at the moment when the value of truth is shattered" (Derrida, 1976, p. 162). While *Troubling the Angels* draws on and dramatizes reoccurring tensions and traditions in feminist ethnography, any reading of such a text is "ordered around its own blind spot" and this is surely doubly so when the text is one's own (Derrida, 1976, p. 164). To privilege a certain text is, in Derrida's (1976) words, exorbitant, by which he means "a wandering thought . . . affected by nonknowledge" that reaches a point beyond "the conscious, voluntary, intentional relationship" of a writer to her time and use of language (pp. 161,158). But "we must begin *wherever we are,*" he says, "[having learned] that it was impossible to justify the point of departure absolutely. *Wherever we are*: in a text where we already believe ourselves to be" (p. 162; emphasis in original). Troubling both habitual frames of representation and deconstructive counterpractices, the book is offered as "modest witness" of a "good enough" ethnography in the making, ethnography as a cultural practice and practice of culture, something to think with rather than a mastery project (Haraway, 1997).

Ironically, such an example courts a situation of being too convinced of its success as an ambivalent failure in a way that recuperates a sense of mastery through the very defense of risky failures.[8] As methodological stances,

reflexive gestures, partial understanding, bewilderment, and getting lost are
rhetorical positions that tend to "confound refutation," and fragmentation of
texts hardly avoids imposing one's interpretation of a fragmented worldview
(Hegeman, 1989). Against such self-consolidations/consolations, my interest
is in the limits of reflexivity and the possibilities of nonmastery as an ethical
move. In this, reflexivity is positioned as about modernist assumptions of
consciousness, intentionality, and cure and displaced by what Derrida has
termed a "double effacement" (1979b, p. 100). Effacement, as some other to
the plenitude of presence, displaces mastery with a recognition that we often
do not know what we are seeing, how much we are missing, what we are not
understanding, or even how to locate those lacks. What is doubly effaced,
then, is both the transparency of language in constructing the referent and
"the narrative of the impossibility of narrative" that is "of the same nature as
what it works against," doing again as it undoes (Miller, 1979. pp. 250, 251).
In order not to be "a bit too masterful and muscular," it undoes itself via "a
ceaseless dissatisfied movement" (Miller, 1979, pp. 251, 252). Eroding privilege and undercutting certainty, both the knower's mastering point of view
and the authority of the metastory "of deconstruction in deconstruction"
(Derrida, 1979b, p. 100) are effaced. Here, the obligation becomes to read the
unreadability of the impossible event, an aporia that sets things in motion:
"What must remain beyond its reach is precisely what revives it at every
moment" (Derrida, 1979b, p. 134).

Staging a set of anxieties that haunts feminist ethnography, the book is
a viewing space punctuated with paradoxes. Working at various levels of
representation, it both uses and troubles the ethnographic genre in order to
give testimony and mark reflexivity as a modernist trap while troubling both
testimony and the angst around reflexivity. Conscious of itself as a system of
conventions and representations, it performs the arbitrariness implicit in the
act of representation. Its aspiration is to consolidate a critical public, both on
the political level of HIV/AIDS support and activism and in the reception
of feminist ethnography as a critical tool, particularly in terms of its "duty to
betray" the seductions of mimetic views of representation: "the mirage of
[the] immediacy of speech" (Derrida, 1976, p. 141).[9]

Pehaps too clever by far in its dizzying involutions and intellectual
somersaults, such a messy text says yes to that which interrupts and exceeds
and renounces its own force toward a stuttering knowledge. The danger is that
it risks "ethically violating the testimony of the other by subsuming her body
or her sentiment to the reductive frames" of our interpretive and textual
moves (Mehuron, 1997, p. 176). Given such complicities, as Derrida (1996a)
notes, the "authentic" witness is necessarily a "false" witness, caught in aporia,
where to succeed is to fail in making the other part of us.

Deconstructive Responsibility: While often assumed to be a nihilistic
undercutting of ethical practice, the primary interest of deconstruction is "in

awakening us to the demands made by the other" (Caputo, 1997c, p. 15). In terms of a responsible deconstruction, how is it possible that *Troubling the Angels* might "be of use" to the women whose stories we tell? Is the violence done by raising issues around the romance of testimonial voice in the crisis of representation enabling or disabling? Can working through familiar narrative forms and everyday language via reflexive experimentation enhance rather than dilute the practical, political intent of feminist ethnography? "What would it be," as Spivak asks, "to learn otherwise, here?" (1994, p. 62)

In June of 1999, I spoke about our book at a conference on women and AIDS in Oklahoma, handed out copies at the women's prison, and engaged with AIDS service care providers and HIV positive women.[10] Continually bought up short by the very tensions I am addressing between feminist imperatives to render women visible and poststructural critiques of representation, I thought much of Foucault's (1997a) challenge that because nothing is innocent and "everything is dangerous . . . we always have something to do" (p. 256). I wondered what we are to do with what we are told in terms of listening for the sense people make of their lives without reverting to "too easy" ideas about voice. How do we avoid practices of usurpative relation to people's stories of lived experience while still troubling experience as a "grand narrative" (Scott, 1992)? How weighty are such academic questions about the limits of representation in the face of the urgency of AIDS in the world?

While the "member check" data included in the Epilogue of the book give some credence to the usefulness of the book in the lives of many of the women we worked with, a different sort of book might have pleased them as much, or more.[11] In refusing to deliver the women to the reader in a linear, tidy tale, in excess of the referent, both more and less than any proper name, Chris and I evoked the "real" through the women's stories while problematizing referentiality. Staging the women "as a slice of the authentic, a piece of the real" (Spivak, 1994, p. 60) while, simultaneously, questioning its own interpretive and textual practices, the book troubles the ruse of presenting the women's stories as transparent language. In addressing issues of responsible engagement, was the member check a "structured alibi for consultation" (Spivak, 1994, p. 63)? In coming to terms with the dangers of such a tack, mimetic realism is not innocent in the way it treats the sign as transparent in privileging representation over signification, reinforces the passivity of the reader, and fails to portray the real as a contradictory linguistic construction. What is our obligation to the people we study? Do we act in their name in the last instance, or to "a greater responsibility than allegiance to a proper name . . . something coming about through the telling" (Spivak, 1994, pp. 41, 46)?

As Derrida teaches us, deconstruction is both remedy and poison (1981). My effort is toward a responsible deconstruction that learns critique from within in order to set to work anew. Assuming that consciousness is not the authority in the last instance (Derrida, 1981, p. 316), my goal is "an analysis that is patient, open, aporetic, in constant transformation, often more fruitful in the recognition of its impasses than in its positions" (Derrida, 1981, p. 322). Drawing on Spivak (1994), who draws on Derrida to address questions of responsibility, my deconstructive methodology is a "setting-to-work . . . bound to good or bad uses, doubled in its acknowledgement" of necessary complicity (p. 28). In formalizing the problematic of responsibility in terms of the relevance of deconstruction to politics, Spivak reminds us that "all complicities are not equivalent" and that "such demonstration can only happen within the intermediary stage" (1994, pp. 63, 23). In other words, one sets to work out of what one knows, but "decisive testing" is in action in "the risks of non-knowledge" (p. 25).

I think what this means is that as much as I would like to return to Oklahoma and see what sense the women I talked to have made of our book, perhaps it is the very questioning engagement of our intervention that is the politics of what we have done. Seeking something not overcoded in terms of received understandings of ethical exchange, including feminist protocols, we have set to work in the mode of deconstruction where accountability and responsibility are about "a persistent effortfulness that makes a 'present' " (Spivak, 1993, p. 156). Attempting "to turn into something doable" the difficult recognition of the stakes of language in telling stories of lived experience, we have tried to write a book that is something other to "precious posturing" (Spivak, 1993, p. 155). This has entailed risking that the testimonial subject can give us what we need instead of what we think we want: not her truth delivered to us in a familiar framework but the truth of the play of frames and the dynamics of presences, absences, and traces as all we have in the undecidability of history.

Conclusion

Even with all these words, I know that I am making a career out of them.

—Rhee, 1999

In working from, with, and for women living with HIV/AIDS, Chris and my book is as much symptom and index as intervention. It is a risky business, this mining of discursive resources toward a kind of knowledge that jolts us out of our familiar habits of mimesis, referentiality, and action (Cohen, 1996). In this account of strategies risked, I have sought the possibilities of research that makes a difference in struggles for social justice while working against the humanist romance of knowledge as cure within a philosophy of consciousness. My sense of responsibility is to move toward innovations leading to new forms, toward negotiation with enabling violence attentive to frame narratives that works against the terrain of controllable knowledge (Spivak, 1993). My interest is in a less comfortable social science, one appropriate to a postfoundational era characterized by the loss of certainties and absolute frames of reference. Using a book full of stuck places and difficult issues of truth, interpretation, and responsibility, I have appropriated contradictory available scripts to create alternative practices of feminist research as a site of being and becoming in excess of intention.

Feminist ethnography is a much-written-on and -about movement. From the consolations of empowerment to a sort of self-abjection at the limit, it is generating itself out of its own impossibilities as it evokes the anxieties that follow the collapse of foundations. Always already swept up in language games that constantly undo themselves, we are all a little lost in finding our way into ethnographic practices that open to the irreducible heterogeneity of the other as we face the problems of doing feminist research in this historical time.

Interlude

The Angel to Philosophy of Science

At the conference, the range of presentations was broad . . . An interesting phenomenon was the fact that South Africans during the times of isolation had developed their own angel [sic] to philosophy of science.

—Newsletter, Centre for Qualitative Research, Psychology Institute, University of Aarhus, Denmark, October, 1995

When I read the above, I was much taken with the misprint that resulted in the "angel to philosophy of science." Somewhat obsessed with angels myself, as a means to trouble familiar categories and logics (Lather, 1997), this final Interlude is a meditation on what an "angel [angle] to philosophy of science" might be made to mean. I do so within the context of all that is involved in examining (post) ethnography as "not something that can be set 'straight' but . . . has to be tracked through its moves and versions, its permeabilities and vulnerabilities, its nervous shifts from one thing to another, its moments of self-possession and dispersal" (Stewart, 1996, p. 9).

Walter Benjamin's (1968) "Theses on the Philosophy of History" is no easy read. Struggling with his backward-facing angel of history suggests what a nonteleological history might look like, a history thought against the consolations of certain meaning and knowing and toward the thought of the limit as a way to make a future. Benjamin's angel of history is a way of both negotiating a relationship to loss and, through its very dangers, steering away from the melodrama and/or easy sentiment attendant upon either a romance of the sublime or a metaphysics of presence. Enacting how language cannot NOT mean and how it leads to identification, subjectivization, and narrative, the angel can be used not to recuperate for a familiar model, but to deconstructively

151

stage the angel as a palimpsest, a failure at containing meaning, a means to
empty out narrative in advance and make it generate itself over its impossibility.

German literary critic Peter Szondi (1978) argues that Benjamin's angel
is the historian facing backwards, emblematic of the crisis of dialectics, a
prophet facing backwards as a break with ideas of progress, learning to read
the harbouring of a future in a past. Werkmeister (1996) sees Benjamin's
angel as the helplessly driven witness of history, shift from enforcer to "witness for the defense" (p. 264), studying history in horror with an angel's
feeble light, blown backwards into the future. Rochlitz (1996) positions
Benjamin's angel as untranslatable without reduction in having much to do
with the weight of history on our lives. Michel Serres (1995b) sees some
party as being over and mobilizes the angel as a resource for being nonmodern,
a sort of quasi object, a hybrid or monster that evokes the anxieties that
follow our triumphs when foundations collapse, displacing not only GOD,
but the place of God.

According to Serres, in the old system, in order to understand, nothing
must move. The new image of knowledge is of turbulence which isn't system
so much as confluence, traversing scales of dimension. Here, Serres argues,
angelology is key: a turbulent array of messengers, tracking and composing
relations outside of defined concepts, producing the grammar of these modes
of relating beyond fetishes of consciousness, essence, being, matter. "We
must invent the place of these relations," Serres writes (1995b, p. 137), as
ground for a new science where philosophy no longer has the right to judge
everything, but the responsibility to create, to invent, to produce what will
foster production, to understand and apply a science in the face of holdovers
and exhaustions. More interested in ethics than demarcation issues, the borders between science and not-science fluctuate constantly. "We are accus-
tomed to abstraction via concepts" as a means to organize stabilities, but this
is about fuzziness and fluctuation, "a foundation with wings" (pp. 112–14).

Foucault's counter-science, Nietzsche's gay science, feminist and other
minoritarian efforts toward a less comfortable social science: all of these are
enactments of a kind of science adequate for our times. Moving from a
narrowly epistemological, universalistic idea of science to a science that in-
tegrates context-dependency with practical deliberation about values toward
praxis, a more expansive idea of science is "simultaneously sociological,
political and philosophical" (Flyvbjerg, 2001, p. 64). Such a science does not
divest experience of its rich ambiguity because it stays close to the complexities and contradictions of existence.

Focusing on practices as event, detecting forces that make life work,
sociality and history are seen as the only foundations we have. Instead of
emulating the natural or "exact" sciences, the goal is getting people to no
longer know what to do so that things might be done differently, so that we

might "produce something that doesn't yet exist" (Foucault, 1991, p. 121). This is the yes of the setting-to-work mode of postfoundational theory that faces unanswerable questions, the necessary experience of the impossible, in an effort to foster understanding, reflection, and action instead of a narrow translation of scientificity.

Afterwords

Still Lost

The Summons of the Archive as Process

Souls were rising, from the earth far below, souls of the dead, of people who had perished, from famine, from war, from the plague, and they floated up, like skydivers in reverse, limbs all akimbo, wheeling and spinning. And the souls of these departed joined hands, clasped ankles, and formed a web, a great net of souls, and the souls were three-atom oxygen molecules, of the stuff of ozone, and the outer rim absorbed them, and was repaired.

Nothing's lost forever.

—Tony Kushner, 1992

And so we come to what Derrida (1976) terms The End of the Book and the questions that continue to haunt a text that has surveyed across the shifts in the social sciences over the last few decades. Using an auto-critique of an example of feminist inquiry, I have explored the implications of such turns for feminist research and the social sciences more generally. In this, I have been particularly interested in how poststructuralism might be used to distinguish between a narrow scientism and an expanded notion of scientificity more capable of sustaining "the vital tensions among the not knowable, the inferential and the empirically verifiable" (Martin, 2001, p. 358).

Despite my refusal to produce the "easy" book—the "as is" collection of the already published—*Getting Lost* is a bit patched. It is perhaps more than one book, maybe three: a picture of the trajectory of my work over 15 years, a book about a book about women living with HIV/AIDS, and a book

155

about feminist methodology with/in the postmodern. The sort of reiterative, citational performance of the text has produced a tangled and self-interruptive archive that "produces as much as it records" (Derrida, 1996b, p. 17) in trying to think with the uncertainties of knowing.[1] The pervasive auto-citation tied to questions of ethical and political import sets me up danger-ously in terms of the relation of my textual practice to postmodern theory, particularly the Lyotardian demand for "small narratives" against the grand narratives of modernism.

Perhaps some new level of narcissism is being approached here. Per-haps it is testimony to how you can say too much about too little.

But just as there is something to the reading of postmodernism to which I am most attracted as that which is about its failure as its grammar (Melville, 2004), there is an insistence that whatever this book is, it is an enactment of its message. Like *Troubling the Angels* in its "everything but the kitchen sink" textuality, *Getting Lost* abstracts a philosophy of inquiry from an archive built up around a study of women living with HIV/AIDS. In this, "it aims to pit what Lyotard calls its 'little expertise' to the task of falling short in such a way as to bear witness notwithstanding to what it must fail to encompass" (quoted in Connor, 2004, p. 67).

To consider how a single study might bear out several decades of twists and turns in theory and methodology is to situate it as a disturbance of scale and proportion. Where to begin with the stuck places in such an effort given Foucault's (1972) caution that "it is not possible for us to describe our own archive, since it is from within these rules that we speak" (p. 130)?

How to Think the Post?

The Old Hot New Thing: When I first moved to Ohio State University in 1988, Bill Taylor, a departmental colleague, welcomed me and cautioned that, eventually, I would become the "old hot new thing." I have thought much of this comment, finding it wise in the ways of the academy and its various fashions. Are we in some new fashion now, of post-post or neopragmatism or the return of the real? Is feminist poststructuralism passé in a world of neopositivisms, hyper-imperialisms, and conservative restorations?

Rather than "the end" or "the return" of this or that in the face of constantly changing historical conditions, what are the possibilities for a sort of "phase" theory of postmodernism/poststructuralism/deconstruction?

The Postmodernist Always Rings Twice:[2] Michael Peters (2004) speaks of "first-generation poststructuralists" (p. 8) whose work has cross-fertilized a wide range of fields. Spivak (1999) writes that the first phase of the argu-ment from poststructuralism was from differance, the "making indeterminate" (p. 426). This first phase of the European development of poststructuralism is now "in its third or fourth generation," spreading out across areas and no longer "largely a French affair" as it is developed and applied, increasingly, around the world.

Lyotard has written of the "double blow" that "includes 'a first excitation, which upsets the apparatus' but 'is not registered.' It remains 'potential, unexploitable and thus ignored by the apparatus,' though this 'absence of form and of transformation is essential to the unconscious affect' recovered in the second blow that repeats the first" (quoted in Rajan, 2002, p. 31). Repetitions and returns of something missed the first time around, "unfolding into a future that must always be folded back into its past" (p. 32): this is a very different temporality than that of successor regimes, end-isms, and apocalyptic breaks.

My central argument has been that the turn that matters in this moment of the post is away from abstract philosophizing and toward concrete efforts to put the theory to work. In her call for putting deconstruction to work, Spivak's (1999) "phase theory" of poststructuralism goes something like this: The future pluperfect of deconstruction's "what will have been said" temporality complicates any linearity. "Third and fourth generations" of "first phases" are interrupted by a return of "first-generation" treatment of the post. Here, distinctions are made between "the end" of, for example, truth, objectivity, and progress and that which might engender examination and reconstruction in the face of the demise of epistemological foundationalism. *This is not about relativism, but about responsibility in not knowing.* It is about complicating reference, not denying it. It is a skepticism not about the "real," but about when language is taken as the real. Is this what is needed in order to generate an intelligibility for poststructuralism, what Spivak terms "an other-directed swerve away from mere philosophical correctness" and toward "the affirmative call or appeal to the wholly other" (p. 426)?

If Spivak is correct that what is entailed is a "setting to work that cannot be defined within the system" (1999, p. 428), how can the "(re)turn of the post" be anything other than a repeat of its failures in the face of so much resistance, misunderstanding, and announcement of its demise?

Its Failure Is Its Grammar: Grasping our thought in time is never easy. Interrupting tidy linearity in how to think postmodernism, Stephen Melville (2004) entertains the idea that its failure *is* its actual grammar (p. 82). In such a reading, its very inability "to establish itself with the kind of authority and centrality" lead it to a state where it "never quite happens" (p. 83). Perhaps its vanishing point is "a consequence of what it is and how it happens" (p. 92). Is this "uneasy inhabitation" (p. 96), exactly, the condition of postmodernity, "now and again . . . more obscure than ever" (p. 82)? Is this the necessary effacement I have been tracking across Derrida for years? What does this mean for the limits as well as possibilities of deconstruction in our particular historical moment?

Working the Limits of Deconstruction
with/in the Rage for Accountability

In looking at the post (re)turn at the site of feminist methodology, perhaps in necessary and productive failure, issues of voice and interpretive responsibility have been a particular tension in this project.

Dosse (1999) has much to say on the importance to the renewal of the social sciences of listening versus the more typical practices of unveiling and forceful interpretation (p. 137). The tension between explanation and understanding (p. 140) arises from both a focus on voices and an understanding that subjects are not transparent to themselves. Respecting the competence of commonsense and people's ability to give meaning to their everyday actions is both imperative and reductionist in reinscribing the ghost of presence. As I worked this tension over the last decade or so, I came to think that perhaps we are all unreliable narrators, researched and researcher alike, given the indeterminacies of language and the workings of power in the will to know. What resulted was a deliberately stumbling approach to the representation of ethnographic voice.

Adele Clarke's (2005) work on grounded theorizing "after the postmodern turn" holds promise of something less stumbling in providing analytical tools to address this tension. Her analytical maps help in "analyzing data cartographically, emphasizing relationality and positionality" (p. 292) in empirical work full of situated theorizings rather than formal universals. Such practices help us see how we are "explicitly located, situated, and historicized" (p. 293) as we deal with "issues of globalization and how things travel . . . open, indeterminate, changing, unstable, unfixed, tenuous, temporary . . . [in producing] analytic snapshots in time and space" (p. 296). In this resituating of a heretofore positivist grounded theorizing, contingencies, relationalities, "serious instabilities," and "the drag of history" (p. 297) are foregrounded and knowing subjects are decentered in an attempt to articulate the social in a way that faces up to the imperialism of our usual ways of doing so. "I suspect I will be working on this for some time" (p. 296), Clarke writes, knowing full well the dangers of systematicity and recipes in the analysis of qualitative data.

Perhaps especially with a tool such as Clarke's situational analysis, it's hard not to get lost here. My point is, exactly, to use that getting lost toward less comfortable, less imperialist ways of knowing. But what of the new scientism that is so much with us now? How can we work the dangers of such practices that are uncertain, incomplete, contingent, tentative, and ambiguous given the present "rage for accountability"?

Speedy (2004) writes of the "killer case study" with policy-shifting impact that we must not lose sight of in the rush to scientistic accounts of scientific legitimacy (p. 45). Kesby reminds us that Foucault's "everything is dangerous" includes "some things are more dangerous than others" (2005, p. 2043). Perhaps we *cannot* afford not to give up on mastery projects in opening ourselves up to the Other via the unwieldiness of projects that are generated by and generative of the very instability that is so difficult to tolerate, let alone learn from. How would this be different from the more typical telling bid to arrest the flux of knowledge?

Biddy Martin (2001) asks what it is to oppose "the imperative to produce an excellence that can be measured, easily administered, made transparent to consumers, and learned/acquired once and for all" in the face of the "incompleteness of Thought and the interminability of pedagogy" (p. 361). Which is the more dangerous in this time of our historical now, and where might we turn for some nonstupid hope?

A Spirituality I Can Bear to Learn From?[3]

Walter's Benjamin's messianic Marxism introduced me to the (re)turn to theology in academic theory. I found such ideas of much use in (re)situating what we think of as quite secular: the salvation narratives of Marxism, feminism, and science itself. I particularly found the angel of history useful in interrupting ways of making sense of the "collective hunger for spirituality" (McHale, 2004, p. 22) alive in the stories of women living with HIV/AIDS. I tracked Derrida's various engagements with what Spivak (2000b) terms "post-secular: . . . the name of an alterity that harbors good and bad—the 'sacred,' if there is any" (p. 33).

From his refusal to situate his work as negative theology to his evocation of "spirit" in *Specters of Marx*, Derrida has moved strongly into the "new intellectual nexus" that some term a "post-religious, post-skeptical . . . post-dualistic" turn in philosophy (Berry, 2004, pp. 174, 171).[4] Levinas, too, figures in such a turn: "It is 'the absolute foreign [that] alone can instruct us' " (quoted in Berry, p. 175).

Part of this "religious turn" is an effort to understand the "foundering of secular confidence" (Berry, 2004, p. 176) at the limits of reason in the face of the often violent revival of fundamentalist religious attitudes, from bombing abortion clinics to the guerrillas/insurgents/terrorists who fight in the name of Islam. Part of it is to try to understand why the U.S. Right has been so much more successful than the Left in galvanizing public opinion and effecting praxis. Spivak (2002), for example, writes:

> I am so irreligious that atheism seems a religion to me. But I now understand why fundamentalists of all kinds have succeeded best in the teaching of the poor . . . One needs some sort of 'licensed lunacy' . . . But

I am influenced by deconstruction and for me, radical alterity cannot be named 'God' in any language . . . 'Licensed lunacy in the name of the unnamable other' then. It took me this long to explain this incomprehensible phrase . . . for a future to come. (pp. 226–27)

The increasing salience of the spiritual in contemporary social and cultural change is no new news to women of color. But one example is Cynthia Dillard's (2006) work on African-American women and spirituality in the context of an academic life. Drawing on a long line of "spiritual striving" from W. E. B. DuBois to Patricia Hill Collins, Dillard puts spirit, Black feminist praxis, and African cultural knowledge at the center of her effort to foster deeper connection in research, service, and teaching.

While my poststructural self gets pretty excited about Cynthia's seeing her African-American identity "melt down like butter," this is about more and different than her finding her way to poststructural insights about shifting identity out of the lived experience of being called a white woman in a Ghanaian market. She writes of coming to a place "beyond double consciousness" in terms of what it means exactly to "be oneself," where she sees her not knowing who she is as an opening into the very sort of relationality she is endorsing.

How can I use my not knowing what to make of all this "spiritual stuff" in a similar way? If I think of Cynthia reading my book and go back to change every "death of God" to something less inflammatory, something less what Levinas termed "apocalyptic ideas or slogans of intellectual high society" (quoted in Sheehan, 2004, p. 25), what would I be doing?

It is the encounter with difference that is the motor of history in postmodernism. To use that encounter toward not being so sure of ourselves is ethics in postmodernism. Western knowledge systems assume the innocence of knowing, grasping, understanding. Levinas has taught us this is a betrayal of the other into the same. The other who refuses to give itself over to such knowledge is our best teacher. This is the other of our own reformulated thinking as well as those we other and those who other us. Our inability to comprehend makes ethics possible. Is this a spirituality I can bear to learn from? What are its lessons in the effort not to consume, but to be with others in indeterminacy and response-ability: what kind of science is this?

What Kind of Science for What Kind of Politics?

In the face of the re-negotiation of American hegemony in the neoliberal regime of globalization, what practices might help develop democratic processes more attuned to antagonisms that cannot be managed by the deliberative, rational, and consensual that so depend on the very certainty that is disappearing (Deutsche, 1996)? A review of the documentary *Gunner Palace*, about U.S. troops in Iraq, carries such lines as "no definition of victory in their future" and "unfortunately, they still have no way to define completing [their mission]" (Gabrenya, 2005, p. F6). A *Newsweek* editorial on economics is structured around the dangers of what we thought we knew (Samuelson, 2005). Calls are out from defense experts for the West to devise "a new way of thinking" in the face of Al-Qaida's decentralized and constantly mutating structure where relations of appropriation and conquest proliferate rather than reduce violence (Robberson, 2004).

This is a new geography where we are all lost to one degree or another. What would it mean to use such times to explore the philosophical and political value of not being so sure? How do we begin to think of what Butler (2001) argues as our need to face up to how not wanting to not know is a violence against the other? How does her call for "a double path in politics" both use and trouble our most fundamental categories in order to see what they yield "when they encounter what is unknown, or not yet known" (p. 23)? What has "the future in its bones," to use C. P. Snow's words (as quoted in Olafson, 2001, p. 7), in terms of the kind of science that might carry authority in such times? What does it mean to "carry authority" in such times?

In situating the social sciences as unmoored as the rest of the culture, this book has argued for a scientificity that is about imperfect information where incompleteness and indeterminacy are assets, more central elements of a scientific posture of getting lost as a way of knowing. Here, the absence of foundations is enabling, opening us to the other. Against the received objectifying, scientistic posture, this is a scientificity of engaged ethics grounded in a permanent facing of the undecidable, an ethical horizon of science more attuned to innovation than "the epistemological quarrel over the conditions of scientificity" (Dosse, 1999, p. 352).

This sort of becoming of the social sciences is a coming into philosophy as well as a philosophy becoming social, a site where one does empirical work in order to trouble it. Bringing philosophy and history and sociology of knowledge together in this task of trying to see how we see and to see what our knowing does in the world entails the ongoing renunciation of imperial mastery positions in all their guises.

This is not about escaping "upwards," abandoning the empirical, but rather about using empirical work as a laboratory toward philosophical understanding and a less dangerous politics. Here, the social sciences become an "investigative workshop" (Dosse, 1999, p. 370), "philosophy by other means" (p. 137) rather than "potentially hard sciences" (p. 211). At the heart of the argument is Beck's (1992) notion of a "reflexive scientization" that replaces the "traditional objectivist accounts of science by a more inclusive science that institutionalizes self-doubt, self-interrogation and self-reflexivity" (Backstrand, 2003, p. 33).

Will we get both better philosophy and better social science out of such practical engagement with the world, a different ontology of knowing, a postepistemological philosophy of science? What is the social and political weight of such efforts?

Questions of Style, Purpose, and Audience

Finally, at least for here and now, I struggle with questions of textual style, purpose and audience.

On the one hand, I have been critiqued in the past (Walker, 1994) for a tendency toward a writing that tries to be its own reading so exhaustively that there is no opening for reading left, so there is no chance for future except for confirmation of a reading that the text has already dictated, a text calculated to account for and include within itself all the readings to which it might be open (Bennington, 2000, p. 138). I have tried in these final words to not account for myself wholly and without remainder. My goal has been to mark the stuck places in my work, the places where I am "still lost."

Surely this includes questions around why we do our work and for what purpose. In *Decolonizing Methodology*, Linda Tuhawai Smith (1999) questions how research-based knowledge remains possible given the global uprising of the marginalized for whom research has historically been "a dirty word." Placing hope in such disappointment and "general shake-up" (Derrida, 2001, p. 69), my effort has been toward a fruitful sense of dislocation in our knowledge projects, "a horizon more ethical than epistemological" (Dosse, 1999, p. 283). Like Adele Clarke (2005), I want to retire to the sidelines the question of whether an ethical social science remains possible (p. 295). Like her, I want to put "differences, complexities and silences at the analytic core" (ibid.), attending to the social as well as to "voices," to the nonhuman as well as the human. I want to attend to the circulations of power and the necessary complicity and, perhaps, inevitable appropriation in service to the panopticon, doing it in order to keep asking who benefits, who loses, how is democracy being enacted in this space (Flyvbjerg, 2001). But how to go about "doing without knowing" (Zerilli, 1998): that is the question that remains at the heart of a book dedicated to situated knowing out of situated doing.

As to the question of who is this written to, who is this "we" of "us" that permeates the text, it is surely Bettie St. Pierre and her "get that book written, I need to read it" encouragement. And it is those like Tineke A. Abma (2002), who uses *Troubling the Angels* to encourage more experimental narrative forms in health sciences research, and Jane Speedy (2004), who does the same with narrative therapy. And it might even be those who use such work to document "extreme postmodernism" and its dangers in our time of audit culture and the rage for accountability.[5]

These are complicated issues at least since Hazel Carby (1982) asked, "What do you mean when you say WE?" from the vantage point of the exclusion of women of color from the idea of a common feminist project. Beatrice Hanssen (2001) asks, "what is a "community of 'we's' " if the "Kantian categorical imperative of unassailable moral obligations" and Rorty's pluralistic "we" of "difference-obliterator" consensus models are no longer tenable (p. 86; see, also, Torgovnick, 1994)?

Given these complications of audience and anti-theory times in a feminism "that can no longer be defined as a coherent project" (Kavka, 2001, p. xii), perhaps *Getting Lost* will not find many "with ears to hear" in these more (neo)pragmatic times. Have such textual experiments had their moment and now it is time to move into feminist work more directly related to policy arenas?

Wanting to leave openings, I mark such issues as not so much about future workings on my part as about where these indeterminacies, puzzlements, and confoundings might travel and with what effect.

To sum up, this book offers a reading of postmodernism toward articulating what is at stake for research-based knowledge in our particular moment. Trying to be attentive to continuities as well as ruptures and discontinuities across the complex operations at play, I have presented such movement as provisional, fragmenting, and heterogeneous. As an effort to identify and amplify what is already begun, this has been a tale of how the postmodern is enacted, constructed in a time and place where the juxtaposition of postmodernism and feminist methodology might found a dynamic out of their divergence in transitioning toward new openings in clearly contested space.

The following chart enacts such a move in comparison with its first version in *Getting Smart*.[6] There, the four columns ended with postmodernism. As I teach my qualitative research students, one can "read" the investments of a chart-maker by what comes at the end, what is situated as "the new best way." The following chart disrupts such tendencies by ending with question marks. It is a product of both Bettie St. Pierre and myself. I include, as well, a chart by a former student, Wanda Pillow, which she developed for use in her own teaching of qualitative research. Her chart, too, is a collaborative project, written with students of her own. It demonstrates the potential for "traveling theory" (Clifford, 1997) and the always revisable that is the best part of what we do for, to, on, and about one another, and with, always with—

Chart 1 Postpositivist New Paradigm Inquiry, Patti Lather and Elizabeth A. St. Pierre (Revised June 2005) Based on Lather, 1991, that was based on Habermas, 1971.

Predict	Understand	Emancipate	Break	Deconstruct	Next??????
*Positivist	*Interpretive	*Critical		*Poststructural Postmodern	*Neopositivist
Mixed Methods	Naturalistic	Neomarxist		Postcolonial	Neopragmatist
	Constructivist	<Feminist>		Postcritical	Citizen Inquiry
	Phenomenological	Critical Race Theory		Posthumanist	Participatory Dialogic Policy Analysis
	Ethnographic	Praxis-oriented		Post-Fordist	Posttheory
	Symbolic Interactionist	<Freirian Participatory Action Research		Queery Theory	Post-post
Interpretive Mixed Methods		Gay & Lesbian Theories		Disability Studies	
		Critical Ethnography		<Discourse Analysis	
				Race-feminist Poststructuralism (Wanda Pillow)	
				Postparadigmatic Diaspora (John Caputo)	
				Post-everything (Fred Erickson)	

*Indicates the term most commonly used   < Indicates cross paradigm movement

*Indicates the term most commonly used

"Break" indicates a shift from the modernist, structural, humanist theories/discourses on the left to the postmodernist, poststructural, post-humanist theories/discourses on the right. In the post theories, all major epistemological, ontological, and methodological concepts (e.g., language, discourse, knowledge, truth, reason, power, freedom, the subject, objectivity, being, reality, method, science) are deconstructed.

NOTE: Though all these paradigms operate simultaneously today, there is an historical sense to their articulation. August Comte (1778–1857) proposed positivism in the nineteenth century; social constructivism is often dated from Peter Berger and Thomas Luckmann's (1966) book, the *Social Construction of Reality*. The emancipatory paradigms grew from the Frankfurt School and the social movements of the 1960s and 1970s; and the post paradigms, from critiques following World War II and the Algerian War, including those of Michel Foucault (1926–1984), Jacques Derrida (1930–2004), and Gilles Deleuze (1925–1995). Paradigm shifts occur as reaction formations to the perceived inadequate explanatory power of existing paradigms. Therefore, someone who works in emancipatory paradigms, for example, is often aware of the theoretical assumptions as well as the critiques of positivism and interpretivism.

Also, some theories that start out in one paradigm change considerably when they are taken up in another; i.e., poststructural feminism is considerably different from liberal, emancipatory feminism. Conventional science is positivist, but when science's assumptions are rethought in interpretive or post paradigms, it is not the same, i.e., **science is not the same in all paradigms in terms of ontology, epistemology, and methodology.**

Chart 2   Major Interpretive Paradigms Chart

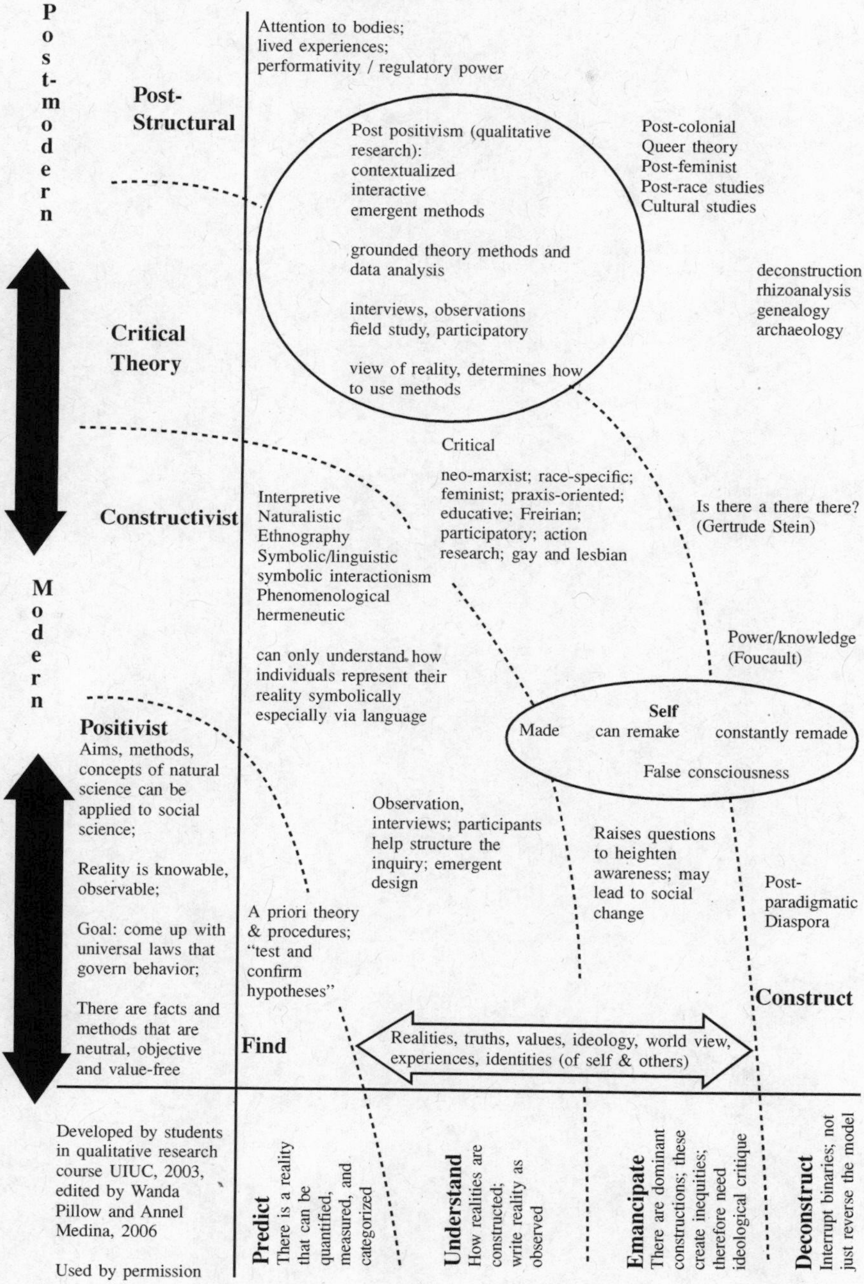

P
o
s
t-
m   **Post-**
o   **Structural**
d
e
r
n

Attention to bodies;
lived experiences;
performativity / regulatory power

Post positivism (qualitative
research):
contextualized
interactive
emergent methods

grounded theory methods and
data analysis

interviews, observations
field study, participatory

view of reality, determines how
to use methods

Post-colonial
Queer theory
Post-feminist
Post-race studies
Cultural studies

deconstruction
rhizoanalysis
genealogy
archaeology

Critical
Theory

Critical

neo-marxist; race-specific;
feminist; praxis-oriented;
educative; Freirian;
participatory; action
research; gay and lesbian

Is there a there there?
(Gertrude Stein)

Constructivist

Interpretive
Naturalistic
Ethnography
Symbolic/linguistic
symbolic interactionism
Phenomenological
hermeneutic

can only understand how
individuals represent their
reality symbolically
especially via language

Power/knowledge
(Foucault)

M
o
d
e
r
n

Self
Made   can remake   constantly remade

False consciousness

Positivist
Aims, methods,
concepts of natural
science can be
applied to social
science;

Reality is knowable,
observable;

Goal: come up with
universal laws that
govern behavior;

There are facts and
methods that are
neutral, objective
and value-free

Observation,
interviews; participants
help structure the
inquiry; emergent
design

Raises questions
to heighten
awareness; may
lead to social
change

Post-
paradigmatic
Diaspora

A priori theory
& procedures;
"test and
confirm
hypotheses"

Find

Construct

Realities, truths, values, ideology, world view,
experiences, identities (of self & others)

Developed by students
in qualitative research
course UIUC, 2003,
edited by Wanda
Pillow and Annel
Medina, 2006

Used by permission

Predict
There is a reality
that can be
quantified,
measured, and
categorized

Understand
How realities are
constructed;
write reality as
observed

Emancipate
There are dominant
constructions; these
create inequities;
therefore need
ideological critique

Deconstruct
Interrupt binaries; not
just reverse the model

Notes

Preface

1. See Weiler, 2001, for discussions of feminist uses of male theorists.
2. Selby's comments are based on a keynote presentation of this early work at the 1993 meeting of the Australian Association of Research in Education, Perth.
3. See Katrial and Sanders, 1989, for how epigraphs can be used in this way.
4. Participants included: Ann Phoenix, Dorthe Staunaes, Jette Kofoect, Nina Lykke, Tine Fristrup, Susan Wright, Yvonne Morck, Dorte Marie Sondergaarde, and myself, Danish Pedagogical University, Copenhagen, September, 2003.
5. Laurel Richardson's (1997) *Fields of Play* is also a model, as is Alice Walker's (1996) *The Same River Twice*. Thanks to Cynthia Dillard for the latter.

Chapter One

1. Charles Taylor defines a social imaginary as the ways we imagine a social space, our expectations, normative notions, and images. It is "the understanding that makes possible practices and a shared sense of legitimacy" (2004, p. 21). It is "the understanding implicit in practice" (p. 26), and it can be transformed into a new context that gives sense to new practices.
2. Gross and Levitt (1994) and Sokal (1998) are the most noted articulations of the backlash against the critiques of science across feminism, multiculturalism, postmodernism, and the social studies of science. See also Koertge, 1998. For Left responses, see Ross, 1996. For "after the science wars," see Ashman and Baringer, 2001.
3. The Nietzschean transvaluation of values involves working the pathos of ruined ideals toward an ethical vitalization. Against those who read him as a nihilist, this move underwrites the new Nietzsche scholarship which positions him as a "proto-deconstructionist" working the ruins of hierarchical binaries toward a healthier being and doing (e.g., Allison, 1985, 2001; Gillespie and Strong, 1988). Judith Butler's work exemplifies this move, as discussed later in this chapter. An example of this sort of inquiry in the context of a reading of U.S. higher education is Readings, 1996.
4. To work "under erasure" involves simultaneously troubling and using the concepts we think we cannot think without. It entails keeping something visible but

crossed out in order to avoid universalizing or monumentalizing it, keeping it as both limit and resource. The classic unpacking of deconstructive logic is Spivak's "Translator's Preface" in Derrida, 1976. For an update, see Caputo, 1997a.

5. Scientificity is sometimes conflated with scientism (see note 12), e.g., Aronowitz (1995), who defines scientificity as not so much the actual practices of science as "the permeation of the standard elements of the scientific attitude into all corners of the social world: seeing is believing; the appeal to 'hard facts' such as statistical outcomes to settle arguments; the ineluctable faith in the elements of syllogistic reasoning" (p. 12). Chapter 3 distinguishes scientificity from scientism and argues for a transvaluation of the former as key in an expanded definition of the social sciences.

6. For more on plateaus, see Deleuze and Guattari, 1987. This is a fold versus a depth model of presenting knowledge, a pragmatics of dissemination to gradually build up by partial pictures the idiom of our history. Plateaus are part of the plethora of conceptual assemblages that Deleuze and Guattari build up in their efforts to devise an open system of philosophy capable of tracking intensities, flux, and movement and undercutting any immediate or totalizing grasp.

7. More elaborated definitional fields pertinent to the social sciences are offered in Lather, 1991; Dickens and Fontana, 1994; Scott and Usher, 1996; Scheurich, 1997; Kreiswirth and Carmichael, 1995; Hollinger, 1994; Haraway, 1997; and, less usefully, Roseneau, 1992, who tends toward a "caricatured deconstruction" that is set up in opposition to construction and portrayed as "deeply conservative or wildly anachronistic" (Wilson, 1998, p. 21). For an entire book arguing the definitional field with a focus on architecture, see Rose, 1991. Hanssen, 2001, is particularly good on the "anti-theory" moment in feminism in terms of the split between critical theorists and postmodernists and the "mediating" role of the neopragmatists as the "newest new" in the "postlinguistic turn" to the local and the contextual.

8. The term "neoliberal" refers to varied developments in political and economic formation. Sometimes related to "globalization," it sets up questions about the nexus of liberalism, policy, and citizenship within a context of post-WWII shifts in the role of Western governments away from laissez-faire economics and toward a state-initiated broadening of economic thinking that diffuses the enterprise-form throughout society as its general organizing principle. Choice, commodity-form, the managerialism of identity and personal and professional relations, all result in "the capitalization of the meaning of life" (Gordon, 1991, 44). For audit culture, see Strathern, 2000.

9. Docherty, 1996; Harris, 1996; McQuillan, 1999.

10. The example of Moi is particularly interesting in terms of feminist work. Her 1999 *What is a Woman?* confronts her poststructural heritage from *Sexual/Textual Politics* (1985) by turning to Simone de Beauvoir, Stanley Cavell, Pierre Bourdieu, and Ludwig Wittgenstein in order to recover the subject of praxis, the situated subject who acts, some third space between the full, liberal human subject and the radically antiessentialist, decentered subject of poststructuralism.

11. But one example would be the ghost of Marx: "It is clear, even if one admits that Marx will disappear for now, that he will reappear one day" (Foucault, in Kritzman, 1988, p. 45).

12. Scientism will be dealt with more extensively in Chapter 3. For purposes of introduction, scientism is the doctrine that science can answer the questions of

morals and meanings originally posed by religion. It draws cultural or philosophical or political conclusions from developments in, particularly, physics and mathematics. As Fuller notes (2001), such a doctrine that science can justify value commitments blurs "the boundaries between 'is' and 'ought,' 'fact' and value,' 'natural' and 'rational,' " and is generally in current disrepute. It is, however, ironically, undergoing a revival as part of the "reenchantment" of science that typifies the more mystical ends of postmodernism "with a fascination with quanta, relativity, and chaos" (p. 187).

13. I take this from Marian Hobson's 1998 book on Derrida where she speaks of "the new new." In addition to academic work, I've seen the phrase used in cultural commentary, for example "The new new thing for 2004" regarding Jaga Jazzist, a Norwegian band that played at the Wexner Center in Columbus, Ohio. Here the "new new" seems to have something to do with hybridities and cultural flows and networks.

14. From Resnov, 1992, title.

15. One example of the continued untroubled currency of this 1986 essay is its reprinting in *Cultural Studies and Education*, 2004, by Gaztambide-Fernandez et al. For a Foucauldian argument about the dangers of academic salvation work, see Popkewitz, 1998.

16. "Mourning Marxism? Philosophical Explorations in Feminism, Poststructuralism and Education," Mary Leach, Patti Lather, Kate McCoy and Wanda Pillow, American Educational Research Association (AERA) annual conference, San Diego, April, 1998.

17. A precedent for such practice is Judith Butler's thanking Donna Haraway for response to an earlier draft of Butler's paper "in a hot tub in Santa Cruz" (1994, p. 173).

18. Excerpts from the taping of this session are in the Chapter 2 Interlude.

19. In an earlier publication, I recast the familiar metaphor so that the "rock" was the need for trustworthiness in data generated by alternative paradigms and the "soft place" was the positivist claim to neutrality and objectivity (Lather, 1986b).

20. These passages are grafted from the work of John Struik on heteronormativity as a ruin (1993a,b).

Chapter One Interlude

1. In a later paper, "White Woman Goes to Africa and Loses Her Voice" (2004d), I wrote of this (mis)identification:

Were such issues not, exactly, mine as a white woman well schooled in US anti-racist politics? Was I performing myself out of "the assumed and unremarked whiteness of feminism" that Handel Wright (2002, p. 3) noted in my work on critical pedagogy? Why did Wright read my work as "perfunctory, indirect, several times removed" (p. 22) in dealing with race while I was read in a South African context as Black? "What's going on here," to echo Patricia Hill-Collins (2000) echoing Marvin Gaye in her writing on Black feminist thought and the politics of postmodernism?

Chapter Two

1. See Foucault, 1984, p. 339.

2. The term "human sciences" comes from Dilthey who differentiated between the human (reflexive, hermeneutic) and natural sciences (Rajan, 2002, p. 111). The term was widely used in France in the 1960s to signal the displacement of philosophy by the theoretical renewal of the social sciences via structuralism. See Dosse, 1999.

3. By quasi-enthnographic, I mean qualitative research that combines sociological fieldwork with aspects of anthropological ethnographic practices.

4. Mascia-Lees, Sharpe and Cohen, 1989; Kondo, 1990; Behar, 1993, 1996; Visweswaran, 1994; Gordon, 1995; Stewart, 1996.

5. Other critiques of the conventions of ethnographic writing birthed by the new ethnography, with its interest in voice, discontinuity, and situatedness, include Kirsch, 1997; Britzman, 1998; and Lather, 2000c.

6. Derridean "play" is like the play in a machine, to move within limits that are both cause and effect. Set against the "work of the negative" of Hegelian thought, it posits the infinite substitution of signifiers, given the demise of a transcendental signified and the absence of absolute determinism. The place of " 'free-play' . . . means that the structure of the machine or the springs, are not so tight, so that you can just try to dislocate: that's what I meant by play" (Derrida, quoted in McGowan, 1991, pp. 104–105). Derridean play unsettles the dominant through pointing to suppressed possibilities in order to supplement or exceed the determinations that order has tried to make stable and permanent. For a textual enactment, see Richardson, 1997.

7. The tensions in feminist methodology around issues of identity, agency, and voice are captured in the contrasting titles of Denise Riley (1988), "*Am I That Name?" Feminism and the Category of "Women" in History* on the problems of "women" as a universalizing category and Laura Lee Downs (1993), "If 'Woman' is Just an Empty Category, Then Why am I Afraid to Walk Alone at Night? Identity Politics Meets the Postmodern Subject."

8. *In Politics of Friendship*, Derrida (1997) writes of the necessity of "the deliberate perversion of the heritage" so that "opposites slide into each other" (pp. 61, 64, 80).

9. The one exception to this was my statement that most of the women did not want to spend their energy being angry at their infectors. Both of the new women took issue with this. A 40-something African-American woman said, "I would have killed him if he weren't already dead." The other, a 67 year old African-American woman diagnosed in 1984 but still quite healthy, talked of her great struggles to not be consumed with anger at her long dead husband for infecting her.

Chapter Two Interlude

1. Elizabeth Ellsworth, Janet Miller, Mimi Orner, Mary Leach, Margo Figgins, P. J. Ford Slack, and myself.

Chapter Three

1. The phrase, physics envy, was used in the *New York Review of Books* as credited to Freud (Flyvbjerg, 2001, pp. 26–27). It is, interestingly, used in the 2002 National Research Council report, *Scientific Research in Education*, without attribution (p. 13).

2. Foucauldian positivity refers to "the codes of language, perception, and practice" that arise for awhile and make possible a particular understanding of "the order of things" (1970, p. xxi). Positivities are some other to "the order of foundations" (p. 340) which has to do with successor regimes, ontologies of continuity, and permanent tables of stable differences. In contrast, the order of positivities is an "analytic of finitude" that historicizes discourse formations within "an ontology without metaphysics" (p. 340). For an elaboration, see Lather, 2004c.

3. For how this "gold standard" is being played out in educational research, see National Research Council report (2002).

4. Distinctions of "exact" and "inexact" science come from Husserl (1970), in reference to the rigor of philosophy given its "inexact" nature.

5. Thomas Sorell, whose 1991 book, *Scientism*, is a general reference, contends that scientism is a relatively new term of abuse laid on those who conceive of science narrowly and hold this narrow view as the one best way of knowing. F. A. Hayek, the economist who first brought the term into wide circulation, "borrows" it from 1936 French usage (1952, p. 207n7). Derrida and Roudinesco (2004) note that the term came into general use around 1911 "to explain and resolve all human phenomena" (p. 207n1). They quote from Lecourt's *Dictionary of the History of Philosophy*: "Scientism is thus a 'discourse on science that claims to abolish philosophy by using the discourse of science itself' " (ibid.).

6. The continued importance of this work is evident in *Philosophy and Methodology of the Social Sciences*, v. 2, edited by Mark Smith (2004). There is a veritable Hayek industry of late, given the implosion of the Keynesian model and a consequent push in economics for a less positivist framework. See, for example, Colonna, Hagemann, & Hamouda, 1991; Frowen, 1997; Fleetwood, 1995; Bouckaert and Godart-van der Kroon, 2000; and Kresge and Wenar, 1994. To track two conjoined postpositivist movements, the Perestroika Movement in political science against mathematization of the field and its progenitor, the postautistic economics movement, see: www.paecon.net.

7. Baez (2005) terms Hayek the " 'hero' of neo-liberals" and argues that the continued turn to Dewey's philosophy of education on the part of progressive educators marks their "fail[ure] to grasp what neo-liberal projects effect in social life" given the globalization of the market (p. 77). Dewey's "critical democracy" that undergirds leftist ideas of schooling seems "out of touch" in terms of the "redirection of conduct" necessary under conditions where life has been redefined in terms of the economic toward "autonomous," "flexible," and "entrepreneurial" (ibid.). Baez's concern is that "progressives have not been inventive enough" (ibid.), to the point of recycling ideas of freedom, democracy, and the public good that have long been appropriated by the neoliberals and their rational choice and human-capital theories. What Baez suggests but does not develop is that Hayek's ideas might fruitfully be more broadly understood as

a Foucauldian "technology of the self" in efforts toward undoing present neoliberal forms of governmentality.

Governmentality is a Foucauldian concept regarding the rationalities of producing social subjects and social order. Sometimes equated with "bio-power," it theorizes how subjects are constituted in relations of power so that they survey themselves into being compliant subjects of modernization. See Clayton, 2000.

8. Stenmark (2001), in his book on scientism, lists several forms, some of which include the "methodological scientism" of the repeatable, observable, and measurable, the "epistemic scientism" where a narrow idea of method is the only road to reliable knowledge, a "rationalistic scientism" where only scientific knowledge is rational knowledge, an "ontological scientism" where everything outside of science is a secondary kind of reality, and, of particular interest, the holding up of science as our best hope for conclusions about sociopolitical values and beliefs. This is a kind of "existential or redemptive scientism" where salvation occurs through science and science alone.

9. See, for example, Alcoff (2000), who resists the "dispersion of philosophical inquiry" into "feminist theory" as opposed to "feminist philosophy" (p. 841).

10. See *The Archeology of Knowledge* (1972, pp. 182–87) for the "thresholds of discursive formations."

11. See Fuller and Collier, 2003, for an explicitly sophistic and dialectical approach to rhetoric in the social studies of science. See, also, Fuller, 1997.

12. In the "science wars," Lacan's mathemes are often held up as a prime example of the "misuse of mathematics" by the human sciences. For the "aggravation" caused to Sokal et al. see Plotnitsky, 2000. But see, Marini, 1992, for an unpacking of mathemes as "a logic that is not a logic" (p. 68) in attempting a theoretical language "that recognizes its uncertainties and contradictions" (p. 69). Mathemes might be looked at as the formalized transmission of not understanding, the formalizing structure of the relationship between terms in order to communicate in shorthand or metaphor the necessary lack of language. Thanks to conversation with Ian Parker and Eric Burman for this "truth of mathemes."

13. McArdle and McWilliam (2005) articulate "ironic research" that has as its goal defamiliarizing terms that are "often presumed to go without saying as real, identifiable conditions of practice" (p. 325). Steven Ward's (1996) genealogy of "self-esteem," for example, is tracked across postwar psychotherapy and experimental psychology to its becoming part of the daily world of educators.

14. The humanities are also seeing a "return of things." See special issue of *Critical Inquiry* (Brown, 2001), which traces ideas back to Heidegger's essay on "The Thing" through recent articulations of "material culture studies." See, also, Daston (2004) for a look at "object studies" that combines physicality and significance across both the sciences and the arts and humanities and Grosz (2001) for a particularly philosophical look at architecture as material culture. Chapter 10 is entitled "The Thing" as she traces "the great thinkers of the thing" from Newton, Descartes, and Kant to Darwin, Nietzsche, Peirce, James, Bergson, Rorty, and Deleuze.

15. In using feminism in the singular, I follow Sara Ahmed et al., the editors of *Transformations: Thinking Through Feminism* (2000) who write:

We are . . . resistant to the assumption that to add an *s* to a term . . . is necessarily to make a substantive commitment to analyze differences. Adding the *s* . . . can easily become a rather tired and liberal gesture, which declares plurality at the level of naming, but which does not then argue the case for differences that cannot be reconciled into this pluralism (p. 20n1).

16. Biddy Martin (2001) uses the Deleuzean "fold" to suggest a way to think where we don't cast out but rather enfold older ideas within newer ones in feminist theory so as to break the relentless "new new" that often typifies academic thought and practice. As she points out, succession need not be conflated with progress and generational antagonism (p. 339).

17. McCall (2005), in her call for a recognition of "the capacity of different methodologies to handle complexity" (p. 1772), turns the table on qualitative (and, more problematically, deconstructive) hegemony in what she terms "research practice in women's studies" (p. 1791) by advocating for the strategic use of advanced quantitative techniques and large data sets as more adequate in dealing with the empirical intersectionality that characterizes the "new inequality" and the public policy arenas involved. This is a postpositivist reinscription that women's studies needs to embrace, McCall argues, more or less successfully to my deconstructive ears. While there is much to be admired in McCall's discussion of intersectionality, she gets in trouble on several fronts: her claim that deconstruction rejects categories, her argument for critical realism against "postmodern relativism," and her proclamation that in postmodernism, ontology is dead, the structural collapsed into the discursive. These rather overrehearsed (mis)understandings of the post are addressed in chapter 5 of this book as well as in Wilson, 1998.

18. As an example of how such terms remain central but increasingly elaborated in terms of "attempt[s] to satisfy the demand for complexity," see Leslie McCall on intersectionality (2005, p. 1773). For reflexivity, see Wanda Pillow (2003).

19. See Spivak, 2002, for a discussion of her work in "the lowest-level rural schools in a mountain province in China" (p. 183) where she is involved in the education of teachers in order to learn to learn from below in a way that is "a re-territorializing of 'the white man's burden'" (p. 190).

Chapter Four

1. While Derrida insists that "deconstruction is not a method" (in Kearney, 1984, p. 124), it can be used to inform an-other logic of critical methodology. At the risk of "methodologizing" it, identifying and then reversing the binary oppositions that structure a text or an argument are the first two steps of deconstruction. The third step is to use the energy of the reversal to think oneself into some third space, some space of "both-and" and "neither-nor" that exceeds the opposing terms of the binary. Deconstruction, then, is an operation of, first, inversion, and then reinscription, a rewriting of the relation between the binary terms toward a more fluid conceptual organization of terms which interrupts a binary logic (Spivak, 1976). Such a

methodologizing approach is tempered by Derrida's famous proclamation that deconstruction is not "a technical operation used to dismantle systems," but something which happens, always already (McDonald, 1985, p. 85).

2. In a 1993 interview, Gayatri Spivak says, "My words are becoming simpler. They are becoming simpler because I can't do anything with the more complicated machinery. It's getting in the way, you know . . . when I'm pushed these days with the old criticism—'Oh! Spivak is too hard to understand!'—I laugh, and I say okay, I will give you, just for your sake, a monosyllabic sentence, and you'll see that you can't rest with it. My monosyllabic sentence is: *We know plain prose cheats*. [laughter] So then what do you do? Shut up? Don't you want to hear some more? And then it becomes much harder" (Danius and Jonsson, 1993, p. 33). Thanks to Bettie St. Pierre for bringing this interview to my attention.

Spivak's recent work tacks "very much from high theory to activist discourse" (Murray, 2003, p. 181) and back again. In this 2003 interview with Murray, she speaks of wearing "like a crown" criticism of "too difficult" writing that might some day come from those involved in her 13-year project to bring education to aboriginal girls "in a corner in rural India" (p. 185). For those from more privileged backgrounds, she assumes a reader willing to work at reading.

3. At a 1994 session of the annual conference of the American Educational Research Assocation on "But Is It Research," organized by Robert Donmoyer, Deborah Britzman concluded her comments with the hope that educational research would become unintelligible to itself. This phrase has "worked like a virus," to quote Kate McCoy quoting performance artist Lauri Anderson. Britzman's statement situates unintelligiblity as an ethical imperative and a political intervention in terms of disrupting the ways we make sense.

4. Arguments regarding the material effects of language are rooted in Althusser's 1971 essay "Ideology and Ideological State Apparatuses." Althusser writes, "An ideology always exists in an apparatus, and its practice or practices. This existence is material" (p. 166). Demonstrating the material existence of ideological beliefs was Althusser's move against the idealism of Hegelian Marxism with its focus on consciousness. His move was, rather, toward the immanence of ideas in the irreducible materiality of discourses, actions, and practices. Hence, the materiality of ideology "interpellates" or "hails" historical subjects so that consciousness becomes an effect rather than cause. This thesis of the materiality of language is key in poststructuralism; see, for example, Montag, 1995.

5. "High theory" refers to the male pantheon of philosophical writing of those such as Kant and Hegel, their critics Nietzsche and Heidegger, and the Marxist variant kept alive in the Frankfurt School, a tradition today carried on by Habermas. In France, the names include Lacan, Althusser, Foucault, Derrida, and Deleuze. Samuel Delany (1994) talks of the "difficult discourse [that] stems historically from the German academic tradition . . . As that tradition moved to France and, finally, produced structuralism and poststructuralism [it] picked up a particularly French accent" (p. 241). Delany goes on about the pleasures of such texts, for example, Derrida: "The reason it's complex is because it's not so much an idea as it is a repeated demonstration of a process, in situation after situation, where meanings that at first glance seem clear, total, and masterable are shown to be undecidable, incomplete, and full of slippage and play" (p. 243).

6. Usher and Edwards (1994) write of correspondence theories as "the powerful modernist position that truth is a matter of 'correspondence' with an outside 'reality' . . . Poststructuralist texts contain within themselves running commentary on and critique of . . . the possibility of knowing the world in a direct and unmediated way—'as it really is' " (pp. 18–19).

7. Albert Oehlen and Christopher Williams, joint presentation, Oehlen Williams 95, Wexner Center for the Arts, Ohio State University, January 26–April 9, 1995.

8. Models I drew from include Bennington and Derrida (1993) and two books by Canadian journalist Brian Fawcett (1989, 1994). Another influence was Joseph McElroy's novel, *Women and Men* (1987), where angel intertexts function as "breathers" and eventually expand in length to take over the text. I was also instructed by the contrasting analyses of the return of angels in postmodernism of McHale (1990) and Bloom (1996).

9. Bettie St. Pierre, e-mail correspondence, July 5, 1995, in response to a presentation of her dissertation research, Ohio State University, 1995. See, also, St. Pierre, 1996.

10. Writing for University of British Columbia course, Analyzing Qualitative Data in the Crisis of Representation, Summer, 1994. This and subsequent student work is quoted with permission.

11. Constructing AIDS: The Epidemic's Second Decade, a course taught by Dr. Ruth Linden, Stanford University, Anthropology Department, Winter, 1996.

12. Behar (1995b) writes of the scene leading up to Esperanza's refusal of the book: her greater enthusiasm for the television that Behar had brought her; tensions around a money order Behar had sent at the family's request; Esperanza's interest in a possible Spanish version of the book. Perhaps most importantly, "I understand that not accepting the book is my *comadre's* way of refusing to be the translated woman" (p. 77).

Chapter Five

1. "Mourning Marxism? Philosophical Explorations in Feminism, Poststructuralism and Education," Mary Leach, Patti Lather, Kate McCoy, Wanda Pillow, and Deborah Britzman, American Educational Research Association (AERA), San Diego, April 1998. The question mark is an homage to a 1972 symposium, Nietzsche Today? where Derrida presented an early version of his *Spurs* (1979) on questions of Nietzsche and the "truth" of woman. For an update, see Gallop, 1997, where she asks "Derrida Today?"

2. "(Mis)Reading Postmodernism: Implications for Educational Research," Elizabeth St. Pierre, Bernadette Baker, Wanda Pillow, Patti Lather, and Kate McCoy, AERA, Seattle, April 2001.

3. Foucault writes: "Maybe the problem of the self is not to discover what it is in its positivity; maybe the problem is not to discover a positive self or the positive foundation for the self. Maybe our problem now is to discover that the self is nothing else than the historical correlation of the technology built in our history. Maybe the problem is to change those technologies . . . to get rid of those technologies, and then, to get rid of the sacrifice which is linked to those technologies. In this case, one of the main political problems nowadays would be, in a strict sense of the word, the politics of ourselves" (1997b, p. 231).

4. In terms of the "return to Marxism" on the part of (some) critical theorists who flirted with the "post" (often under the sign of "critical postmodernism") but who now see it as an accommodation/complicity with dominant powers, see Hill, McLaren, Cole, and Rikowski, 2002. For a history of post-Marxism, see Sim, 2000. For an argument that this (re)articulation of Marxism as animated by a critique of poststructuralism creates yet another layer of gendered trackings in the continued articulation of the intersections/tensions of critical pedagogy and feminist thought and practice, see Lather, 1998. Whether such internecine battles regarding critical pedagogy as a largely masculinized space remain interesting to the parties involved and, far more importantly, to the field itself, the future pluperfect of deconstruction's "what will have been said" temporality suggests that such debates might be fruitfully viewed as a generational footnote.

5. Some examples of "applied Derrida" in educational research include program evaluation (Stronach and MacLure, 1997), philosophy of education (Garrison and Leach, 2001), various feminist poststructural interventions (St. Pierre and Pillow, 2000; special issue of *Qualitative Studies in Education* on "Poststructuralist Lines of Flight in Australia," guest edited by Bronwyn Davies, 17(1), 2004); pedagogy (Trifonas, 2000); and practitioner-oriented research in nursery teaching and math education (Brown and Jones, 2001). A particularly rich collection is Biesta and Egea-Kuehne, 2001, *Derrida & Education*.

6. For a historical survey of the weight of the natural science model on educational research, particularly via a narrowed psychology, see Lagemann, 2000.

7. Rooney (1995) writes about Althusser's reading of Marx as marked by discrepancies, repetitions, hesitations, and uncertainties, always beginning again, a doubling between historical situatedness and political interestedness, in short, reading as a necessarily guilty rather than innocent practice.

Chapter Six

1. At the Twenty-Fifth Nobel Conference at Gustavus Adolphous College in St. Peter, Minnesota, in 1989 on The End of Science, feminist philosopher, Sandra Harding, put it this way:

> As we study our world today, there is an uneasy feeling that we have come to the end of science, that science, as a unified, objective endeavor is over . . . This leads to grave epistemological concerns. If science does not speak about extrahistorical, universal laws, but is instead social, temporal and local, then there is no way of speaking of something real beyond science that science merely reflects (quoted in Kiziltan, Bain, and Canizares, 1990, p. 354).

2. I use the term exemplar not as a cookbook or "the best of," but as concrete illustrations of a number of abstract qualities. They are not used in the Kuhnian sense of paradigmatic cases that dominate a research community's sense of both normal and revolutionary science. To the contrary, my exemplars are, except for Agee and Evans, a quite idiosyncratic selection from the work of friends and dissertation students with

which I happen to be familiar. Like Mishler (1990), I offer them as resources, "spring-boards" (p. 422).

3. Welchman (1989), writing of dadaism and surrealism in art, says of the diagram: "The diagram is, therefore, always useful and yet equally futile; it can only come into being as the will-to-use, but it only exists to be modified, to be altered, or enacted, or scratched (broken up)" (p. 92).

Chapter Seven

1. This chapter has benefited from the intersections of my work with that of my Ohio State University colleagues Thomas Piontek and Nancy Johnson. For critiques of Western feminist ethnography, see Behar, 1993, 1996; Visweswaran, 1994; Behar and Gordon, 1995; Stewart, 1996.

2. Van Maanen, 1988, 1995; Behar, 1993, 1996; Richardson, 1994, 1997; Behar and Gordon, 1995.

3. Restoration Hardware, an upscale tool-and-home-furnishing chain is about the store-as-autobiography in its folksy pitch for such items as "deeply personal" sandwich spreaders (*Columbus Dispatch*, Feb. 23, 1997). For a critique of empathy, see Caruth and Keenan 1995. Empathy is about sameness: "[e]mpathy is what the public is supposed to learn to feel, but it solidifies the structure of discrimination. . . . Its structure is something that somehow elides thinking about death. Something is not confronted there, when you think you're understanding or empathizing in a certain way" (pp. 264, 269).

4. Behar, 1996, approaches these issues.

5. Deleuze and Felix Guattari and their theories of becoming and topology/cartography are interruptive of the more typical ontologically-driven Western theories of being and typology (Deleuze and Guattari, 1987). As theorists of knowledge, power, and desire, they shift philosophy in ways that use Nietzsche and Baruch Spinoza toward a nonsystematic system of concepts, a sort of "geophilosophy" that provides tools for thinking differently within and against dominant discourses.

6. An advance flier for the book delineates the very diffuse sense of multiple audience to which the book is addressed: "**Troubling the Angels** invites multiple ways of reading and grappling with the HIV virus, for personal and professional caregivers, families and friends, students of health, disease, and methodologies, and those living with HIV/AIDS."

7. My thinking in this section is inspired by Malini Johar Schueller's (1992) critique of James Agee's *Let Us Now Praise Famous Men*, where she situates Agee as paternalistic and liberal in his idealization of those whose stories he tells but, nevertheless, as opening up of a space for subverting narrow and consensual definitions of the tenant farmers who people his book.

8. As noted by an anonymous reviewer of an earlier version of this chapter.

9. My thinking here is inspired by a review of the art of David Reeb, whose work addresses historical painting and the problem of testimony, particularly around the Intifada (See Itamar Levy, "Eye-Witness" [Review of David Reeb: Paintings 1982–1994], Tel Aviv Museum of Art, catalogue 7/94). Thanks to Nurit Coehn-Evron.

10. Women and AIDS Second Regional Conference, June 14, 1999, Tulsa. Representatives from nine states attended; 59 sponsors and supporters were listed in

the conference program; 50 scholarships were given out to maximize attendance by
HIV+ women.

11. One example would be *Breaking the Walls of Silence* (ACE Program
Members, 1998), which grew out of an HIV/AIDS peer-counseling program at the
maximum security women's prison at Bedford Hills, New York. Eight years in the
making and another three years to press, the book combines the Freirian emphasis on
empowerment and the knowledge-sharing of its "behind-the-scenes" editor, Kathy
Boudin, a former member of the Weather Underground, with personal testimony from
women in prison and curriculum guidelines for nine education and counseling work-
shops. For a review, see Kaplan, 1999. Another example would be *A Positive Life:
Portraits of Women Living with HIV/AIDS* (1997), a book of photographs and interviews by Mary Berridge and River Huston, which Piontek (2000) contrasts with the
narrative strategies of *Troubling the Angels.*

Chapter Seven Interlude

1. From report on 14th International Human Science Research Conference,
Midrand, South Africa, August 21–25, 1995, written by Ingunn Hagen, Dan Yngve
Jacobsen, and Birthe Loa Knizek. Another example is Gary Hill, "Remarks on Color,"
1994, where he made a movie of his young daughter reading excerpts from Ludwig
Wittgenstein's book of the same name regarding the inadequacies of language and
how we are always between understanding and not understanding where she read
angels instead of angles. Tate Modern, July, 2006.

Afterwords

1. My thinking about archives comes from O'Driscoll, 2002, particularly his
reading of Derrida's *Archive Fever*, 1996b.

2. This subtitle is from Adair, 1992.

3. Subtitle is adapted from Weems and Lather, 2000.

4. "Negative theology" is defined by Caputo (1997c) as a "learned unknowing" (p. 55), as he goes on at some length to distinguish Derrida's work as this but
also more and other. In *Of Spirit* (1989), Derrida delineates a Heideggerian
postspirituality as two moves. The first move is against the traditional concept of
"spirit," where it is resituated as not about interiority but about being in the world. The
second move is a return, in a deconstructed sense, to where the ghost or other of what
it was is doubled, not in opposition but in "something beyond itself" (p. 24). This is
a sort of "fall" into question marks (p. 28) that brings history and materiality to bear
on the question of "spirit."

5. National Research Council report, 2002, p. 25. Bettie St. Pierre has had
t-shirts made up that say "Xtreme postmodernist," including page number of NRC report.

6. In terms of the limits of such charts: "[S]uch a structuralist diagram ignores
the volatility—and indeed excessiveness—of the figures, which in practice exclude
any heuristic containment, and contaminate or combine with rather than exclude one
another. Indeed . . . [such diagrams] often draw on more than one figure of thought,
using them to complicate and supplement one another, or discovering that one figure
generates or is already inhabited by another" (Rajan and O'Driscoll, 2002, p. 4).

Bibliography

Abma, Tineke A. 2002. "Emerging Narrative Forms of Knowledge Representation in the Health Sciences: Two Texts in a Postmodern Context." *Qualitative Health Research* 12(1): 5–27.

ACE Program Members. 1998. *Breaking the Walls of Silence: AIDS and Women in a New York State Maximum-Security Prison.* Woodstock, N.Y.: Overlook.

Adair, Gilbert. 1992. *The Postmodernist Always Rings Twice: Reflections on Culture in the 90's.* London: Fourth Estate.

Agee, James, and Walker Evans. 1988. *Let Us Now Praise Famous Men.* Boston: Houghton Mifflin.

Ahmed, Sara, Jane Kilby, Celia Lury, Maureen McNeil, and Beverley Skeggs, eds. 2000. *Transformations: Thinking through Feminism.* London: Routledge.

Albanese, Denise. 1996. *New Science, New World.* Durham, N.C.: Duke University Press.

Alcoff, Linda. 1989. "Justifying Feminist Social Science." In *Feminism and Science*, edited by Nancy Tuana, pp. 85–103. Bloomington: Indiana University Press.

———. 2000. "Review Essay: Philosophy Matters: A Review of Recent Work in Feminist Philosophy." *Signs* 25(3): 841–82.

Allison, David B., ed. 1985. *The New Nietzsche.* Cambridge, Mass.: MIT Press.

———. 2001. *Reading the New Nietzsche.* Lanham, Md.: Roman and Littlefield.

Althusser, Louis. 1971. *Lenin and Philosophy and Other Essays.* Translated by B. Brewster. New York: Monthly Review Press.

Altieri, Charles. 1990. "The Powers and Limits of Oppositional Postmodernism." *American Literary History* 2: 443–81.

Angus, Ian, and Lenore Langsdorf, eds. 1993. *The Critical Turn: Rhetoric and Philosophy in Postmodern Discourse.* Carbondale: Southern Illinois University Press.

Antonio, Robert. 2000. "After Postmodernism: Reactionary Tribalism." *American Journal of Sociology* 9: 154–63.

Apple, Michael. 2001. *Educating the 'Right' Way: Markets, Standards, God, and Inequality.* New York: Routledge.

Aronowitz, Stanley. 1995. "Bringing Science and Scientificity Down to Earth." *Cultural Studies Times* 1(3): 12, 14.

Ashmore, Keith M., and Philip S. Baringer, eds. 2001. *After the Science Wars*. London: Routledge.

Babich, Babette. 1994. *Nietzsche's Philosophy of Science: Reflecting Science on the Ground of Art and Life*. Albany: State University of New York Press.

Bachelard, Gaston. 1949. *Le Rationalisme Applied*. Paris: University Presses of France.

Backstrand, Karin. 2003. Civic Science for Sustainability: Reframing the Role of Experts, Policy-Makers and Citizens in Environmental Governance. *Global Environmental Politics* 3(4): 24–41.

Baez, Benjamin. 2005. "Schools and the Public Good: Privatization, Democracy, Freedom, and 'Government.'" *Journal of Curriculum Theorizing* 21(2): 63–82.

Baker, Peter. 1995. *Deconstruction and the Ethical Turn*. Gainesville: University Press of Florida.

Bal, Mieke. 2001. "Enfolding Feminism." In *Feminist Consequences: Theory for the New Century*, edited by Elisabeth Bronfen and Misha Kavka, pp. 321–52. New York: Columbia University Press.

Balibar, Etienne. 1995. *The Philosophy of Marx*. London: Verso.

Bataille, Georges. 1988/1954. *Inner Experience*. Albany: State University of New York Press.

Baudrillard, Jean. 1987. *Forget Foucault*. New York: Semiotext(e).

———. 1983. The Precession of Simulacra. In *Simulations*. Translated by Paul Foss, Paul Patton, and Philip Beitchman, pp. 1–79. New York: Semiotext(e).

Beck, Ulrich. 1992/1986. *Risk Society: Towards a New Modernity*. Translated by Mark Ritter. London: Sage.

Behar, Ruth. 1993. *Translated Woman: Crossing the Border with Esperanza's Story*. Boston: Beacon.

———. 1995a. "Introduction: Out of Exile." In *Women Writing Culture*, edited by R. Behar and D. Gordon, pp. 1–32. Berkeley and Los Angeles: University of California Press.

———. 1995b. "Writing in My Father's Name: A Diary of Translated Woman's First Year." In *Women Writing Culture*, edited by R. Behar and D. Gordon, pp. 65–84. Berkeley and Los Angeles: University of California Press.

———. 1996. *The Vulnerable Observer: Anthropology that Breaks Your Heart*. Boston: Beacon.

Behar, Ruth, and Deborah Gordon, eds. 1995. *Women Writing Culture*. Berkeley and Los Angeles: University of California Press.

Belenky, Mary Field, Blythe McVicker Clinchy, Nancy Rule Goldberger, and Jill Mattuck Tarule. 1986. *Women's Ways of Knowing: The Development of Self, Voice, and Mind*. New York: Basic Books.

Benjamin, Walter. 1968/1940. "Theses on the Philosophy of History." In *Illuminations*, edited by H. Arendt, pp. 253–64. New York: Schocken Books.

———. 1977. *The Origin of German Tragic Drama*. Translated by John Osborne. London: Verso.

———. 1989. "N [Re the Theory of Knowledge, Theory of Progress]. In *Benjamin: Philosophy, History, Aesthetics*, edited by Gary Smith, pp. 43–83. Chicago: University of Chicago Press.

Bennett, Tony. 1990. *Outside Literature*. London: Routledge.

———. 1992. "Putting Policy into Cultural Studies." In *Cultural Studies*, edited by Larry Grossberg, Cary Nelson, and Paula Treichler, pp. 23–37. London: Routledge.

Bennington, Geoffrey. 2000. *Interrupting Derrida*. London: Routledge.

Bennington, Geoffrey, and Jacques Derrida. 1993. *Jacques Derrida*. Chicago: University of Chicago Press.

Berger, Peter, and Thomas Luckmann. 1966. *The Social Construction of Reality: A Treatise in the Sociology of Knowledge*. Garden City, Neb.: Doubleday.

Berridge, Mary, and River Huston. 1997. *A Positive Life: Portraits of Women Living with HIV*. Philadelphia: Running Press.

Berry, Philippa. 2004. "Postmodernism and Post-Religion." In *The Cambridge Companion to Postmodernism*, edited by Steven Connor, pp. 168–81. Cambridge: Cambridge University Press.

Best, Steven, and Douglas Kellner. 1997. *The Postmodern Turn*. New York: Guilford Press.

Beyer, Lanny, and Daniel Liston. 1992. "Discourse or Moral Action: A Critique of Postmodernism." *Educational Theory* 42(4): 371–93.

Biesta, Gert, and Denise Egea-Kuehne, eds. 2001. *Derrida & Education*. London: Routledge.

Blanchot, Maurice. 1982. *The Space of Literature*. Translated by Ann Smock. Lincoln: University of Nebraska Press.

———. 1986. *The Writing of the Disaster*. Translated by Ann Smock. Lincoln: University of Nebraska Press.

Bloom, Harold. 1975. *A Map of Misreading*. New York: Oxford University Press.

———. 1996. *Omens of Millennium: The Gnosis of Angels, Dreams and Resurrection*. New York: Riverhead Books.

Borgmann, Albert. 1992. *Crossing the Postmodern Divide*. Chicago: University of Chicago Press.

Bottomore, Tom. 1983. *A Dictionary of Marxist Thought*. Oxford: Blackwell Reference.

Bouckaert, Boudewijn, and Annette Godart-van der Kroon, eds. 2000. *Hayek Revisited*. Cheltenham, U.K.: Edward Elgar.

Bourdieu, Pierre. 1990. *In Other Words: Essays Toward a Reflexive Sociology*. New York: Polity Press.

Braidotti, Rosi. 2005. "A Critical Cartography of Feminist Post-Postmodernism." *Australian Feminist Studies* 20(47): 169–80.

Brantlinger, Patrick, and D. Ulin. 1993. "Policing Nomads: Discourse and Social Control in Early Victorian England." *Cultural Critique* 25: 33–64.

Britzman, Deborah. 1991. *Practice Makes Practice: A Critical Study of Learning to Teach*. Albany: State University of New York Press.

———. 1995. "The Question of Belief: Writing Poststructural Ethnography." *Qualitative Studies in Education* 8(3): 233–42.

———. 1997. "The Tangles of Implication." *Qualitative Studies in Education* 10(1): 31–37.

———. 1998. *Lost Subjects, Contested Objects: Towards a Psychoanalytic Inquiry of Learning*. Albany: State University of New York Press.

———. 2000. "If the Story Cannot End: Deferred Action, Ambivalence, and Difficult Knowledge." In *Between Hope and Despair: Pedagogy and the Remembrance of Historical Trauma*, edited by Roger Simon, Sharon Rosenberg, and Claudia Eppert, pp. 27–57. Lanham, Md.: Rowman and Littlefield.

———. 2003. *After-Education: Anna Freud, Melanie Klein, and Psychoanalytic Histories of Learning*. Albany: State University of New York Press.

Brown, Bill. 2001. "Thing Theory." *Critical Inquiry*, special issue on Things, 28(1): 1–22.

Brown, Tony, and Liz Jones. 2001. *Action Research and Postmodernism: Congruence and Critique*. Buckingham: Open University Press.

Brown, Wendy. 1995. "Wounded Attachments: Late Modern Oppositional Political Formations." In *The Identity in Question*, edited by John Rajchman, pp. 199–228. New York: Routledge.

Brunette, Peter, and David Wills. 1994. *Deconstruction and the Visual Arts: Art, Media, Architecture*. Cambridge: Cambridge University Press.

Bryant, Miles. 2004. "Forcing Change in Educational Research." TEA/SIG, Division A, AERA, Fall, 11(2): 5.

Burczack, Ted. 1994. "The Postmodern Moments of F. A. Hayek's Economics." *Economics and Philosophy* 10: 31–58.

Butler, Judith. 1993a. "Poststructuralism and Postmarxism." *diacritics* 23(4): 3–11.

———. 1993b. *Bodies That Matter: On the Discursive Limits of "Sex."* New York: Routledge.

———. 1994. "Bodies That Matter." In *Engaging With Irigaray: Feminist Philosophy and Modern European Thought*, edited by C. Burke, N. Schor, and M. Whitford, pp. 141–74. New York: Columbia University Press.

———. 1995. "For a Careful Reading." In *Feminist Contentions: A Philosophical Exchange*, edited by S. Benhabib, J. Butler, D. Cornell, and N. Fraser, pp. 124–44. New York: Routledge.

———. 2001. "The Question of Social Transformation." In *Women and Social Transformation*, edited by Elizabeth Beck-Gernsheim, Judith Butler, and Lidia Pulgvert, pp. 1–28. Translated by Jacqueline Vaida. New York: Peter Lang.

———. 2003. "Values of Difficulty." In *Just Being Difficult? Academic Writing in the Public Arena*, edited by Jonathan Culler and Kevin Lamb, pp. 199–215. Stanford, Calif.: Stanford University Press.

———. 2004. *Undoing Gender*. New York: Routledge.

Caputo, John. 1993. "On Not Circumventing the Quasi-Transcendental: The Case of Rorty and Derrida." In *Working Through Derrida*, edited by Gary Madison, pp. 147–69. Evanston, Ill.: Northwestern University Press.

———, ed. 1997a. *Deconstruction in a Nutshell: A Conversation with Jacques Derrida*. New York: Fordham University Press.

———. 1997b. *The Prayers and Tears of Jacques Derrida: Religion without Religion*. Bloomington: Indiana University Press.

———. 1997c. "Dreaming of the Innumerable: Derrida, Drucilla Cornell, and the Dance of Gender." In *Derrida and Feminism: Recasting the Question of Woman*, edited by Ellen Feder, Mary Rawlinson, and Emily Zakin, pp. 141–60. New York: Routledge.

Carby, Hazel. 1982. "White Women Listen! Black Feminism and the Boundaries of Sisterhood." In *The Empire Strikes Back: Race and Racism in 70's Britain*, edited by Centre for Contemporary Culture Studies, University of Birmingham, pp. 183–211. London: Hutchinson.

Caruth, Cathy, and Thomas Keenan. 1995. "The AIDS Crisis Is Not Over: A Conversation with Gregg Bordowitz, Douglas Crimp, and Laura Pinsky." In *Trauma: Explorations in Memory*, edited by Cathy Caruth, pp. 256–72. Baltimore: Johns Hopkins University Press.

Cartwright, Nancy. 1999. *The Dappled World: A Study of the Boundaries of Science.* Cambridge: Cambridge University Press.

Casey, Kathleen. 1995. "The New Narrative Research in Education." In *Review of Research in Education, 1995–96,* v. 21, edited by Michael Apple, pp. 211–53. Washington, D.C.: AERA.

Cavell, Stanley. 1976. *Must We Mean What We Say?* Cambridge, England: Cambridge University Press.

Chow, Rey. 1991. "Postmodern Automatons." In *Feminists Theorize the Political,* edited by Judith Butler and Joan Scott, pp. 101–20. New York: Routledge.

Cixous, Helene. 1993. *Three Steps on the Ladder of Writing.* New York: Columbia University Press.

Clarke, Adele. 2005. *Situational Analysis: Grounded Theory After the Postmodern Turn.* Thousand Oaks, Calif.: Sage.

Clayton, Daniel. 2000. "Governmentality." In *The Dictionary of Human Geography,* edited by Ron Johnston, Derek Gregory, Geraldine Pratt, and Michael Watts, pp. 318–19. Oxford: Blackwell.

Clifford, James. 1983. "On Ethnographic Authority." *Representations* 1(2): 118–46.

———. 1997. *Routes: Travel and Translation in the Late Twentieth Century.* Cambridge, Mass.: Harvard University Press.

Clifford, James, and George Marcus, eds. 1986. *Writing Culture: The Poetics and Politics of Ethnography.* Berkeley and Los Angeles: University of California Press.

Clough, Patricia. 1992. *The Ends of Ethnography.* Thousand Oaks, Calif.: Sage.

Cohen, Tom. 1996. "The Ideology of Dialogue: The Bakhtin/De Man (Dis)Connection." *Cultural Critique* 33(Spring): 41–86.

Colonna, Marina, Harald Hagemann, and Omar Hamouda, eds. 1994. *Capitalism, Socialism and Knowledge: The Economics of F. A. Hayek.* Volume II. Brodfield, Vt.: Edward Elgar.

Con Davis, Robert. 1990. "Woman as Oppositional Reader: Cixous on Discourse." In *Gender in the Classroom: Power and Pedagogy,* edited by Susan Gabriel and I. Smithson, pp. 96–111. Urbana: University of Illinois Press.

Connor, Steven. 2004. "Postmodernism and Literature." In *The Cambridge Companion to Postmodernism,* edited by Steven Connor, pp. 62–81. Cambridge: Cambridge University Press.

Constas, Mark. 1998. "Deciphering Postmodern Educational Research." *Educational Researcher* 27(9): 37–42.

Critchley, Simon. 1992. *The Ethics of Deconstruction.* Oxford: Blackwell.

———. 2001. *Continental Philosophy: A Very Short Introduction.* Oxford: Oxford University Press.

Cronbach, Lee, and Paul Meehl. 1955. "Construct Validity in Psychological Tests." *Psychological Bulletin* 52: 281–302.

Croce, Arlene. 1994. "Discussing the Undiscussable." *The New Yorker*, December 26, 54–60. Reprinted in *The Crisis of Criticism*, edited by Maurice Berger, pp. 15–29. New York: New Press. 1998.

Cudd, Ann E. 2001. "Objectivity and Ethno-Feminist Critiques of Science." In *After the Science Wars*, edited by Keith M. Ashman and Philip S. Baringer, pp. 80–97. London: Routledge.

Cullenberg, Stephen, Jack Amariglio, and David F. Fuccio, eds. 2001. *Postmodernism, Economics and Knowledge*. London: Routledge.

Danius, Sara, and Stefan Jonsson. 1993. "An Interview with Gayatri Chakravorty Spivak." *boundary 2* 20(2): 24–50.

Daston, Lorraine, ed. 2004. *Things That Talk: Object Lessons from Art and Science*. Cambridge, Mass.: MIT Press.

Davidson, Arnold. 1997. "Structures and Strategies of Discourse: Remarks toward a History of Foucault's Philosophy of Language." In *Foucault and His Interlocutors*, edited by A. Davidson, pp. 1–17. Chicago: University of Chicago Press.

Davis, Dawn Rae. 2002. "(Love Is) the Ability of Not Knowing: Feminist Experience of the Impossible in Ethical Singularity." *Hypatia* 17(1): 145–61.

De Caro, Mario, and David Macarthur. 2004. *Naturalism in Question*. Cambridge, Mass.: Harvard University Press.

De Certeau, Michel. 1984. *The Practice of Everyday Life*. Berkeley and Los Angeles: University of California Press.

Delany, Samuel. 1994. *Silent Interviews: On Language, Race, Sex, Science Fiction and Some Comics*. Hanover, N.H.: Wesleyan University Press.

Deleuze, Giles. 1992. "What is a Dispositif?" In *Michel Foucault Philosopher*, pp. 159–68. Translated by Timothy Armstrong. New York: Routledge.

———. 1993. *The Fold: Leibniz and the Baroque*. Translated by T. Conley. Minneapolis: University of Minnesota Press.

Deleuze, Gilles, and Felix Guattari,. 1983. *On the Line*. Translated by J. Johnson. New York: Semiotexte.

———. 1987. *A Thousand Plateaus: Capitalism and Schizophrenia*. Translated by Brian Massumi. Minneapolis: University of Minnesota Press.

De Man, Paul. 1983. *The Blindness of Insight: Essays in the Rhetoric of Contemporary Criticism*. Minneapolis: University of Minnesota Press.

———. 1986. *The Resistance to Theory*. Minneapolis: University of Minnesota Press.

Denzin, Norm. 1989. *The Research Act*, 3rd ed. Englewood Cliffs, N.J.: Prentice-Hall.

Derrida, Jacques. 1976/1967. *Of Grammatology*. Translated by Gayatri Spivak. Baltimore, Md.: Johns Hopkins University Press.

———. 1978/1966. "Structure Sign and Play in the Discourse of the Human Sciences." In *Writing and Difference*, pp. 278–93. Translated by Alan Bass. Chicago: University of Chicago Press.

———. 1979a/1978. *Spurs: Nietzsche's Styles*. Translated by Barbara Harlow. Chicago: University of Chicago Press.

———. 1979b. "Living On." Translated by James Hulbert. In *Deconstruction and Criticism*, by Harold Bloom, Paul de Man, Jacques Derrida, Geoffrey Hartman, and J. Hillis Miller, pp. 75–76. New York: Seabury.

————. 1981. *Dissemination*. Translated by Barbara Johnson. Chicago: University of Chicago Press.

————. 1982/1972. *Margins of Philosophy*. Translated by Alan Bass. Chicago: University of Chicago Press.

————. 1989. *Of Spirit: Heidegger and the Question*. Translated by Geoffrey Bennington and Rachel Bowlby. Chicago: University of Chicago Press.

————. 1991. *Cinders*. Lincoln: University of Nebraska Press.

————. 1992a. *Acts of Literature*. Edited by Derek Attridge. New York: Routledge.

————. 1992b. *The Other Heading*. Translated by Pascale-Anne Brault and Michael B. Naas. Bloomington: Indiana University Press.

————. 1993. "The Rhetoric of Drugs: An Interview." *differences* 5(1): 1–25.

————. 1994. *Specters of Marx: The State of the Debt, the Work of Mourning, and the New International*. Translated by Peggy Kamuf. New York: Routledge.

————. 1995. *Points: Interviews, 1974–1994*. Edited by Elizabeth Weber. Translated by Peggy Kamuf et al. Stanford, Calif.: Stanford University Press.

————. 1996a. "By Force of Mourning." *Critical Inquiry* 22(2): 71–92.

————. 1996b. *Archive Fever: A Freudian Impression*. Translated by Eric Prenowitz. Chicago: University of Chicago Press.

————. 1996c. "*As If* I Were dead: An Interview with Jacques Derrida." In *Applying: To Derrida*, edited by John Brannigan, Ruth Robbins, and Julian Wolfreys, pp. 212–26. London: MacMillan.

————. 1997. *Politics of Friendship*. Translated by George Collins. London: Verso.

————. 1999. *Adieu to Emmanuel Levinas*. Translated by Pascale-Anne Brault and Michael Naas. Stanford, Calif.: Stanford University Press.

————. 2001. "A Certain 'Madness' Must Watch over Thinking: Interview with Francois Ewald." In *Derrida and Education*, edited by Gert Biesta and Denisa Egea-Kuehne, pp. 55–76. London: Routledge.

Derrida, Jacques, and Elisabeth Roudinesco. 2004. *For What Tomorrow: A Dialogue*. Translated by Jeff Fort. Stanford, Calif.: Stanford University Press.

Deutsche, Rosalind. 1996. *Evictions*. Cambridge, Mass.: MIT Press.

de Vries, Hilary. 1992. "A Playwright Spreads His Wings." *Los Angeles Times*, 25 October.

Dickens, David, and Andrea Fontana, eds. 1994. *Postmodernism & Social Inquiry*. New York: Guilford Press.

Dillard, Cynthia. 2006. *On Spiritual Strivings: Transforming an African American Woman's Academic Life*. Albany: State University of New York Press.

Dillon, Millicent. 1980. "Conversation with Michel Foucault." *The Threepenny Review* 1(1): 5.

Dirks, Nicholas, Geoff Eley, and Sherry Ortner. 1994. "Introduction." In *Culture/ Power/History: A Contemporary Reader in Social Theory*, edited by Nicholas Dirks, Geoff Eley, and Sherry Ortner, pp. 3–45. Princeton, N.J.: Princeton University Press.

Docherty, Thomas. 1996. *After Theory*. Edinburgh: Edinburgh University Press.

Dosse, Francis. 1999. *Empire of Meaning: The Humanization of the Social Sciences*. Translated by Hassan Melehy. Minneapolis: University of Minnesota Press.

Downs, Laura Lee. 1993. "If 'Woman' Is Just an Empty Category, Then Why Am I
    Afraid to Walk Alone at Night? Identity Politics Meets the Postmodern Sub-
    ject." *Comparative Studies in Society and History* 35(2): 414–37.
Duncker, Patricia. 1999. "Jurassic Feminism Meets Queer Politics." In *Post-Theory:
    New Directions in Criticism,* edited by Martin McQuillan, Graeme MacDonald,
    Robin Purves, and Stephan Thomson, pp. 51–62. Edinburgh: Edinburgh Uni-
    versity Press.
Duttmann, Alexander Garcia. 1993. "What Will Have Been Said about AIDS?" *Public*
    7: 95–114.
Elam, Diane. 1994. *Feminism and Deconstruction: Ms. en abyme.* London: Routledge.
Eley, Geoff. 1996. "Is All the World a Text? From Social History to the History of
    Society Two Decades Later." In *The Historic Turn in the Human Sciences,*
    edited by Terrence J. McDonald, pp. 193–243. Ann Arbor: University of Michi-
    gan Press.
Ellison, Julie. 1996. "A Short History of Liberal Guilt." *Critical Inquiry* 22(2):
    344–71.
Ellsworth, Elizabeth. 1989. "Why Doesn't This Feel Empowering? Working through
    the Repressive Myths of Critical Pedagogy." *Harvard Educational Review* 59(3):
    297–325.
———. 1997. *Teaching Positions.* New York: Teachers College Press.
Fawcett, Brian. 1986. *Cambodia: A Book for People Who Find Television Too Slow.*
    New York: Collier Books.
———. 1994. *Gender Wars: A Novel and Some Conversation about Sex and Gender.*
    Toronto: Somerville House Publishing.
Fay, Brian. 1987. *Critical Social Science.* Ithaca, N.Y.: Cornell University Press.
Fekete, John. 1995. "Postmodernism and Cultural Studies: On the Utopianization of
    Heterotopia." In *Constructive Criticism: The Human Sciences in the Age of
    Theory,* edited by Martin Kreiswirth and Tom Carmichael, pp. 201–19. Toronto:
    University of Toronto Press.
Felman, Shoshona. 1987. *Jacques Lacan and the Adventure of Insight: Psychoanalysis
    in Contemporary Culture.* Cambridge, Mass.: Harvard University Press.
Felman, Shoshona, and Dori Laub. 1992. *Testimony: Crises of Witnessing in Litera-
    ture, Psychoanalysis, and History.* New York: Routledge.
Fine, Arthur. 1986. *The Shaky Game: Einstein, Realism and the Quantum Theory.*
    Chicago; University of Chicago Press.
Fine, Michelle. 1992. *Disruptive Voices: The Possibilities of Feminist Research.* Ann
    Arbor: University of Michigan Press.
Fish, Stanley. 1994. *There's No Such Thing as Free Speech . . . And It's a Good Thing
    Too.* Oxford: Oxford University Press.
Fiske, John. 1996. "Black Bodies of Knowledge: Notes on an Effective History."
    Cultural Critique 33(Spring), 185–212.
Fleetwood, Steve. 1995. *Hayek's Political Economy: The Socio-Economics of Order.*
    London: Routledge.
Flyvbjerg, Bent. 2001. *Making Social Science Matter: Why Social Inquiry Fails and
    How It Can Succeed Again.* Cambridge: Cambridge University Press.

Foley, Douglas. 1998. "On Writing Reflexive Realist Narratives." In *Being Reflexive in Critical Educational and Social Research*, edited by Geoffrey Shacklock and John Smyth, pp. 110–29. London: Falmer Press.

Fonow, Mary Margaret, and Judith Cook, eds. 1991. *Beyond Methodology: Feminist Research as Lived Experience*. Bloomington: Indiana University Press.

———. 2005. "Feminist Methodology: New Applications in the Academy and Public Policy." *Signs* 30(4): 2211–36.

Foster, Hal. 1996. *The Return of the Real: The Avant-Garde at the End of the Century*. Cambridge, Mass.: MIT Press.

Foucault, Michel. 1970/1966. *The Order of Things: An Archaeology of the Human Sciences*. New York: Vintage Books.

———. 1972. *The Archaeology of Knowledge and the Discourse on Language*. Translated by A. M. Sheridan. New York: Pantheon.

———. 1977. *Language, Counter-Memory, Practice*. Edited by Donald Bouchard. Ithaca, N.Y.: Cornell University Press.

———. 1980. *Power/Knowledge: Selected Interviews and Other Writings, 1972–1977*. Edited and translated by Colin Gordon. New York: Pantheon.

———. 1983. "On the Genealogy of Ethics: An Overview of Work in Progress." In *The Foucault Reader*, edited by Paul Rabinow, pp. 340–72. New York: Pantheon.

———. 1984. "Preface to the *History of Sexuality*." In *Foucault Reader*, vol. 2, edited by Paul Rabinow, pp. 333–39. New York: Pantheon.

———. 1988. "Truth, Power, Self: An Interview with Michel Foucault, October 25, 1982." In *Technologies of the Self: A Seminar with Michel Foucault*, edited by Luther Martin, Huck Gutman, and Patricia Hutton, pp. 9–15. Amherst: University of Massachusetts Press.

———. 1991/1981. *Remarks on Marx: Conversations with Duccio Trombadori*. New York: Semiotext(e).

———. 1997a. "On the Genealogy of Ethics." In *The Essential Works of Michel Foucault, 1954–1984: Ethics*, vol. 1, edited by Paul Rabinow, pp. 253–80. New York: New Press.

———. 1997b. "Christianity and Confession." In *The Politics of Truth/Michel Foucault*, edited by Sylvere Lothringer and Lysa Hochroth, pp. 199–236. New York: Semiotext(e).

———. 1998. *Aesthetics, Method, and Epistemology*. Edited by James D. Faubion. New York: New Press.

Fraser, Nancy. 1989. *Unruly Practices: Power, Discourse and Gender in Contemporary Social Theory*. Minneapolis: University of Minnesota Press.

Fritzman, J. M. 1990. "Lyotard's Paralogy and Rorty's Pluralism: Their Differences and Pedagogical Implications." *Educational Theory* 40(3): 371–80.

Frowen, Stephen F., ed. 1997. *Hayek: Economist and Social Philosopher*. London: MacMillan.

Fuller, Steve. 1997. *Science*. Minneapolis: University of Minnesota Press.

———. 2001. "The Reenchantment of Science: A Fit End to the Science Wars?" In *After the Science Wars*, edited by Keith M. Ashman and Philip S. Baringer, pp. 183–208. London: Routledge.

Fuller, Steve, and James Collier. 2003. *Philosophy, Rhetoric, and the End of Knowledge: A New Beginning for Science and Technology*. Hillsdale N.J.: Lawrence Earlbaum.

Fuss, Diana. 1996. "Look Who's Talking, or If Looks Could Kill." *Critical Inquiry* 22(2): 383–92.

Gabardi, Wayne. 2000. *Negotiating Postmodernism*. Minneapolis: University of Minnesota Press.

Gallagher, Kathleen. 2001. "The Staging of Qualitative Research: Authorship, Ownership, and Artistic Expression in Social Science Inquiry." *Journal of Curriculum Theorizing* 17(3): 145–56.

Gabrenya, Frank. 2005. March 25. "Filmmaker Captures Anxiety of Soldiers." *Columbus Dispatch*, 25 March, F6.

Gallop, Jane. 1991. *Around 1981: Academic Feminist Literary Theory*. New York: Routledge.

———. 1997. " 'Women' " in Spurs and Nineties Feminism." In *Derrida and Feminism: Recasting the Question of Woman*, edited by Ellen Feder, Mary Rawlinson, and Emily Zakin, pp. 7–20. New York: Routledge.

Garber, Marjorie, Beatrice Hanssen, and Rebecca Walkowitz, eds. 2000. *The Turn to Ethics*. New York: Routledge.

Garrison, James. 1994. "Realism, Deweyan Pragmatism, and Educational Research." *Educational Researcher* 23(1): 5–14.

Garrison, James, and Mary Leach. 2001. "Dewey after Derrida." In *Handbook of Research on Teaching*, 4th ed., edited by Virginia Richardson, pp. 69–81. Washington, D.C.: AERA.

Gaztambide-Fernandez, Ruben, Heather Harding, and Tere Sorde-Marti, eds. 2004. *Cultural Studies and Education: Perspectives on Theory, Methodology, and Practice*. Cambridge. Mass.: Harvard Educational Review.

Geertz, Clifford. 1980. "Blurred Genres." *The American Scholar* 49: 165–79.

Gilbert-Rolfe, Jeremy. 1995. *Beyond Piety: Critical Essays on the Visual Arts, 1986–1993*. Cambridge: Cambridge University Press.

Gillespie, Michael Allen, and Tracy B. Strong, eds. 1988. *Nietzsche's New Seas: Explorations in Philosophy, Aesthetics and Politics*. Chicago: University of Chicago Press.

Giroux, Henry. 1992. "Language, Difference and Curriculum Theory: Beyond the Politics of Clarity." *Theory into Practice* 31(3): 219–27.

Godzich, Wlad. 1994. *The Culture of Literacy*. Cambridge. Mass.: Harvard University Press.

Gordon, Colin. 1991. "Governmental Rationality: An Introduction." In *The Foucault Effect: Studies in Governmentality*, edited by G. Burchell, C. Gordon, and P. Miller, pp. 1–51. Chicago: University of Chicago Press.

Gordon, Deborah. 1995. "Border Work: Feminist Ethnography and the Dissemination of Literacy." In *Women Writing Culture*, edited by Ruth Behar and D. Gordon, pp. 373–89. Berkeley and Los Angeles: University of California Press.

Gramsci, Antonio. 1971. *Selections from the Prison Notebooks of Antonio Gramsci*. Edited and translated by Quintin Hoare and G. Smith. New York: International Pub.

Greene, Maxinne. 1994. "Epistemology and Educational Research: The Influence of Recent Approaches to Knowledge." In *Review of Research in Education*, edited by L. Darling-Hammond, pp. 423–64. Washington, D.C.: AERA.

Gross, Paul, and Norman Levitt. 1994. *Higher Superstition: The Academic Left and its Quarrels with Science*. Baltimore, Md.: Johns Hopkins University Press.

Grosz, Elizabeth. 2001. *Architecture from the Outside: Essays on Virtual and Real Space*. Cambridge, Mass.: MIT Press.

Habermas, Jurgen. 1971/1968. *Knowledge and Human Interests*. Translated by Jeremy J. Shapiro. Boston: Beacon Press.

Hacking, Ian. 1983. *Representing and Intervening: Introductory Topics in Philosophy of Natural Sciences*. New York: Cambridge University Press.

———. 1991. "How Should We Do the History of Statistics?" In *The Foucault Effect: Studies in Governmentality*, edited by Graham Burchell, Colin Gordon, and Peter Miller, pp. 181–96. Chicago: University of Chicago Press.

———. 2002. *Historical Ontology*. Cambridge, Mass.: Harvard University Press.

Hanley, Charles J. 2005. "Experts Say No End in Sight to War on Terror." *The Monitor* [McAllen, Texas], 10 July, 15A.

Hansen, Miriam. 1996. "Schindler's List is Not Shoah." *Critical Inquiry* 22: 292–312.

Hanssen, Beatrice. 2001. "Whatever Happened to Feminist Theory?" In *Feminist Consequences: Theory for the New Century*, edited by Elisabeth Bronfen and Misha Kavka, pp. 58–98. New York: Columbia University Press.

Haraway, Donna. 1988. "Situated Knowledges: The Science Question in Feminism and the Privilege of Partial Perspective." *Feminist Studies* 14(3): 575–99.

———. 1991. *Simians, Cyborgs, and Women: The Reinvention of Nature*. New York: Routledge.

———. 1997. *Modest witness@second Millennium: Feminism and Technoscience*. New York: Routledge.

Harding, Sandra, ed. 1987. *Feminist Methodology*. Bloomington: Indiana University Press.

———. 1991. *Whose Science? Whose Knowledge? Thinking Through Women's Lives*. Ithaca, N.Y.: Cornell University Press.

———. ed. 1993. *The "Racial" Economy of Science*. Bloomington: Indiana University Press.

Harris, Wendell, ed. 1996. *Beyond Poststructuralism: The Speculations of Theory and the Experience of Reading*. University Park: Pennsylvania State University Press.

Hartsock, Nancy. 1987. "Rethinking Modernism: Minority vs. Majority Theories." *Cultural Critique* 7: 187–206.

Harvey, David. 1989. *The Condition of Postmodernity*. Oxford: Basil Blackwell.

Haver, William. 1996. *The Body of This Death: Historicity and Sociality in the Time of AIDS*. Stanford, Calif.: Stanford University Press.

Hayek, Friedrich August. 1952. *The Counter-Revolution of Science: Studies in the Abuse of Reason*. Glencoe, Ill.: Free Press.

Hayles, N. Katherine. 1990. *Chaos Bound: Orderly Disorder in Contemporary Literature and Science*. Ithaca, N.Y.: Cornell University Press.

Hebdige, Dick. 1996. "Style: From Subculture to High Culture," talk sponsored by the Center for Interdisciplinary Studies in Art and Design, Wexner Center for the Arts, Ohio State University, January 31.

Hegeman, Susan. 1988. "History, Ethnography, Myth: Some Notes on the 'Indian-Centered' Narrative." *Social Text* 23(Fall/Winter): 144–60.

Hill, Dave, Peter McLaren, Mike Cole, and Glenn Rikowski. 2002. *Marxism Against Postmodernism in Educational Theory*. Lanham, Minn.: Lexington Books.

Hill-Collins, Patricia. 2000. "What's Going on? Black Feminist Thought and the Politics of Postmodernism." In *Working the Ruins: Feminist Poststructural Theory and Methods in Education*, edited by Elizabeth St. Pierre and Wanda Pillow, pp. 41–73. New York: Routledge.

Hobson, Marian. 1998. *Jacques Derrida: Opening Lines*. London: Routledge.

Holland, Eugene. 1993. *Baudelaire and Schizoanalysis: The Sociopoetics of Modernism*. Cambridge: Cambridge University Press.

Hollinger, Robert. 1994. *Postmodernism and the Social Sciences: A Thematic Approach*. Thousand Oaks, Calif.: Sage.

Honderich, Ted, ed. 2005. *The Oxford Companion to Philosophy*. Oxford: Oxford University Press.

hooks, bell. 1992. "Eating the Other: Desire and Resistance." In *Black Looks: Race and Representation*, edited by bell hooks, pp. 21–49. Boston: South End Press.

Howe, Kenneth. 1998. "The Interpretive Turn and the New Debate in Education." *Educational Researcher* 27(8): 13–20.

———. 2004. "A Critique of Experimentalism." *Qualitative Inquiry* 10(1): 42–61.

Hoy, David Couzens. 2004. *Critical Resistance: From Poststructuralism to Post-Critique*. Cambridge, Mass.: MIT Press.

Husserl, Edmund. 1970. *The Crisis of European Sciences and Transcendental Phenomenology: An Introduction to Phenomenological Philosophy (1934–37)*. Translated by David Carr. Evanston, Ill.: Northwestern University Press.

Hutcheon, Linda. 1989. *The Politics of Postmodernism*. New York: Routledge.

Irigaray, Luce. 1985. *The Sex Which is Not One*. Translated by C. Porter and C. Burke. Ithaca, N.Y.: Cornell University Press.

———. 1993. *An Ethics of Sexual Difference*. Translated by Carolyn Burke and Gillian C. Gill. London: Athlone Press.

Jameson, Fredric. 1998. *The Cultural Turn: Selected Writings on the Postmodern, 1983–1998*. London: Verso.

Jewett, Andrew. 2003. "Science & the Promise of Democracy in America." *Daedalus* Fall: 64–70.

Joeres, Ruth. 1992. "Editorial: On Writing Feminist Academic Prose." *Signs* 17(4): 701–704.

Johnson, Barbara. 1981. "Translator's Introduction." In *Dissemination*, by Jacques Derrida, pp. vii–xxxiii. London: Athlone Press.

Johnson, Nancy. 1997. "Subverting the Rhetorical Tradition through the Feminist Imagination." Conference proposal, "From Boundaries to Border Lands: Intersections of Feminism(s) and Rhetoric(s)." Oregon State University, Corvallis, September.

Juhasz, Alexandra. 1999. "They Said We Were Trying to Show Reality—All I Want to Show Is My Video: The Politics of the Realist Feminist Documentary." In *Collecting Visible Evidence*, edited by Jane Gaines and Michael Renov, pp. 190–215. Minneapolis: University of Minnesota Press.

Kaplan, Abraham. 1964. *The Conduct of Inquiry: Methodology for Behavioral Sciences*. San Francisco: Chandler.

Kaplan, Esther. 1999. "Life Sentences." [Review of *Breaking the Walls of Silence: AIDS and Women in a New York State Maximum Security Prison*]. *Women's Review of Books* 16(8): 17–18.

Karamcheti, Indira. 1992. "The Business of Friendship" [Review of *Friends, Brothers and Informants: Fieldwork Memoirs of Banaras*, by Nita Kumar]. *Women's Review of Books* 9(12): 16–17.

Katriel, Tamar, and Robert E. Sanders, eds. 1989. "The Meta-Communicative Role of Epigraphs in Scientific Text Construction." In *Rhetoric in the Human Sciences*, edited by Herbert W. Simons, pp. 183–94. London: Sage.

Kavka, Misha. 2001. "Introduction." In *Feminist Consequences: Theory for the New Century*, edited by Elisabeth Bronfen and Misha Kavka, pp. ix–xxvi. New York: Columbia University Press.

Kearney, Richard. 1984. *Dialogues with Contemporary Continental Thinkers: The Phenomenological Heritage.* Manchester: Manchester University Press.

Keenan, Thomas. 1997. *Fables of Responsibility: Aberrations and Predicaments in Ethics and Politics.* Palo Alto, Calif.: Stanford University Press.

Kesby, Mike. 2005. "Retheorizing Empowerment through Participation as a Performance in Space: Beyond Tyranny to Transformation." *Signs* 30(4): 2037–66.

Kincheloe, Joe, and Peter McLaren. 1994. "Rethinking Critical Theory and Qualitative Research." In *Handbook of Qualitative Research*, edited by Norman Denzin and Y. Lincoln, pp. 138–57. Thousand Oaks, Calif.: Sage.

Kirsch, Gesa. 1997. "Multi-Vocal Texts and Interpretive Responsibility." *College English* 59(2): 191–202.

Kiziltan, Mustafa, William Bain, and Anita Canizares. 1990. "Postmodern Conditions: Rethinking Public Education." *Educational Theory* 40(3): 351–70.

Knauft, Bruce. 1994. "Pushing Anthropology Past the Post: Critical Notes on Cultural Anthropology and Cultural Studies as Influenced by Postmodernism and Existentialism." *Critique of Anthropology* 14(2): 117–52.

Koertge, Noretta. 1998. *A House Built on Sand: Exposing Postmodernist Myths about Science.* New York: Oxford University Press.

Kofman, Sarah. 1988. "Baubo: Theological Perversion and Fetishism." In *Nietzsche's New Seas: Explorations in Philosophy, Aesthetics, and Politics*, edited by M. A. Gillespie and T. Strong, pp. 175–202. Chicago: University of Chicago Press.

———. 1993. *Nietzsche and Metaphor.* Translated by Duncan Large. Stanford, Calif.: Stanford University Press.

Komar, Kathleen. 1987. *Transcending Angels: Rainer Maria Rilke's Duino Elegies.* Lincoln: University of Nebraska Press.

Kondo, Dorinne. 1990. *Crafting Selves: Power, Gender, and Discourses of Identity in a Japanese Workplace.* Chicago: University of Chicago Press.

Kostkowska, Justyna. 2004. " 'To Persistently Not Know Something Important': Feminist Science and the Poetry of Wislawa Szmborska." *Feminist Theory* 5(2): 185–203.

Kreiswirth, Martin, and Thomas Carmichael, eds. 1995. *Constructive Criticism: The Human Sciences in the Age of Theory.* Toronto: University of Toronto Press.

Krell, David. 2000. *The Purest of Bastards: Works of Mourning, Art, and Affirmation in the Thought of Jacques Derrida.* University Park: Pennsylvania State University Press.

Kresge, Stephen, and Leif Wenar, eds. 1994. *Hayek on Hayek: An Autobiographical Dialogue.* Chicago: University of Chicago Press.

Kristeva, Julia. 1978–79. "Postmodernism and Periphery." *Third Text* 2: 1–8.

Kritzman, Lawrence D., ed. 1988. *Michael Foucault: Politics, Philosophy, Culture: Interviews and other Writings, 1977–1984*. New York: Routledge.

Kulchyski, Peter. 1992. "Primitive Subversions: Totalization and Resistance in Native Canadian Politics." *Cultural Critique* 21 (Spring): 171–96.

Kushner, Tony. 1992. *Angels in America, Part Two: Perestroika*. New York: Theatre Communications Group.

Kvale, Steiner. 1989. "To Validate is to Question." In *Issues of Validity in Qualitative Research*, edited by Steiner Kvale, pp. 73–92. Lund, Sweden: Studentliterature.

Ladwig, James. 1996. *Academic Distinctions: Theory and Methodology in the Sociology of School Knowledge*. New York: Routledge.

Lagemann, Ellen. 2000. *An Elusive Science: The Troubling History of Education Research*. Chicago: University of Chicago Press.

Laspina, James Andrew. 1998. *The Visual Turn and the Transformation of the Textbook*. Mahwah, N.J.: Lawrence Erlbaum.

Lather, Patti. 1986a. "Research as Praxis." *Harvard Educational Review* 56(3): 257–77.

———. 1986b. "Issues of Validity in Openly Ideological Research: Between a Rock and a Soft Place." *Interchange* 17(4): 63–84.

———. 1991. *Getting Smart: Feminist Research and Pedagogy with/in the Postmodern*. New York: Routledge.

———. 1992a. "Post-Critical Pedagogies: A Feminist Reading." In *Feminisms and Radical Pedagogy: A Reader*, edited by Carmen Luke and Jennifer Gore, pp. 120–37. London: Routledge.

———. 1992b. "Critical Frames in Educational Research: Feminist and Poststructural Perspectives. *Theory into Practice* 31(2): 1–13.

———. 1993a. "Fertile Obsession: Validity after Poststructuralism." *The Sociological Quarterly* 34(4): 673–93.

———. 1993b. "The Politics and Ethics of Feminist Research: Researching the Lives of Women with HIV/AIDS." Paper presented at the Ethnography and Education Research Forum, Philadelphia, February.

———. 1994a. "Staying Dumb? Feminist Research and Pedagogy with/in the Postmodern." In *After Postmodernism*, edited by Herb Simons and Michael Billig, pp. 101–32. Thousand Oaks, Calif.: Sage.

———. 1994b. "Dada Practice: A Feminist Reading" [response to Stephanie Kirkwood Walker's review of *Getting Smart*]. *Curriculum Inquiry* 24(2): 181–88.

———. 1995. "Troubling Angels: Interpretive and Textual Strategies in Researching the Lives of Women with HIV/AIDS." *Qualitative Inquiry* 1(1): 41–68.

———. 1996. "Troubling Clarity: The Politics of Accessible Language." *Harvard Educational Review* 66(3): 525–45.

———. 1998. "Critical Pedagogy and Its Complicities." *Educational Theory* 48(4): 487–97.

———. 2000a. "Drawing the Line at Angels." In *Working the Ruins: Feminist Poststructural Theory and Methods in Education*, edited by Elizabeth St. Pierre and Wanda Pillow, pp. 284–311. New York: Routledge.

———. 2000b. "Reading the Image of Rigoberta Menchu: Undecidability and Language Lessons." *Qualitative Studies in Education* 13(2): 153–62.

———. 2000c. "Against Empathy, Voice and Authenticity." In *Transgressive Methodology*, special issue of *Women, Gender and Research*, v.4, Copenhagen, 16–25.

————. 2004a. "This *Is* Your Father's Paradigm: Government Intrusion and the Case of Qualitative Research in Education." *Qualitative Inquiry* 10(1): 15–34.

————. 2004b. "Scientific Research in Education: A Critical Perspective." *Journal of Curriculum and Supervision* 20(1): 14–30, and *British Educational Research Journal* 30(6): 759–72, joint publication.

————. 2004c. "Foucauldian "Indiscipline" as a Sort of Application: Qu(e)er(y)ing Research/Policy/Practice." In *Dangerous Coagulations: The Uses of Foucault in the Study of Education*, edited by Bernadette M. Baker and Katharina E. Heyning, pp. 279–304. New York: Peter Lang.

————. 2004d. "Ethics Now: White Woman Goes to Africa and Loses Her Voice." Paper presented at the annual meeting of the American Educational Research Association, San Diego, April.

Lather, Patti, and Chris Smithies. 1997. *Troubling the Angels: Women Living With HIV/AIDS*. Boulder: Westview/HarperCollins.

Lather, Patti, and Pam Moss. 2005. "Introduction: Implications of the *Scientific Research in Education* Report for Qualitative Inquiry." *Teachers College Record* 107(1): 1–3.

Latour, Bruno. 1993. *We Have Never Been Modern*. Translated by Catherine Porter. Cambridge, Mass.: Harvard University Press.

————. 1999. *Pandora's Hope: Essays on the Reality of Science Studies*. Cambridge, Mass.: Harvard University Press.

————. 2000. "When Things Strike Back: A Possible Contribution of Science Studies to the Social Sciences." *British Journal of Sociology* 51(1): 107–24.

————. 2004. "Why Has Critique Run Out of Steam? From Matters of Fact to Matters of Concern." *Critical Inquiry* 30(2): 225–48.

Lawson, Tony. 1997. *Economics and Reality*. London: Routledge.

Leach, Mary. 1992. "Can We Talk? A Response to Burbules and Rice." *Harvard Educational Review* 62(2): 257–71.

Lecercle, Jean-Jacques. 1990. *The Violence of Language*. London: Routledge.

Lefebvre, Henri. 1991. *The Production of Space*. Oxford: Basil Blackwell.

Lenzo, Kate. 1995. "Validity and Self-Reflexivity Meet Poststructuralism: Scientific Ethos and the Transgressive Self." *Educational Researcher* (May):17–23, 45.

Leslie, Esther. 2000. *Walter Benjamin: Overpowering Conformism*. London: Pluto.

Leupin, Alexandre. 1991. "Introduction: Voids and Knots in Knowledge and Truth. In *Lacan & the Human Sciences*, edited by A. Leupin, pp. 1–23. Lincoln: University of Nebraska Press.

Levinson, Marjori. 1995. "Pre- and Post-Dialectical Materialisms: Modeling Praxis without Subjects and Objects." *Cultural Critique* (Fall): 111–27.

————. 1998. "Posthumous Critique." In *In Near Ruins: Cultural Theory at the End of the Century*, edited by Nicholas B. Dirks, pp. 257–94. Minneapolis: University of Minnesota Press.

Levy, Itamar. 1994. "Eye-Witness [Review of *David Reeb: Paintings 1982–1994*]." Tel Aviv: Tel Aviv Museum of Art, July 1994, 125–30.

Lincoln, Yvonna, and Egon Guba. 1985. *Naturalistic Inquiry*. Newbury Park, Calif.: Sage.

Litvak, Joseph. 1997. "Strange Gourmets: Sophistication, Theory and the Novel." In *Novel Gazing: Queer Readings in Fiction*, edited by Eve Kosofsky Sedgwick, pp. 74–93. New York: Routledge.

Lofaro, Michael, ed. 1992. *James Agee: Reconsiderations*. Knoxville: University of Tennessee Press.

Lorde, Audre. 1984. *Sister Outsider*. Trumansburg, N.Y.: Crossing.

Lubiano, Wahnemma. 1991. "Shuckin' off the African-American Native Other: What's 'Po-mo' Got To Do With It?" *Cultural Critique* (Spring): 49–186.

Lutz, Catherine. 1993. "Social Contexts of Postmodern Cultural Analysis." In *Postmodern Contentions: Epochs, Politics, Space*, edited by John Paul Jones III, Wolfgang Natter, and Theodore Schatzki, pp. 137–64. New York: Guilford Press.

Lyotard, Jean-Francois. 1984. *The Postmodern Condition: A Report on Knowledge*. Translated by G. Bennington and B. Massumi. Minneapolis: University of Minnesota Press.

MacLure, Maggie. 2004. "Towards a 'Gothic' Sensibility in Educational Research: Methods as Phantasmagoria." Paper presented at the annual meeting of the American Educational Research Association, San Diego, April.

Malabou, Catherine, and Jacques Derrida. 2004. *Counterpath: Traveling with Jacques Derrida*. Translated by David Wills. Stanford, Calif.: Stanford University Press.

Marcus, George. 1993. Interviewed in "Inside Publishing." *Lingua Franca*, July/August, 13–15.

———. 1994. "What Comes (Just) After 'Post'? The Case of Ethnography." In *The Handbook of Qualitative Research*, edited by Norman Denzin and Yvonna Lincoln, pp. 563–74. Thousand Oaks, Calif.: Sage.

———. 1997. "Critical Cultural Studies as One Power/Knowledge Like, Among, and in Engagement with Others." In *From Sociology to Cultural Studies*, edited by Elizabeth Long, pp. 399–425. London: Blackwell.

Marcus, George, and Richard Fischer. 1986. "A Crisis of Representation in the Human Sciences." In *Anthropology as Cultural Critique: An Experimental Moment in the Human Sciences*, pp. 7–16. Chicago: University of Chicago Press.

Marini, Marcelle. 1992. *Jacques Lacan: The French Context*. Translated by Anne Tomiche. New Brunswick, N.J.: Rutgers University Press.

Martin, Biddy. 2001. "Success and Its Failures." In *Feminist Consequences: Theory for the New Century*, edited by Elisabeth Bronfen and Misha Kavka, pp. 353–80. New York: Columbia University Press.

Marx, Karl. 1975. *Early Writings*. London: Penguin.

Mascia-Lees, Francis, Patricia Sharpe, and Colleen Cohen. 1989. "The Postmodernist Turn in Anthropology: Cautions from a Feminist Perspective." *Signs* 15(1): 7–33.

McArdle, Felicity, and Erica McWilliam. 2005. "From Balance to Blasphemy: Shifting Metaphors for Researching Early Childhood Education." *Qualitative Studies in Education* 18(3): 323–36.

McCall, Leslie. 2005. "The Complexity of Intersectionality." *Signs* 30(3): 1771–1800.

McCoy, Kate. 1997. "Killing the Father/Becoming Uncomfortable with the Mother Tongue: Rethinking the Performative Contradiction." *Educational Theory* 47(4): 489–500.

McDonald, Christie, ed. 1985. *The Ear of the Other: Texts and Discussion with Jacques Derrida*. Lincoln: University of Nebraska Press.

McDonald, Terrence J., ed. 1996. *The Historic Turn in the Human Sciences*. Ann Arbor: University of Michigan Press.

McElroy, Joseph. 1987. *Women and Men: A Novel*. Normal, Ill.: Dalkey Archive Press.

McGee, Patrick. 1992. *Telling the Other: The Question of Value in Modern and Postcolonial Writing*. Ithaca, N.Y.: Cornell University Press.

McGowan, John. 1991. *Postmodernism and Its Critics*. Ithaca, N.Y.: Cornell University Press.

McGuigan, Jim. 2001. "Problems of Cultural Analysis and Policy in the Information Age." *Cultural Studies/Critical Methodologies* 1(2): 190–219.

McHale, Brian. 1990. *Constructing Postmodernism*. New York: Routledge.

———. 2004. *The Obligation Toward the Difficult Whole: Postmodernist Long Poems*. Tuscaloosa: University of Alabama Press.

McLaren, Peter, and R. Farahmandpur. 2000. "Reconsidering Marx in Post-Marxist Times: A Requiem for Postmodernism?" *Educational Researcher* 29(3): 25–33.

McQuillan, Martin, Graeme MacDonald, Robin Purves, and Stephan Thomson, eds. 1999. *Post-Theory: New Directions in Criticism*. Edinburgh: Edinburgh University Press.

McWilliam, Erica Lenore. 1992. *In Broken Images: A Postpositivist Analysis of Student Needs Talk in Pre-service Teacher Education*. Unpublished dissertation, University of Queensland.

———. 1993. " 'Post' Haste: Plodding Research and Galloping Theory." *British Journal of Sociology of Education* 14(2): 199–205.

Mehan, Hugh. 1995. "CAE Presidential Address: Resisting the Politics of Despair." *Anthropology and Education Quarterly* 26: 239–50.

Mehuron, Kate. 1997. "Sentiment Recaptured: The Performative in Women's AIDS Testimonies." In *Feminist Interpretations of Jacques Derrida*, edited by Nancy Holland, pp. 165–92. University Park: Pennsylvania State University Press.

Meiners, Erica. 1994. Course writing for Education 508B, Data Analysis in the Crisis of Representation, University of British Columbia, Summer.

Melville, Stephen. 1986. *Philosophy Beside Itself: On Deconstruction and Modernism*. Minneapolis: University of Minnesota Press.

———. 1996. "Color Has Not Yet Been Named: Objectivity in Deconstruction." In *Seams: Art as Philosophical Content*, edited by J. Gilbert-Rolfe, pp. 129–46. Amsterdam: G&B Arts.

———. 2004. "Postmodernism and Art: Postmodernism Now and Again." In *The Cambridge Companion to Postmodernism*, edited by Steven Connor, pp. 82–96. Cambridge: Cambridge University Press.

Menchu, Rigoberta. 1984. *I, Rigoberta Menchu: An Indian Woman in Guatemala*. Edited by Elisabeth Burgos-Debray. Translated by Ann Wright. London: Verso.

Miller, J. Hillis. 1979. "The Critic as Host." In *Deconstruction and Criticism*, by Harold Bloom, Paul de Man, Jacques Derrida, Geoffrey Hartman, and J. Hillis Miller, pp. 217–53. New York: Seabury.

Miller, Toby. 1993. *The Well-Tempered Self: Citizenship, Culture, and the Postmodern Subject*. Baltimore: Johns Hopkins University Press.

Mishler, Elliot. 1990. "Validation in Inquiry-guided Research: The Role of Exemplars in Narrative Studies." *Harvard Educational Review* 60(4): 415–42.

Moi, Toril. 1985. *Sexual/Textual Politics: Feminist Literary Theory*. New York: Methuen.

———. 1988. "Feminism, Postmodernism, and Style: Recent Feminist Criticisms in the United States." *Cultural Critique*, 9: 3–22.

———. 1999. *What Is a Woman? and Other Essays*. Oxford: Oxford University Press.

Mol, Annemarie. 2002. *The Body Multiple: Ontology in Medical Practice*. Durham, N.C.: Duke University Press.

Montag, Warren. 1995. " 'The Soul is the Prison of the Body': Althusser and Foucault, 1970–1975." *Yale French Studies* 88: 53–77.

Morris, Michael. 1992. *The Good and the True*. Oxford: Clarendon Press.

Murray, Stuart J. 2003. "The Politics of the Production of Knowledge: An Interview with Gayatri Chakravorty Spivak." In *Just Being Difficult? Academic Writing in the Public Arena*, edited by Jonathan Culler and Kevin Lamb, pp. 181–98. Stanford, Calif.: Stanford University Press.

Mykhalovskiy, Eric. 1996. "Reconsidering Table Talk: Critical Thoughts on the Relationship Between Sociology, Autobiography and Self-indulgence." *Qualitative Sociology* 19(1): 131–51.

Nagele, Rainer. 1991. *Theatre, Theory, Speculation: Walter Benjamin and the Scenes of Modernity*. Baltimore, Md.: Johns Hopkins University Press.

Nash, June. 1997. "When Isms Become Wasms: Structural Functionalism, Marxism, Feminism and Postmodernism." *Critique of Anthropology* 17(1): 11–32.

National Research Council. 2002. *Scientific Research in Education*. Edited by Richard J. Shavelson and Lisa Towne. Washington, D.C.: NRC.

Nealon, Jeffrey. 1993a. *Double Reading: Postmodernism After Deconstruction*. Ithaca, N.Y.: Cornell University Press.

———. 1993b. "Thinking/Writing the Postmodern: Representation, End, Ground, Sending." *boundary 2* 20(1): 221–41.

Nelson, John, Allen Megill, and Donald McCloskey, eds. 1987. *The Rhetoric of the Human Sciences: Language and Argument in Scholarship and Public Affairs*. Madison: University of Wisconsin Press.

Nicholson, Linda, ed. 1990. *Feminism/Postmodernism*. New York: Routledge.

Nietzsche, Friedrich. 1974/1887. *The Gay Science*. Translated by Walter Kaufmann. New York: Vintage.

Niranjana, Tejaswini. 1992. *Siting Translation: History, Post-Structuralism and the Colonial Context*. Berkeley and Los Angeles: University of California Press.

Norris, Christopher. 1984. *The Deconstructive Turn: Essays in the Rhetoric of Philosophy*. London: Methuen.

———. 1996. *Reclaiming Truth: Contribution to a Critique of Cultural Relativism*. Durham, N.C.: Duke University Press.

———. 2003. "Truth After Theory." In *life.after.theory*, edited by Michael Payne and John Schad, pp. 78–114. London: Continuum.

Oakley, Ann. 2003. "Research Evidence, Knowledge Management and Educational Practice: Early Lessons from a Systematic Approach." *London Review of Education* 1(1): 21–33.

Ockman, Joan, ed. 2000. *The Pragmatist Imagination: Thinking About "Things in the Making."* New York: Princeton Architectural Press.

O'Driscoll, Michael. 2002. "Derrida, Foucault, and the Archiolithics of History." In *After Poststructuralism: Writing the Intellectual History of Theory*, edited by

T. Rajan and M. O'Driscoll, pp. 284–309. Toronto: University of Toronto Press.

Olafson, Frederick. 2001. *Naturalism and the Human Condition*. London: Routledge.

Ormiston, Gayle. 1990. "Postmodern Differends." In *Crisis in Continental Philosophy*, edited by Arleen Dallery and C. Scott, pp. 235–83. Albany: State University of New York Press.

Orner, Mimi. 1992. "Interrupting the Call for Student Voice in 'Liberatory' Education." In *Feminisms and Critical Pedagogy*, edited by C. Luke and J. Gore, pp. 74–89. New York: Routledge.

Osborne, Thomas, and Nikolas Rose. 1999. "Do the Social Sciences Create Phenomena? The Example of Public Opinion Research." *British Journal of Sociology* 50(3): 367–96.

Outhwaite, William. 1994. *Habermas: A Critical Introduction*. Lincoln: University of Nebraska Press.

Patai, Daphnai. 1991. "U.S. Academics and Third World Women: Is Ethical Research Possible?" In *Women's Words: The Feminist Practice of Oral History*, edited by S. Gluck and D. Patai, pp. 137–54. New York: Routledge.

———. 1994. "Sick and Tired of Scholars' Nouveau Solipsism." *The Chronicle of Higher Education*, 23 February, A52.

Payne, Michael, and John Schad, eds. 2003. *life.after.theory*. London: Continuum.

Pefanis, Julian. 1991. *Heterology and the Postmodern: Bataille, Baudrillard, and Lyotard*. Durham: Duke University Press.

Peters, Michael, and Nick Burbules. 2004. *Poststructuralism and Educational Research*. Boulder: Rowman and Littlefield.

Phillips, D. C., and Nicholas Burbules. 2000. *Postpositivism and Educational Research*. Lanham, Md.: Rowman and Littlefield.

Picart, Caroline Joan. 1999. *Resentment and the "Feminine" in Nietzsche's Politico-Aesthetics*. University Park: Pennsylvania State University Press.

Piercy, Marge. 1973. *To Be of Use: Collected Poems*. Garden City, N.Y.: Doubleday.

Pillow, Wanda. 2000. "Deciphering Attempts to Decipher Postmodern Educational Research." *Educational Researcher* 29(5): 21–24.

———. 2003. "Confession, Catharsis, or Cure? Rethinking the Uses of Reflexivity as Methodological Power in Qualitative Research." *Qualitative Studies in Education* 16(2): 175–96.

Piontek, Thomas. 1999. "Telling the Stories of Women with HIV/AIDS: Feminism and the Limits of Representation." The National Women's Studies Association Annual Conference, Albuquerque, June 1999.

———. 2000. "Language and Power in Postmodern Ethnography: Representing Women with HIV/AIDS." In *Hybrid Spaces: Theory, Culture, Economy*, edited by Johannes Angermüller, Katharina Bunzmann, and Christina Rauch, pp. 97–112. Hamburg, Germany: LIT. (Distributed in North America by Transaction Publishers/Rutgers University.)

Pippin, Robert. 1988. "Irony and Affirmation in Nietzsche's *Thus Spoke Zarathustra*." In *Nietzsche's New Seas*, edited by M. A. Gillespie and T. Strong, pp. 45–71. Chicago: University of Chicago Press.

Pitt, Alice. 1998. "Qualifying Resistance: Some Comments on Methodological Dilemmas." *Qualitative Studies in Education* 11(4): 535–53.

Pitt, Alice, and Deborah Britzman. 2003. "Speculations on Qualities of Difficult Knowledge in Teaching and Learning: An Experiment in Psychoanalytic Research." *Qualitative Studies in Education* 16(6): 755–76.

Plotnitsky, Arkady. 2000. "On Lacan and Mathematics." In *Lacan in America*, edited by Jean-Michel Rabate, pp. 247–76. New York: Other Press.

Polkinghorne, Donald. 1988. *Narrative Knowing and the Human Sciences*. Albany: State University of New York Press.

Popkewitz, Thomas. 1998. "The Culture of Redemption and the Administration of Freedom as Research." *Review of Educational Research* 65(1): 1–34.

Poster, Mark. 1989. *Critical Theory and Poststructuralism: In Search of a Context*. Ithaca, N.Y.: Cornell University Press.

Prado, C. G. 1995. *Starting with Foucault: An Introduction to Genealogy*. Boulder, Colo.: Westview Press.

Probyn, Elspeth. 2000. "Shaming Theory, Thinking Dis-connections." In *Transformations: Thinking through Feminism*, edited by Sara Ahmed et al., pp. 48–60. London: Routledge.

Putnam, Hilary. 1978. *Meaning and the Moral Sciences*. London: Routledge.

Quinby, Lee. 1991. *Freedom, Foucault, and the Subject of America*. Boston: Northeastern University Press.

Rabinowitz, Paula. 1992. "Voyeurism and Class Consciousness: James Agee and Walker Evans, *Let Us Now Praise Famous Men*." *Cultural Critique* 21(Spring): 143–70.

Radhkrishnan, Rajagopalan. 1996. *Diasporic Mediations: Between Hope and Location*. Minneapolis: University of Minnesota Press.

Rajan, Tilottama. 2002. *Deconstruction and the Remainders of Phenomenology: Sartre, Derrida, Foucault, Baudrillard*. Stanford, Calif.: Stanford University Press.

Rajan, Tilottama, and Michael J. O'Driscoll. 2002. "Introduction." In *After Poststructuralism: Writing the Intellectual History of Theory*, edited by T. Rajan and M. O'Driscoll, pp. 3–21. Toronto: University of Toronto Press.

Rajchman, John. 1991. *Philosophical Events: Essays of the 80's*. New York: Columbia University Press.

Ransom, John. 1997. *Foucault's Discipline: The Politics of Subjectivity*. Durham, N.C.: Duke University Press.

Readings, Bill. 1996. *The University in Ruins*. Cambridge, Mass.: Harvard University Press.

Redner, Harry. 1987. *The Ends of Science: An Essay on Scientific Authority*. Boulder and London: Westview Press.

Renov, Michael. 1992) "Lost, Lost, Lost: Mekas as Essayist." In *To Free the Cinema: Jonas Mekas and the New York Underground*, edited by David E. James, pp. 215–39. Princeton, N.J.: Princeton University Press.

Rhee, Jeong Eun. 1999. Qualifying examination, Ohio State University, November 1999.

Richardson, Laurel. 1992 "The Consequences of Poetic Representation: Writing the Other, Rewriting the Self." In *Investigating Subjectivity: Research on Lived Experience*, edited by Carolyn Ellis and Michael Flaherty, pp. 125–40. Newbury Park, Calif.: Sage.

———. 1994. "Writing: A Method of Inquiry." In *The Handbook of Qualitative Research*, edited by Norman Denzin and Yvonna Lincoln, pp. 516–29. Thousand Oaks, Calif.: Sage.

———. 1997. *Fields of Play: Writing an Academic Life.* Brunswick, N.J.: Rutgers University Press.

Riley, Denise. 1988. *"Am I That Name?" Feminism and the Category of "Women" in History.* Minneapolis: University of Minnesota Press.

Rilke, Rainer. 1989. *The Selected Poetry of Rainer Maria Rilke.* Translated and edited by S. Mitchell. New York: Vintage International.

Robberson, Tod. 2004. "Al-Qaida's Intentions Difficult to Discern." *Centre Daily Times* (State College, Penn.), 27 March, A3.

Robinson, Jill. 1994. "White Woman Researching/Representing 'Others': From Anti-apartheid to Postcolonialism?" In *Writing Women and Space: Colonial and Postcolonial Geographies*, edited by Ann Blunt and Gillian Rose, pp. 197–226. New York: Guilford.

Rochlitz, Rainer. 1996. *The Disenchantment of Art: The Philosophy of Walter Benjamin.* New York: Guilford.

Rooney, Ellen. 1989. *Seductive Reasoning: Pluralism as the Problematic of Contemporary Literary Theory.* Ithaca, N.Y.: Cornell University Press.

———. 1995. "Better Read than Dead: Althusser and the Fetish of Ideology." *Yale French Studies* 88: 183–200.

Rorty, Richard, ed. 1967. *The Linguistic Turn: Recent Essays in Philosophical Method.* Chicago: University of Chicago Press.

———. 2001. "History of Science: Studied Ambiguity." *Science*, v. 293, issue 5539, 28 September.

Rosaldo, Renato. 1993. "After Objectivism." In *The Cultural Studies Reader*, edited by Simon During, pp. 104–17. London: Routledge.

Rose, Margaret. 1991. *The Post-Modern and the Post-Industrial: A Critical Analysis.* Cambridge: Cambridge University Press.

Rosen, Charles. 1977. "The Ruins of Walter Benjamin." Review of *The Origin of German Tragic Drama*. *The New York Review of Books*, 27 October and 10 November, 31–40 and 30–38.

Roseneau, Paula. 1992. *Post-Modernism and the Social Sciences: Insights, Inroads, and Intrusions.* Princeton, N.J.: Princeton University Press.

Ross, Andrew, ed. 1996. *Science Wars.* Durham, N.C.: Duke University Press.

Samuelson, Robert J. 2005. "Time to Toss the Textbook." *Newsweek*, 27 June, 39.

Sawiki, Jana. 1988. "Feminism and the Power of Foucauldian Discourse." In *After Foucault: Humanistic Knowledge, Postmodern Challenges*, edited by Jonathan Arac, pp. 161–78. New Brunswick, N.J.: Rutgers University Press.

———. 1991. *Disciplining Foucault: Feminism, Power, and the Body.* New York: Routlege.

Schad, John. 2003a. "Preface: What Are We After?" In *life.after.theory*, edited by Michael Payne and John Schad, pp. ix–xi. London: Continuum.

———. 2003b "Epilogue: Coming Back to 'Life.'" In *life.after.theory*, edited by Michael Payne and John Schad, pp. 168–89. London: Continuum.

Scheurich, James. 1995. "A Postmodern Review of Research Interviewing." *Qualitative Studies in Education* 8: 239–52.

———. 1996. "The Masks of Validity: A Deconstructive Investigation." *Qualitative Studies in Education* 9(1): 49–60.

———. 1997. *Postmodern Methodology*. London: Falmer.

Schrift, Alan. 1995. *Nietzsche's French Legacy: A Genealogy of Poststructuralism*. New York: Routledge.

Scott, Charles. 1996. *On the Advantages and Disadvantages of Ethics and Politics*. Bloomington: Indiana University Press.

Scott, Charles, and Robin Usher, eds. 1996. *Understanding Educational Research*. London: Routledge.

Scott, Joan. 1992. "Experience." In *Feminists Theorize the Political*, edited by Joan Scott and Judith Butler, pp. 22–40. New York: Routledge.

Schueller, Malini Johar. 1992. *The Politics of Voice: Liberalism and Social Criticism from Franklin to Kingston*. Albany: State University of New York Press.

Seidman, Steve, and Jeffrey Alexander, eds. 2001. *The New Social Theory Reader*. New York: Routledge.

Selby, Jane. 2004. "Working Divides between Indigenous and Non-Indigenous: Disruptions of Identity." *Qualitative Studies in Education* 17(1): 143–56.

Serres, Michel. 1982. *Hermes: Literature, Science, Philosophy*. Edited by J. Harari and D. Bell. Baltimore, Md.: Johns Hopkins University Press.

———. 1995a/1993. *Angels a Modern Myth*. Translated by Francis Cowper. Paris/ New York: Flammarion.

Serres, Michel, with Bruno Latour. 1995b/1990. *Conversations on Science, Culture, and Time*. Translated by R. Lapidus. Ann Arbor: University of Michigan Press.

Shamdasani, Sonu. 1994. "Introduction: The Censure of the Speculative." In *Speculations after Freud: Psychoanalysis, Philosophy and Culture*, edited by Sonu Shamdasani and Michael Munchow, pp. xi–xvii. London and New York: Routledge.

Sharrock, Wes, and Rupert Read. 2002. *Kuhn: Philosopher of Scientific Revolution*. Cambridge: Polity.

Sheehan, Paul. 2004. "Postmodernism and Philosophy." In *The Cambridge Companion to Postmodernism*, edited by Steven Connor, pp. 20–42. Cambridge: Cambridge University Press.

Sim, Stuart. 2000. *Post-Marxism: An Intellectual History*. London: Routledge.

Simon, Roger, and Don Dippo. 1986. "On Critical Ethnographic Work." *Anthropology and Education Quarterly* 17(4): 195–202.

Simons, Herb, ed. 1990. *The Rhetorical Turn: Invention and Persuasion in the Conduct of Inquiry*. Chicago: University of Chicago Press.

Skeggs, Beverley. 2000. "Introduction." In *Transformations: Thinking through Feminism*, edited by Sara Ahmed et al., pp. 27–32. London: Routledge.

Smith, Mark, ed. 2004. *Philosophy and Methodology of the Social Sciences*, v. 2. London: Sage.

Sokal, Alan D. 1998. *Fashionable Nonsense: Postmodern Intellectuals' Abuse of Science*. New York: Picador.

Sollers, Philippe. 1983. *Writing and the Experience of Limits*. Edited by D. Hayman. Translated by P. Barnard and D. Hayman. New York: Columbia University Press.

Solnit, Rebecca. 2005. *A Field Guide to Getting Lost*. London: Viking.

Sommer, Doris. 1994. "Resistant Texts and Incompetent Readers." *Poetics Today* 15(4): 523–51.

Sorell, Tom. 1991. *Scientism: Philosophy and the Infatuation with Science*. London: Routledge.

Spanos, William. 1993. *The End of Education: Toward Posthumanism*. Minneapolis: University of Minnesota Press.

Speedy, Jane. 2004. "Living a More Peopled Life: Definitional Ceremony as Inquiry into Psychotherapy 'Outcomes.' " *The International Journal of Narrative Therapy and Community Work* 3: 43–53.

Spillers, Hortense. 1994. "The Crisis of the Negro Intellectual: A Post-Date." *boundary 2* 21(3): 65–116.

Spivak, Gayatri. 1976. "Translator's Preface." In *Of Grammatology*, by Jacques Derrida, pp. ix–xc. Baltimore, Md.: Johns Hopkins University Press.

———. 1987. *In Other Worlds: Essays on Cultural Politics*. New York: Routledge.

———. 1988. "Can the Subaltern Speak?" In *Marxism and the Interpretation of Culture*, edited by Cary Nelson and Larry Grossberg, pp. 271–313. Urbana: University of Illinois Press.

———. 1991. "Theory in the Margin: Coetzee's *Foe* reading Defoe's *Crusoe/Roxana*." In *Consequences of Theory*, edited by Jonathan Arac and B. Johnson, pp. 154–80. Baltimore, Md.: Johns Hopkins University Press.

———. 1992. "French Feminism Revisited: Ethics and Politics." In *Feminists Theorize the Political*, edited by Judith Butler and Joan Scott, pp. 54–85. New York: Routledge.

———. 1993. *Outside in the Teaching Machine*. New York: Routledge.

———. 1994. "Responsibility." *boundary 2* 21(3): 19–64.

———. 1999. *A Critique of Postcolonial Reason: Toward a History of the Vanishing Present*. Cambridge, Mass.: Harvard University Press.

———. 2000a. "Claiming Transformation: Travel Notes With Pictures." In *Transformations: Thinking through Feminism*, edited by Sara Ahmed et al., pp. 119–30. London: Routledge.

———. 2000b. "From Haverstock Hill Flat to U.S. Classroom." In *What's Left of Theory? New Work on the Politics of Literary Theory*, edited by Judith Butler, John Guilory, and Kendall Thomas, pp. 1–39. New York: Routledge.

———. 2002. "Righting Wrongs." In *Human Rights, Human Wrongs: The Oxford Amnesty Lectures 2001*, edited by Nicholas Owen, pp. 168–227. Oxford: Oxford University Press.

Sprinkler, Michael. 1993. "Politics and Friendship: An Interview with Jacques Derrida." In *The Althusserean Legacy*, edited by A. Kaplan and M. Sprinkler, pp. 183–231. London: Verso.

Stacey, Judith. 1988. "Can There Be a Feminist Ethnography?" *Women's Studies International Forum* 11: 163–82.

Stanfield, John. 1994. "Ethnic Modeling in Qualitative Research." In *Handbook of Qualitative Research*, edited by Norman Denzin and Yvonna Lincoln, pp. 175–88. Thousand Oaks, Calif.: Sage.

Stengers, Isabelle. 1997. *Power and Invention: Situating Science*. Minneapolis: University of Minnesota Press.

Stenmark, Mikael. 2001. *Scientism: Science, Ethics and Religion*. Sydney: Ashgate.

Stewart, Kathleen. 1996. *A Space on the Side of the Road: Cultural Poetics in an "Other" America*. Princeton, N.J.: Princeton University Press.

Stockton, Kathryn Bond. 1992. "Bodies and God: Poststructuralist Feminists Return to the Fold of Spiritual Materialism." *boundary 2* 19(2): 113–49.

Stone, M. W. F., and Jonathan Wolff, eds. 2000. *The Proper Ambition of Science*. London: Routledge.

St. Pierre, Elizabeth. 1995. *Arts of Existence: The Construction of Subjectivity in Older White Southern Women*. Unpublished dissertation, Ohio State University.

———. 1997a. "Methodology in the Fold and the Irruption of Transgressive Data." *Qualitative Studies in Education* 10(2): 175–89.

———. 1997b. "Circling the Text: Nomadic Writing Practices. *Qualitative Inquiry* 10(3): 403–17.

———. 2000. "The Call for Intelligibility in Postmodern Educational Research." *Educational Researcher* 29(5): 25–28.

St. Pierre, Elizabeth, and Wanda Pillow, eds. 2000. *Working the Ruins: Feminist Poststructural Practice and Theory in Education*. New York: Routledge.

Strathern, Marilyn, ed. 2000. *Audit Cultures: Anthropological Studies in Accountability, Ethics and the Academy*. London: Routledge.

Stronach, Ian, and Maggie MacLure. 1997. *Educational Research Undone: The Postmodern Embrace*. Buckingham, U.K.: Open University Press.

Struik, John. 1993a. "Bodies in Trouble and the Problem of Sexual Practices." Paper presented at the Queer Sites Conference, Toronto, Ontario.

———. 1993b. "Queer Cures." Bergamo Curriculum Theorizing Conference, Dayton Ohio, October.

Szondi, Peter. 1978. "Hope in the Past: On Walter Benjamin." *Critical Inquiry* (Spring): 491–506.

Taylor, Charles. 2004. *Modern Social Imaginaries*. Durham, N.C.: Duke University Press.

Teigas, Demeetrium. 1995. "The Critique of Scientism." In *Knowledge and Hermeneutic Understanding: A Study of the Habermas-Gadamer Debate*, edited by D. Teigas, pp. 3–22. London: Associated University Presses.

Tiedemann, Rolf. 1989. "Historical Materialism or Political Messianism? An Interpretation of the Theses 'On the Concept of History.' " In *Benjamin: Philosophy, History, Aesthetics*, edited by G. Smith, pp. 175–202. Chicago: University of Chicago Press.

Tomlinson, Hugh. 1989. "After Truth: Post-modernism and the Rhetoric of Science." In *Dismantling Truth: Reality in the Post-Modern World*, edited by Hilary Lawson and L. Appignanesi, pp. 43–57. New York: St. Martin's Press.

Torgovnick, Marianna. 1994. "The Politics of 'We.' " In *Eloquent Obsessions: Writing Cultural Criticism*, edited by M. Torgovnick, pp. 260–78. Durham, N.C.: Duke University Press.

                                      203

Trifonas, Peter. 2000. *The Ethics of Writing: Derrida, Deconstruction and Pedagogy*. Boulder, Colo.: Rowan and Littlefield.

Tuhiwai-Smith, Linda. 1999. *De-Colonizing Methodology: Research and Indigenous Peoples*. London: Zed Books.

Uebel, Thomas E. 2000. "Some Scientism, Some Historicism, Some Critics: Hayek's and Popper's Critiques Revisited." In *The Proper Ambition of Science*, edited by M. W. F. Stone and Jonathan Wolff, pp. 151–73. London: Routledge.

Ulmer, Gregory. 1989. *Teletheory: Grammatology in the Age of Video*. New York: Routledge.

Usher, Robin, and R. Edwards. 1994. *Postmodernism and Education*. London: Routledge.

Van Loon, Joost. 2001. "Ethnography: A Critical Turn in Cultural Studies." In *Handbook of Ethnography*, edited by Paul Atkinson, Amanda Coffey, Sara Delamont, John Lofland, and Lyn Lofland, pp. 273–84. London: Sage.

Van Maanen, John. 1988. *Tales of the Field: On Writing Ethnography*. Chicago: University of Chicago Press.

———. 1995. "An End to Innocence: The Ethnography of Ethnography." In *Representation in Ethnography*, edited by J. Van Maanen, pp. 1–35. Thousand Oaks Calif.: Sage.

Visweswaran, Kamala. 1988. Defining Feminist Ethnography. *Inscriptions*, 3/4: 27–46.

———. 1994. *Fictions of Feminist Ethnography*. Minneapolis: University of Minnesota Press.

Walker, Alice. 1996. *The Same River Twice: Honoring the Difficult*. New York: Scribner.

Walker, Stephanie Kirkwood. 1994. "Canonical Gestures." *Curriculum Inquiry* 24: 171–80.

Ward, Graham. 2000. *Theology and Contemporary Critical Theory*, second edition. Houndmills: Palgrave.

Ward, Steven. 1996. "Filling the World with Self-Esteem: A Social History of Truth-Making." *Canadian Journal of Sociology* 21(1): 1–23.

Watney, Simon. 1994. *Practices of Freedom: Selected Writing on HIV/AIDS*. Durham, N.C.: Duke University Press.

Weems, Lisa, and Patti Lather. 2000. "A Psychoanalysis We Can Bear to Learn From" [Review of Deborah Britzman, *Lost Subjects, Contested Objects: Toward a Psychoanalytic Inquiry of Learning*, SUNY, 1998]. *Educational Researcher* 29(6): 41–42.

Weiler, Kathleen, ed. 2001. *Feminist Engagements: Reading, Resisting, and Revisioning Male Theorists in Education and Cultural Studies*. New York: Routledge.

Weiner, Gaby. 1994. *Feminisms in Education: An Introduction*. Buckingham and Philadelphia: Open University Press.

Welchman, John. 1989. "After the Wagnerian Bouillabaisse: Critical Theory and the Dada and Surrealist Word-Image." In *The Dada and Surrealist Word-Image*, edited by Judi Freeman, pp. 57–95. Cambridge, Mass.: MIT Press.

Werckmeister, O. K. 1982. "Walter Benjamin, Paul Klee, and the Angel of History." *Oppositions*, 7: 103–25.

Whitford, Margaret. 1991. *Luce Irigaray: Philosophy in the Feminine*. London: Routledge.

Willinsky, John. 2001. "The Strategic Education Research Program and the Public Value of Research." *Educational Researcher* 30(1):2 5–14.

Wilson, Elizabeth. 1998. *Neural Geographies: Feminism and the Microstructure of Cognition*. New York: Routledge.

Winant, Howard. 1990. "Gayatri Spivak on the Politics of the Subaltern." *Socialist Review*, 20(3): 81–97.

Winch, Peter. 1990. *The Idea of a Social Science and its Relation to Philosophy*. London: Routledge.

Woodbrooks, Catherine. 1991. *The Construction of Identity Through the Presentation of Self: Black Women Candidates Interviewing for Administrative Positions at a Research University*. Unpublished dissertation, Ohio State University.

Woolgar, Steve. 1988. *Science: The Very Idea.* London: Tavistock.

Wright, Handel. 2002. "Homies Don't Play Posties, Homies Don't Play Neos: Black Ambivalent Elaboration and the End(s) of Critical Pedagogy." Paper presented at the annual meeting of the American Educational Research Association, New Orleans, April 2002.

Wylie, Alison. 2002. *Thinking from Things: Essays in the Philosophy of Archaeology*. Berkeley and Los Angeles: University of California Press.

Young, Robert. 1990. *White Mythologies: Writing History and the West*. London: Routledge.

Zerilli, Linda. 1998. "Doing Without Knowing: Feminism's Politics of the Ordinary." *Political Theory* 26(4): 435–58.

Ziarek, Ewa. 2001. *An Ethics of Dissensus: Postmodernity, Feminism, and the Politics of Radical Democracy*. Stanford, Calif.: Stanford University Press.

Index

Abma, Tineke A., 162
accountability, 2, 110–11
  Derrida on, 109
  rage for, 18, 158–59, 162
  See also responsibility
Agee, James, 37, 51, 56, 72, 121–22,
    177n7
agency, x, 16, 41, 107, 170n7
Ahmed, Sara, 172n15
AIDS. *See* HIV disease
Alcoff, Linda, 172n9
Alexander, Jeffrey, 34
Althusser, Louis, 2, 5, 69, 104, 174n4,
    176n7
Anderson, Lauri, 174n3
angel(s), 43, 45–47, 54, 57, 88, 90–91,
    138, 140, 155
  Derrida on, 111
  of history, xi, 42, 91, 132, 151–53
  Serres on, xi, 94, 152
  Smithies on, 27–28
  validity of, 91, 131–33
  See also Troubling the Angels
anger, 170n9
Angus, Ian, 2
anti-intellectualism, 86
aporia(s), 15, 43, 105, 106, 137
  of exemplarity, 145–46
  praxis of, 4, 107
Apple, Michael, 15, 26
Aronowitz, Stanley, 168n5
audit culture, 2, 6, 12, 162
authenticity, 75, 147

authority, 161
  counter-practices of, 120–28
  ethnographic, 37
  legitimation and, 18, 118, 158–59
  objectivity and, 126

Babich, Babette, 87, 88
Backstrand, Karin, 161
Baez, Benjamin, 64, 171n7
Baker, Peter, 2
Bataille, Georges, viii
Baudrillard, Jean, 47, 121
Beck, Ulrich, 161
Behar, Ruth, 93
Belsey, Catherine, 84
Benjamin, Walter, vii, viii, 3, 7, 40,
    110, 120, 140
  angel of history and, xi, 42, 91, 132,
    151–53
  on getting lost, 1, 13
  "indolence of the heart" and, 143
  on mourning, 11
  theology and, 42, 43, 159
  "Theses on the Philosophy of
    History," 10, 43, 151
  on truth, 10, 83
Bennett, Tony, 2, 103, 120
Bennington, Geoffrey, 47, 111, 162, 175n8
Berridge, Mary, 178n11
Berry, Philippa, 159
Best, Steven, 2
Beyer, Lanny, 113–15
Blanchot, Maurice, 92, 94, 144

205

214 Index

stuck places, xi, 15–16, 30
subjectivism, 72
subversive repetition, 33–48
successor regimes, 8, 25–26
Szmborska, Wislawa, 75
Szondi, Peter, 152

Taylor, Bill, 156
Taylor, Charles, 167n1
terrorism, xii, 12, 159–61
textwork, 34, 40–42, 47
theology, 2, 60, 132
    Benjamin and, 42, 43, 159
    negative, 178n4
    Spivak on, 159–60
theory
    anti, 168n7
    end of, 3, 5–6
    "galloping," 18
    high, 85, 89, 174n2, 174n5
    post, 5
thing, the, 172n14
Tiedemann, Rolf, 109–10
Tomlinson, Hugh, 7
Too Big, 47, 87, 96
translators, 86, 92–93
transparency, 28, 72, 77, 83, 105, 147
    Delany on, 174n5
    in *Let Us Now Praise Famous Men,* 122
    Spivak on, 174n2
    in *Troubling the Angels,* 83–86
transvaluation, 10, 18, 167n3
Troubling the Angels (Lather &
        Smithies), vii–ix, xii, 156, 162
    double(d) practices of representation
        in, 39–40
    e-mail updates to, 97–100
    ethnography of, 33–36, 135–49
    fieldwork of, 44–47
    headwork of, 42–43
    interview on, 23–31
    naked methodology and, 49–57
    praxis under erasure in, 109–11
    publicity flier for, 35
    reflexivity in, 86–89
    reunion for, 79–82

textwork of, 40–42
transparency in, 83–86
truth, 119
    Benjamin on, 10, 83
    Foucault and, 6
    naked, 77
    Nietzsche and, 16, 77, 141
    regime of, 120
    understanding of, 85

Uebel, Thomas, 64
Ulmer, Gregory, 124
uncanniness, 86
unconscious, 16
    of knowledge, 60
    of sciences, 48
under erasure, 2, 14, 27–28, 107–9
universalism, 72
"unnatural sciences," 40, 61
Usher, Robin, 175n6

validity, xi, 24, 117–29
    ironic, 121–22, 128
    paralogical, 122–23, 128
    rhizomatic, 124–25, 128–29
    of tears, 141
    transgressive, 120, 128–29
    voluptuous, 125–29
"Validity of Angels" (Lather), 91,
        131–33
Van Loon, Joost, 104, 106
Van Maanen, John, 2, 39
    realist tales of, 24, 89
    on "vanity ethnography," 29–30, 44,
        92, 137
Vienna Circle, 66
Visweswaran, Kamala, 17, 37, 38, 41
voice(s), x, 41, 46, 52, 170n7
    analytical, 29
    ethnography and, 35–38
    limits of, 75, 136–37
    Marcus on, 41
    multiple, 83, 87, 114
    race and, 96
    romance of, 27, 137